Women's Global Health

Women's Global Health

Norms and State Policies

Edited by Lyn Boyd-Judson and Patrick James

LEXINGTON BOOKS
Lanham • Boulder • New York • Toronto • Plymouth, UK

Published by Lexington Books
A wholly owned subsidiary of Rowman & Littlefield
4501 Forbes Boulevard, Suite 200, Lanham, Maryland 20706
www.rowman.com

10 Thornbury Road, Plymouth PL6 7PP, United Kingdom

British Library Cataloguing in Publication Information Available

Library of Congress Cataloging-in-Publication Data

Women's global health : norms and state policies / edited by Lyn Boyd-Judson and Patrick James.
p. cm.
Includes bibliographical references and index.
ISBN 978-0-7391-8888-0 (cloth : alk. paper) -- ISBN 978-0-7391-8889-7 (electronic)
I. Boyd-Judson, Lyn, 1964- editor of compilation. II. James, Patrick, 1957- editor of compilation.
[DNLM: 1. Women's Health--legislation & jurisprudence. 2. Public Policy. 3. Social Control, For-
mal. 4. World Health--legislation & jurisprudence. WA 33.1]
RA564.85
362.1082--dc23
2013033424

∞™ The paper used in this publication meets the minimum requirements of American
National Standard for Information Sciences Permanence of Paper for Printed Library
Materials, ANSI/NISO Z39.48-1992.

Printed in the United States of America

Contents

v

Chapter One

Women's Global Health, Norms and State Policies

Lyn Boyd-Judson and Patrick James

OVERVIEW

For women around the globe, health has become the central intersection of the personal and the political; their bodies effectively become the arena for policy debates about population, poverty, reproduction, and morality. On the academic side of things, a comprehensive assessment of health for women can inform debates underway in a wide range of disciplines. This includes public health, most obviously, but also political science, economics, sociology, anthropology, and other fields. Moreover, the contents of this volume are intended to advance the interdisciplinary fields of ethics, women's studies, and international studies. Results from the research reported here may even turn out to have implications for a wider range of disciplines in the humanities, social sciences, and natural sciences.

Our volume seeks to answer interlocking questions with implications for knowledge in the preceding fields, along with relevance to policy: How do the laws and policies of a nation-state affect women's health? Is the state invested in these issues because women are seen to be bearers and nurturers of future citizens? Or are there other concerns such as economic development, human welfare, or religious ideology that shape this engagement? What are the current and historical responsibilities of the state in addressing women's health issues? How can they be measured and improved upon, and how do we approach the underlying ethical issues in practical and useful ways for women around the globe? Toward the end of this chapter, these

1

queries will be streamlined into three general questions to which the contributing chapters will respond through a range of perspectives, methods, and
substantive interests.

This volume brings together a collection of papers originally given at a
colloquium at the University of Southern California: "The Ethics of State
Involvement in Women's Health," March 2010. The volume continues with
seven chapters containing case studies of an international organization and
states in the developed and developing worlds. A final chapter offers conclusions from the editors.

This introductory chapter includes four additional sections. First, concept
formation is pursued. What is meant by global health and women's global
health, respectively? The second section identifies the focus of the volume
within the vast agenda of women's global health. Chapter summaries appear
in the third section. Fourth, and finally, a few thoughts are offered prior to the
point of departure for the case studies in chapters 2 through 8.

PROBLEMS OF CONCEPT FORMATION

Within a rapidly changing world, new policy challenges and attendant academic fields of interest are likely to arise. At one point or another, consensus
can be expected to develop on the boundaries of one area from another. This
is not yet the case for either global health or women's global health, fields
that right now seem to be growing like Topsy. An "upsurge of interest" in
studying and participating in global health is clear to see (Macfarlane et al.
2008: 383). Given so many entrants to the field, with points of origin from an
expanding array of disciplines, problems of concept formation are an understandable by-product. In an authoritative review of activities at academic
institutions, Macfarlane and others (2008: 384) find "no common understanding of the term global health." Thus it seems prudent to invest a minimal amount of space to a debate over the finer points of definition, especially
given the current project's emphasis on relevance to policy.

One definition of global health with high intuitive plausibility, along with
institutional legitimacy, comes from the US National Academy of Sciences,
put forward specifically by the Institute of Medicine (IOM) (quoted in Macfarlane et al. 2008: 385): [1]

> Health problems, issues, and concerns that transcend national boundaries, may
> be influenced by circumstances or experiences in other countries, and are best
> addressed by cooperative actions, and solutions.

The definition possesses face validity because it draws attention to matters of
possibly global scope. While Western in origin, the definition does not impose a specific vision with regard either to policy or responsibility for prob-

lems, issues and concerns. This concept formation, moreover, suggests that transnational cooperation is required to meet the challenges entailed by the quest for global health. Thus the definition can provide a foundation for later operational rendering of women's global health, the main focus of this volume.

Consider more directly the meaning of women's global health. Logically, given the difficulty in obtaining consensus over the meaning of global health, it cannot be any easier to identify agreement on a concept that obviously requires even more specific designation. Moreover, women's health "has attracted increasing attention in public health circles, as well as in clinical medicine" (Inhorn 2006: 345). Thus women's global health also is increasing in scope and complexity. An expanding agenda, in turn, makes it more likely that a concerted effort to define women's global health would meet with roadblocks as exponents of one field or another seek ownership of the concept as understood within their discipline.

All things considered, the pragmatic way of handling the challenge posed by defining women's global health is to adopt an encompassing concept formation that eschews reductionism. Specifically, the approach here seeks to minimize the risk that potentially important sources of insight are missed as a result of defining women's global health in a restrictive way that derives from any one field—even medicine.

Where, then, to begin? Perhaps without peer in its scope is the ethnographic project reviewed by Inhorn (2006). With more than 150 volumes, this project, which brings together the research efforts of literally hundreds of scholars from around the globe, stands as the most comprehensive effort by anthropologists to identify patterns in women's health. In fact, Inhorn's (2006: 345) article is entitled "Defining Women's Health." The choice of this project as the source for an operational definition of women's global health, with dimensions identified on the basis of the themes derived by Inhorn (2006) from its many volumes, is the best available for a study that is interdisciplinary and seeks to avoid any kind of premature closure.

Table 1.1 conveys twelve themes derived from more than 150 studies conducted over the course of twenty-five years (Inhorn 2006: 347). Perhaps the most obvious implication of this summary table is that a significant number of disciplines have the potential to add further depth of understanding and explanation to these highly encompassing themes. Terms such as reproductive essentialization, cultural construction, medicalization, biomedical hegemony, state, and subjectivities have links to various fields. The table's implicit direction toward inclusiveness is true in a qualitative sense as well; it is not difficult to review its themes and imagine further contributions from disciplines that span the natural sciences, social sciences, and humanities because diverse empirical and normative concerns are interwoven throughout the themes.

Table 1.1.   Defining Women's Health: A Dozen Messages from 157 Ethnographies

1. The power to define women's health
2. The reproductive essentialization of women's lives
3. The cultural construction of women's bodies
4. The increasing medicalization of women's lives
5. The increasing biomedical hegemony over women's health
6. The production of health by women
7. The health-demoting effects of patriarchy
8. The intersectionality of race, class, gender (etc.) in women's health
9. The state intervenes in women's health
10. The politics of women's health
11. The importance of women's local moral worlds
12. The importance of understanding women's subjectivities

Source: Inhorn (2006: 347)

Reinforcing this effective call for inclusiveness in the study of women's global health are the mandates conveyed by leading academic and policy-oriented institutions. A summary of featured items from the websites of the Institute for Global Health (IGH) (2013) at USC, the Global Health Institute (GHI) (2013) at the University of California, and the Global Health Policy Center (GHPC) (2013) at the Center for Strategic and International Studies will prove quite informative. While many other institutions could be surveyed, the contents described momentarily are consistent with an overall trend toward expansiveness in the agenda of women's global health.

USC's IGH (2013) offers a wide range of publications. Connections with women's health appear across the board and encompass a range of material and ideational concerns. HIV/AIDS, along with sexual and reproductive health and rights, are prominent examples in connection with women's global health. The GHI (2013) at the University of California, which includes a "Center for Expertise in Women's Health and Empowerment," suggests an inclusive approach through its name alone. Indeed, GHI's basic statement includes the following assertion: "To make major improvements in women's health, you can't look solely through a medical lens, so we're really trying to look more creatively and innovatively at how to achieve better health for women through less traditional mechanisms." Along similar lines, consider the points included by GHPC (2013) in its summary of an interview with Joyce Banda, President of Malawi. The president emphasized the importance of economic empowerment of women vis-à-vis effective family planning while also talking about the significance of education for girls, along with more traditional concerns in women's health such as counteracting maternal mortality. In sum, the interview with President Banda reveals a panoramic sense of women's health as something that goes beyond medical care alone and enters into a range of public policies.

When reflecting on academic research and practice, it is impossible to sum up so many diverse perspectives in a succinct definition of women's public health. It seems much better to facilitate further study by acknowledging that, in operational terms, women's global health is an elaboration of global health as defined by IOM: Women's global health is a network of problems, issues and concerns, material and physical, which must be met through cooperative actions and solutions at the state level and beyond. Table 1.1, which conveys women's global health in multiple dimensions that reflect a range of disciplines, thereby creates the context for the current enterprise.

Focus

Given that a full consideration of women's global health in all its dimensions is beyond the scope of any given study, what is the intended specific contribution of the present volume? The overarching goal is to assess women's global health in terms of *norms and state policies.*[2] Within the vast literature touching on women's global health, no previous study combines these concerns. Moreover, the timing for such an investigation would seem just right. Policies and laws affecting reproduction, sexuality, child welfare, domestic violence and other aspects of women's global health, writ large, have been proliferating in recent years. A focus on women's health, with a cross-national agenda that focuses on the roles played by norms and state policies, naturally will have implications for the important issues of rights, access to resources, and governance.

Given the range of subject matter and approaches available, the volume does not apply a single theoretical framework throughout its contents. Instead, respective chapters draw upon concepts from various disciplines, most notably political science and anthropology, and interdisciplinary fields, notably ethics, women's studies, and international studies. Thus, at the level of theory, the current project can be described as deliberately eclectic. This is in keeping with the preceding review of women's global health as a concept: the contributors to this project eschew any sense of orthodoxy, seeing it as premature, while obviously not dismissing the results of studies that might adopt a specific theoretical framework to see what insights it can bring.

With respect to eclecticism, return now to the themes from Table 1.1, which can be taken as an attempt to map women's global health in multiple dimensions. The current study obviously fits in most directly with the ninth theme, which focuses on how the state intervenes in women's health. Concern with state policies also makes the volume relevant to the first theme about women's health, which focuses on the power to define it.

Given the volume's focus on norms in addition to state policies, connections with even more themes from the table also will come into play. Marinova and James, in their chapter, identify health-demoting effects of patriarchy, the seventh theme. The chapter by Thoradeniya connects with the eleventh theme, on women's local moral worlds. And virtually all chapters in some ways touch on the twelfth theme, which pertains to understanding women's subjectivities. It would not be difficult to point out more connections, but the overall point is clear: The current study, which connects with many of the themes identified by an ethnographic mapping of the study of women's global health, would not obviously benefit from imposition of a particular framework borrowed from a given discipline.

Chapter Outlines

Chapter 2 explores ethical tensions involved in global health promotion efforts by international organizations and states and considers the extent to which these global initiatives contribute to significant disparities in the global health status of men and women. To this end, the chapter considers the degree to which three aspects of the global health regime exacerbate sex and gender differentials in global health.

First, the chapter looks at the evolution of international responses to women, gender, and global health within the United Nations system. It turns out that global health initiatives led by UN organs and affiliated agencies have evolved from a narrow focus on women's fertility and maternal health to a much broader formulation of women's health rights. Still, UN actors tend to equate gender with women's issues alone. As a result, the UN unintentionally neglects health challenges that disproportionately affect men and, at the same time, inadequately considers the gender constraints that shape women's health-seeking behavior and health outcomes. Second, the chapter finds that the human right to health is formulated in largely gender-neutral terms. When international human rights law departs from formal gender neutrality, it does so in a way that presumes women and children as the primary groups vulnerable to particular global health inequities and gender inequities. At first glance, this departure from strict gender neutrality appears to work in favor of women. However, the chapter raises questions about whether or not rights-based instruments are effective tools for advancing women's health. Third, and finally, the chapter examines funding gaps in global health aid. Available data on global health aid indicates that some diseases, notably HIV/AIDS, receive funding that is disproportionate to the morbidity or mortality caused by these illnesses. Conversely, health challenges that pose significant threats to women, including maternal/reproductive health and poverty-related health problems, are under-funded. In this regard, the evidence suggests a gap in global health expenditures that works to the disadvantage of women's health.

Chapter 3 focuses on social norms and policies with regard to prostitution and human trafficking in three Western European states. The chapter explores the question of why countries in the same geographic region, with similar socio-economic development and adherence to regional and international treaties, have adopted different approaches to prostitution. In 1999, Sweden pioneered the so-called "abolitionist" approach, which outlaws prostitution and imposes penalties on the buyers, while the Netherlands and Germany have legalized and regulated prostitution since 2000 and 2002, respectively, which epitomizes the regulationist or "sex work" approach.

Inquiry into the social norms underpinning these divergent policies reveals three very different normative approaches, notably a difference between the Dutch and the German rationale for legalization. The chapter begins by drawing from literature on norms from International Studies, including feminist scholarship, and proceeds to examine the three different normative contexts for the legislation, providing an overview of the passage of the legislation. Utilizing government documents from Sweden, the Netherlands, and Germany in the course of analysis, the chapter concludes by finding that the *normative context* accounts for contrasting policies among the three countries. The chapter examines the normative implications of the regulationist and abolitionist approaches, keeping in mind that codification of ethical principles holds two-fold significance: as a reflection of social customs, and as a major influence on the social fabric and future efforts at gender equality.

Chapter 4 focuses on morality and legality with specific attention to abortion-related health issues. A substantial literature establishes that, globally, when abortion is illegal, women's health suffers both directly (from illegal abortions and pregnancy) and indirectly (from impacts of poverty). This research seems, however, to "stop at the door" of the legality of abortion— assuming that making abortion legal will solve most if not all of these problems.

However, is that assumption justified? Are the positive effects for women's health the same across countries that legalize abortion? In particular, this chapter explores three hypotheses about policy-related results. First, it looks at whether the positive impact of legal abortion is tempered in places where poverty is extreme. Second, it looks at whether the *degree* of abortion legality (i.e., the situations in which abortion remains effectively illegal) affects the positive health results of legalizing abortion. Third, and finally, controlling both for poverty and the degree of legality, the chapter asks whether the grounds on which abortion became legal impact upon the health benefits of legalization.

Most of this chapter focuses on the third of the preceding hypotheses. Time-lagged analysis of statistical data about abortion laws and health in 30 countries, paired with comparative case analyses from Mozambique and Tanzania, is used to reveal an important difference. States that use justifications which retain the taboo on abortion (such as privacy, rape, and third-party decision-making) obtain fewer health benefits than states whose justifications transgress the prohibition. The chapter concludes with insights about what this question tells us for the relationship between jurisprudence and women's material benefit in abortion law around the world.

Chapter 5 focuses on U.S. family planning policy and the Global Gag Rule (GGR). U.S. leadership in international family planning entails both positive and negative consequences. On the positive side, the United States is the principal funder for many programs through the United States Agency for International Development (USAID) and the United Nations Population Fund (UNFPA). On the negative side, this allows Washington to exert significant control over many aspects of family planning around the world. And U.S. rules and regulations can and frequently do change dramatically with each new presidential administration. Shifting policies result in the internal politics of one country—the United States—being played out in women's lives and access to family planning around the globe.[3] More pointedly, women's bodies and lives around the world are the venue where the often contentious domestic politics of the United States are acted out.

This dynamic tension will be examined through the lens of the GGR, which is enacted and rescinded with the changing of U.S. presidents. President George W. Bush re-imposed the GGR—that no U.S. family planning assistance can be provided to foreign NGOs that use funding from any other source to perform abortions in cases other than a threat to the woman's life, rape, or incest; provide counseling and referral for abortion; or lobby to make abortion legal or more available in their country. President Obama rescinded the GGR soon after taking office.

Loss of family planning funds and services when the GGR is in place has been well-documented.[4] This chapter analyzes the present situation of President Obama lifting the order, and implications for family planning around the world, now and in the future. Potential strategies for lifting or limiting U.S. control, sustaining funding, and enacting a fairly permanent set of rules and regulations will be examined.

Chapter 6 investigates the ethics of state policies that restrict access to infant formula. Of particular interest is the impact of such policies on women's and children's health. To begin, the World Health Organization (WHO) and United Nations Children's Fund (UNICEF) recommend that all infants be breastfed, regardless of their socio-economic status, risk of disease, or other potentially mitigating circumstances. Children who are breastfed are more likely to survive at least to the age of five, have stronger immune systems and are better nourished. Breastfeeding also is beneficial to the mother, helping her bond with her child and return to her pre-pregnancy weight, reducing obesity. Despite the risks inherent to choosing infant formula over breastfeeding, in most countries women have the right to decide which method of infant feeding on which to rely. The assumption is that a mother will balance her rights to bodily autonomy and self-determination with her child's right to adequate nutrition.

Many manufacturers, in an effort to promote the infant formula market during the mid-to-late 1990s, employed unethical marketing techniques that led mothers to prefer infant formula over breastmilk. There have since been both national and international reactions to this profit-driven marketing at the expense of the health of infants. Most countries adopted laws and policies regulating the promotion of infant formula by corporations, in an effort to police these subversive tactics and ensure that mothers are able to make decisions regarding infant feeding based on unadulterated evidence.

Recent efforts in Iran to promote breastfeeding and prevent mothers from using infant formula, however, have crossed the line from promoting child and maternal health to forcing government mandates on the bodies of women and children. The law in Iran (and under debate in several countries) makes it illegal to access infant formula without a prescription obtained from a doctor, who must first determine the medical necessity in its use. From both public health, legal, and rights-based perspectives, this move to enforce breastfeeding as the only option is a step backwards in relation to women's rights to control their bodies, children's rights to nutrition, and mothers' abilities to thrive in social, political, and economic society.

Chapter 7 examines the government-sponsored Janani Suraksha Yojana (JSY) Maternal Health Financing Scheme in India as a case study in ethics and global health promotion. An estimated 358,000 maternal deaths occurred worldwide in 2008, a thirty-four percent decline from the 1990 levels of 500,000. However, developing countries continued to account for ninety-nine percent of the deaths, with Sub-Saharan Africa and South Asia contributing to eighty-seven percent (313,000). Significant numbers of maternal deaths occur among populous countries in Asia: India, Indonesia, and Bangladesh, which are among the eleven countries where sixty-five percent of all maternal deaths occurred in 2008.

In April 2005, the government of India launched JSY (Safe Motherhood scheme), which is an integral component of the National Rural Health Mission. JSY is a conditional cash transfer scheme—to incentivise women of low socio-economic status to deliver in a health facility. There is also provision for reimbursement for transport and incentives to Accredited Social Health Activists for encouraging mothers to have institutional deliveries. The focus is on states that have high maternal mortality and low rates of institutional delivery—the eight empowered action group states of Bihar, Madhya

Pradesh, Uttar Pradesh, Rajasthan, Jharkhand, Chhatisgarh, Orissa, and Utta-ranchal.

This chapter will describe the components and performance of the Janani Suraksha Yojana scheme. Findings from reviews conducted after a three-year implementation period—including awareness of JSY, payments to ben-eficiaries, the outcomes and recommendations to improve its operational and financial management—will be presented. The public health ethics of the government-sponsored program to promote maternal and neonatal care at a period of greatest vulnerability and the role of the state to promote equity within the health system also are assessed.

Chapter 8 explores the ethics behind the new shift in women's health in modern Sri Lanka; a policy of "beyond reproduction," which was marked with the establishment of Well Woman Clinics (WWC) in 1996.[5] The central function of WWCs is to facilitate early detection of common, non-communi-cable diseases among women who are past their reproductive age, hence the term "beyond reproduction." Sri Lanka was the first to establish a govern-ment WWC program in South Asia. Fundamental questions arise about this innovative policy: What does "beyond reproduction" mean to women in Sri Lanka? How do they comprehend this modern concept? In short, what are the ethical considerations of the state and women's understanding of their bodies with regard to the establishment of WWCs?

Following its independence in 1948, Sri Lanka started designing its poli-cies in line with development discourse from the West, which perceived population growth as a major hindrance to development. Thus women's health and their bodies, especially reproduction, became the linchpin of poli-cy formulation. Further, women's understanding of the body as a concept was challenged by both international and national policy formulations. In Sri Lanka "women's health" is predominantly a territory confined to policy-makers and medical professionals, while "women's body" is specific to the territory of social scientists, anthropologists, and feminists. By bringing these two concepts—women's health and body—into a single analytical frame-work, the chapter engages in a discursive analysis to understand the ethical considerations and tensions between international policy and national level provisions with regard to establishment of WWCs in Sri Lanka. An ethno-graphic research component of in-depth interviews and oral histories in a selected Medical Officer of Health (MOH) area in Sri Lanka brings out the interplay between policy and practice at a grassroots level.

Chapter 9, the volume's conclusion, puts together the theory and evidence from the preceding chapters to answer three overarching questions:

- How do laws and policies of international organizations and states impact upon women's health?

- In what ways should states and international organizations consider altering their policies to impact more favorably on women's health?
- What norms can and should guide the provision of women's global health?

Tentative answers to these questions will advance the study of women's global health significantly. The integrated approach of this volume—a global focus, along with assessment of the actions from governments and the principal international organization of states— is regarded as the most promising path toward greater understanding and ultimately better policies and outcomes.

A FEW THOUGHTS AT THE POINT OF DEPARTURE

Women's global health is a vast, even amorphous, field of study. It is expanding so rapidly that prudence suggests the value of carrying out research in a pragmatic way on the basis of an inclusive definition that possesses face validity. The chapters that follow cover material consistent with the multidimensional sense of women's public health identified by a review of numerous ethnographic studies. This inclusive approach, in turn, lines up with the basic concept of global health as put forward by the IOM of the U.S. National Academy of Sciences, which represents the mainstream of research. Thus the chapters that follow reflect an inclusive and pragmatic approach toward carrying out research on women's global health.

REFERENCES

Global Health Institute. 2013. http://ucghi.universityofCalifornia.edu.
Global Health Policy Center. 2013. ttp://www.smartglobalhealth.org.
Inhorn, Marcia C. 2006. "Defining Women's Health: A Dozen Messages from More than 150 Ethnographies." *Medical Anthropology Quarterly* 20: 345-378. Institute for Global Health. 2013. http://globalhealth.usc.edu.
Macfarlane, Sarah B., Marian Jacobs and Ephata E. Kaaya. 2008. "In the Name of Global Health: Trends in Academic Institutions." *Journal of Public Health Policy* 29: 383-401.

NOTES

1. Macfarlane et al. (2008: 384) identify tropical medicine and international health as concepts antecedent to global health.

2. While the focus of the volume is on women's health, references to men's health will appear at certain points for purposes of comparison.

3. This same issue is played out in the regulations surrounding the provision of the U.S. President's Emergency Plan for AIDS Relief (PEPFAR) funds and antiretroviral drugs.

4. See http://www.populationaction.org/globalgagrule/Summary.shtml for some country-specific data.

5. This is from the Annual Report on Family Health, Sri Lanka, 2004-2005, Colombo, 2007, p.31. WWCs were established in Sri Lanka with the support from UNFPA, as a direct consequence of the UN Population Conference in Cairo, in 1994. By the end of 2005, 397 WWCs were functioning in the country, mostly based at MOH offices. The number of women attending has increased from 61,707 in 2004 to 74,165 in 2005. However, Family Health Bureau (FHB) notes that "still it is only a fraction of the target population."

Chapter Two

Closing the Gender Gap in Global Health

Debra L. DeLaet

INTRODUCTION

Significant disparities in the health status of men and women exist around the globe. These differences reflect what can be characterized as a gender gap in global health. This gender gap reflects a complicated, sometimes paradoxical, reality. Although women have higher life expectancy than men, they face specific health challenges resulting from gender norms that devalue women and exacerbate poverty-related challenges that affect women's quality of life. Conversely, despite economic and social benefits conferred by gender norms that privilege men globally, men face many health disadvantages, perhaps most notably lower life expectancies in every region of the world.

This chapter begins with an overview of data that demonstrates the existence of this multifaceted gender gap in global health and also considers the underlying causes of disparities. Subsequently, the chapter examines the extent to which these inequities are embedded in global norms governing health promotion and in health initiatives. To this end, the chapter considers the extent to which three aspects of the global health regime contribute to or exacerbate the gender gap in global health.

First, the chapter looks at the evolution of international responses to women, gender, and global health within the United Nations system. The chapter shows that global health initiatives led by UN organs and affiliated agencies have evolved from a narrow focus on women's fertility and maternal health to a much broader formulation of women's health rights. Despite broadening of the UN's focus, its global health initiatives remain rooted in an approach that conflates gender with biological sex and remains focused almost exclusively on women's issues alone. As a result, the UN fails to consider the gender constraints that shape women's health-seeking behavior and health outcomes and, at the same time, neglects health challenges that disproportionately affect men.

Second, the chapter considers the extent to which the human right to health under international law is gender neutral. It finds that the human right to health is formulated in largely those terms. When international human rights law departs from formal gender neutrality, it does so in a way that presumes women and children as the primary groups vulnerable to particular global health inequities and gender inequities. At first glance, this departure from strict gender neutrality appears to work in favor of women. However, the chapter raises questions about whether or not rights-based instruments are effective tools for advancing women's, or men's, health.

Third, and finally, the chapter examines funding gaps in global health aid. Available data on global health aid indicates that some diseases, notably HIV/AIDS, receive funding that is disproportionate to the morbidity or mortality caused by these illnesses. Conversely, health challenges that pose significant threats to women, including maternal/ reproductive health and poverty-related health problems, are under-funded. In this regard, the evidence suggests a gap in global health aid that may work to the disadvantage of women's health.

A GENDER GAP IN GLOBAL HEALTH

Significant differentials characterize the health status of men and women around the globe. Several indicators used to measure health status, including life expectancy (United Nations Development Programme [UNDP], 2009), health-adjusted life expectancy (World Health Organization [WHO] 2009) and disability-adjusted life years (WHO 2008), demonstrate these health disparities. Health disparities between men and women are complicated and work in different directions depending on the health indicator under consideration. In some cases, women are at a health disadvantage in comparison to men, but other indicators suggest that men suffer worse health outcomes.

Women, on average, have a higher life expectancy than men. In 2007, the global average female life expectancy was seventy years; for men, average life expectancy was sixty-five. These global averages differ significantly according to levels of economic development. In high-income countries, female life expectancy is eighty-two years while male life expectancy is only seventy-seven years. Female life expectancy is seventy-four years in upper-middle-income states, compared to only sixty-seven years for males. The gap between female and male life expectancy narrows somewhat in lower-middle-income countries. Women, on average, can expect to live seventy years in these countries, whereas men can expect to live sixty-seven years. The gap narrows further in low-income countries, where women can expect to live fifty-eight years compared to fifty-five years for men (WHO 2009). As these figures indicate, women's greater longevity is especially pronounced in the developed world. For example, in developed countries, more than twice as many women than men live to over the age of eighty (Buvinic et al. 2006: 197). That said, it is notable that women's health advantage in life expectancy holds across levels of economic development.

The same female health advantage holds true across all regions of the world. Women can expect to live longer lives in Europe, the Americas, the Arab States, South-East Asia, Africa, the Eastern Mediterranean region, and the Western Pacific Region (WHO 2009). Some interesting data emerges when life expectancy is examined within specific regions. The starkest gap in life expectancy between women (74.4) and men (65.4) emerges in Central and Eastern Europe and the Commonwealth of Independent States, where women can expect to live almost ten years longer than men. The gap between women and men is smallest in Sub-Saharan Africa, where female life expectancy is 52.5 compared to 50.4 for men (WHO 2009: 44). According to United Nations Development Programme (UNDP) data for 2007, male life expectancy was higher than female life expectancy in only two countries: Afghanistan (43.5 for women versus 43.6 for men) and Swaziland (44.8 for women compared to 45.7 for men.). Taken together, WHO and UNDP data on life expectancy demonstrate a striking if surprising pattern of greater longevity for women that holds across the globe.

Health-adjusted life expectancy (HALE) is the number of years a newborn infant could expect to live if prevailing patterns of age-specific mortality rates at the time of birth were to stay the same throughout the child's life (UNDP 2009). Estimates follow the same pattern as life expectancy indicators. However, the gap between men and women is smaller in HALE estimates. The 2007 health-adjusted life expectancy for women globally was sixty-one years; this figure is just fifty-eight years for men. This pattern again holds across levels of economic development. In high-income countries, females have a health-adjusted life expectancy of seventy-two years compared to sixty-eight years for males. In upper-middle-income countries, women can expect to live sixty-three years in good health in comparison to fifty-eight years for men. Once again, the gap between men and women narrows somewhat at lower levels of economic development. Females have a HALE of sixty-two years in lower-middle-income countries whereas men can be expected to live sixty years in good health. The gap is narrowest in low-income countries where a female HALE is forty-nine years compared to a male HALE of forty-eight years (WHO 2009: 44).

HALE estimates indicate that the female health advantage on this indicator holds across regions of the world. As is the case with life expectancy in general, women have higher health-adjusted life expectancy in Africa, the Americas, South-East Asia, Europe, the Eastern Mediterranean Region, and the Western Pacific Region. However, the gap between men and women on HALE indicators across all regions is smaller than the gap between men and women in measures of general life expectancy.

Individual countries show the most interesting discrepancies between life expectancy and HALE indicators. Unlike life expectancy measures, which show a male advantage over females in only Afghanistan and Swaziland, males have higher HALE estimates in a number of countries: Bangladesh, Botswana, the Central African Republic, Pakistan, Qatar, Tajikistan, Tonga, and Zimbabwe. In numerous other countries, Afghanistan, Bahrain, Benin, Cameroon, Chad, Kuwait, Mali, Mozambique, Nepal, Nigeria, Sudan, Swaziland, Tuvalu, United Arab Emirates, and United Republic of Tanzania, HALE estimates for men and women are identical. The male advantage in HALE is not large in the cases where it exists—typically just one or two years (WHO 2009: 36-43). Nevertheless, the shift is notable and suggests that HALE estimates, which incorporate variables related to the quality and not just longevity of life, are more likely to capture the effects of variables that have negative effects on women's health.

Compared to basic estimates of life expectancy, HALE indicators represent a more nuanced measure of human health that incorporates not simply gaps in health outcomes but also indicators related to health experiences and quality of life. However, even HALE measures must be evaluated with a certain degree of caution about what they tell us about health inequities between men and women. For one thing, HALE indicators are based on just fifty national health surveys that themselves reflect self-reporting of health status from different populations (Mathers et al. 2003: 437). Feminist IR work in other areas indicates that women's concerns and issues often are under-represented in international processes and programming, even when they are designed with the intention of facilitating women's inclusion. Thus, it is highly likely that HALE indicators underestimate illnesses and health challenges that limit the number of years women around the globe can expect to live in full health (Mathers et al. 2003: 448). Thus, despite the fact that HALE represents an improvement over life expectancy as a measure of health, we need to delve more deeply into the data to understand the nature and extent of the gender gap in global health.

One way in which to accomplish this objective is to look at "lost" healthy life expectancy which is the difference between total life expectancy and HALE (Mathers et al. 2003: 439). When lost years of health are examined, the global patterns in life expectancy and HALE are reversed, and global health disadvantages for women become more apparent. At a global level, women have, on average, nine lost years of healthy life expectancy compared to seven lost years for men. This pattern holds across levels of economic development. The estimated number of lost years of health for females is highest in upper-middle-income countries, where women lose an average of eleven years of good health; males in these countries lose an average of nine years of good health. In low-income countries, the number of lost years of good health drops to nine for females and seven for males. Women in all regions of the world share this health disadvantage relative to men. In every region, women lose eight or nine years of good health whereas male lost healthy life expectancy ranges from six to eight (WHO 2009: 44). As this data indicates, women have higher morbidity than men even though they have greater average life expectancy as well as higher health-adjusted life expectancy. "In other words," according to Buvinic et al. (2006: 197), "women spend about fifteen percent of their lives in unhealthy conditions and men spend twelve percent." Thus, higher levels of morbidity mean that women lose more years of healthy life than men, changing the direction of the gender gap in global health.

Women also experience different burdens of disease, as measured in DALYs, which indicate the number of years of health life lost due to particular diseases and injuries. In this way, DALYs reflect the relative contributions of various diseases and injuries to variations in HALE (WHO 2009: 439). Globally, men have a slightly higher burden of disease (as measured in DALY losses) than women. In 2001, approximately fifty-two percent of DALY losses were attributed to males (Buvinic et al. 2006: 197). However, it should be noted that the burden of disease carried by women and men varies by region and age group. Males have a higher burden of disease in every region of the world, except South Asia, where women carry 50.1 percent of the disease burden. In Europe, the male burden of disease is 54.8 percent. In age cohorts, the most notable shift in this general pattern is for women between the ages of 5–29. In this age cohort, girls and women lose more DALYs than boys and men. In all other age groups, boys/men experience a higher proportion of DALY losses. This pattern holds across groupings of countries according to levels of economic development (Buvinic et al. 2006: 197).

Although men experience a slightly higher burden of disease in general, women and men suffer disproportionately from different kinds of illnesses, as measured by years lost due to disability (YLD). YLD measures the "equivalent years of life lost through time spent in states of less than full health." (WHO 2008: 36). For both men and women, unipolar depressive disorders account for the highest proportion of YLD. However, the percentage of years lost due to disability is only 8.3 percent for men compared to 13.4 percent for women. The second major contributor to YLD for men, alcohol use disorders, account for 6.8 percent of lost years of health. Other major causes of YLD losses for males include adult-onset hearing loss (4.8

percent), refractive errors (4.7 percent), schizophrenia (2.8 percent), cataracts (2.7 percent), bipolar disorder (2.5 percent), chronic obstructive pulmonary disease (2.4 percent), asthma (2.2 percent), and falls (2.2 percent). For women, refractive errors (4.6 percent) are the second major cause of YLD, followed by adult-onset hearing loss (4.3 percent), cataracts (3.2 percent), osteoarthritis (3.1 percent), schizophrenia (2.6 percent), anemia (2.4 percent), bipolar disorder (2.3 percent), birth asphyxia and birth trauma (2.3 percent), and Alzheimer and other dementia (1.9 percent) (WHO 2008: 37).

As these data show, different sets of illnesses are more likely to affect the health experiences and outcomes of women and men. Women have higher disease prevalence for certain illnesses, such as osteoarthritis and Alzheimer's Disease, that result, in part, from women's average higher life expectancy. Additionally, maternal conditions stemming from pregnancy and birth-related complications contribute significantly to women's burden of disease. Men have significantly higher prevalence rates of alcohol-related disorders. Injuries contribute disproportionately to men's burden of disease, and men are also more prone to suffer from heart disease and coronary artery disease. Such differences result from a complicated interplay of biological and sociocultural factors as will be explored in the subsequent section.

The major causes of burden of disease for women vary according to the income levels of countries. In high-income countries, the top five causes of DALY losses in women include unipolar depressive disorders, migraine, health problems associated with alcohol use, bipolar disorders, and schizophrenia. In low-income countries, the major causes of DALY losses for women are HIV/AIDS, tuberculosis, abortion complications, schizophrenia, and maternal sepsis (WHO 2008: 46). Conditions specific to women comprise a significant proportion of their burden of disease. Globally, maternal conditions (including maternal hemorrhage, maternal sepsis, hypertensive disorders, obstructed labor, obstetric fistula, and complications from unsafe abortions) contribute to 2.8 percent of women's DALY losses (Buvinic et al. 2006: 199). Over 500,000 women die each year due to complications from pregnancy and childbirth; most of these deaths would be preventable with adequate public health interventions (UNDP 2003: 9). Neoplasms, including breast and cervical cancer, contribute to 1.1 percent of DALY losses for women (Buvinic et al. 2006: 199). In terms of shared health conditions, women suffer much higher rates of depression; they are roughly twice as likely as men to experience depression. In Sub-Saharan Africa, teenage girls are anywhere from five to sixteen times more likely than teenage boys to become infected with HIV/AIDS. Women also have higher disease prevalence for certain illnesses, such as Alzheimer's, osteoporosis, and arthritis, due to their average higher life expectancy (Buvinic et al. 2006: 196). Injuries contribute disproportionately to men's burden of disease, and men are also more prone to suffer from ischemic heart disease, and coronary artery disease. A significant proportion of the global male burden of disease—2.7 percent of DALY losses—results from war and violence (Buvinic et al. 2006: 209). Men also have significantly higher prevalence rates of drug and alcohol-related disorders (WHO 2008: 36).

The causes of male and female mortality globally reveal both disparities and similarities in the health experiences of women and men. At the global level, cardiovascular disease is the major cause of death for both men (26.8 percent) and women (31.5 percent). Globally, other major causes of male mortality are infectious and parasitic diseases (16.7 percent), cancers (13.4 percent), unintentional injuries (8.1 percent), respiratory infections (7.1 percent), and respiratory diseases (6.9 percent). After cardiovascular disease, the major causes of death for females include infections and parasitic diseases (15.6 percent), cancers (11.8 percent), respiratory infections (7.4 percent) and respiratory diseases (6.8 percent) (WHO 2008: 10).

As these data indicate, cardiovascular disease is a major cause of mortality for both men and women. Perhaps surprisingly, cardiovascular disease is the cause of a higher percentage of deaths among women than men. This discrepancy might be explained by the fact that women have higher average life expectancy. (Prior to the onset of menopause, hormonal differences between women and men lead to lower rates of cardiovascular disease in women that disappear in postmenopausal women.) Additionally, the high rate of male mortality due to unintentional injuries affects the overall rate of male mortality from other causes. In turn, the high rate of death from unintentional injuries among men can be attributed to the gendered phenomena that men are both more likely to engage in work that has high rates of associated injury as well as the fact that men are more likely to engage in risky behavior leading to injury. The fact that infectious disease is a major cause of death for both men and women reflects the reality that communicable illnesses still constitute a significant proportion of disease in developing areas where the majority of the world's population lives. Men have higher mortality rates across all regions, which can be attributed in large part to high male mortality due to injuries. Although this pattern holds around the globe, sex differentials in mortality rates are apparent across regions. Differences are most pronounced in Africa where females have significantly higher mortality due to communicable illnesses, maternal and nutritional conditions. Overall, HIV/AIDS causes 40 percent of female deaths in Africa compared to the 14 percent of deaths resulting from maternal conditions. Communicable illnesses are also the major cause of mortality for African men, but they are less likely to die from communicable illnesses than women. Males in Africa have a somewhat higher mortality resulting from injuries. In Europe, cardiovascular disease and injury are major causes of male mortality. Men face much higher mortality rates than women in the Eastern Mediterranean region due to injuries. In South-East Asia, minimal differences between men and women manifest in mortality rates due to communicable illnesses. Men have slightly higher mortality rates due to non-communicable illnesses and injuries. In Latin America and the Caribbean, injuries are a major cause of death for men, contributing to higher male mortality rates in this region.

A final indicator that underscores a serious global health disadvantage for women is the surplus male population in the developing world. Approximately 50.3 percent of the world's 6.2 billion people are male, whereas roughly 49.7 percent are female. Records of live births across all societies indicate a "natural" sex ratio of 103–106 male births for every 100 female births. In China today, this ratio is 124 to 100 in favor of boys. India, South Korea, Singapore, and Taiwan have similarly distorted sex ratios. These sex ratios indicate a male surplus population. Globally, estimates suggest that 100 million women are "missing" from the total global population ("The Worldwide War on Baby Girls" 2010). The discrepancy results from gender-biased practices in areas of the developing world, most notably sex-selective abortion and the killing of girls in infancy. These practices stem from cultural preferences for boys in many societies. The neglect of female children, dowry violence, and other forms of domestic violence also contribute to surplus male population across the globe. This "gender paradox"—of longer average female life expectancy and health-adjusted life expectancy but a lower percentage of women in the world's total population—is concentrated largely in the developing world (Buvinic et al. 2006: 197). High-income countries have a higher proportion of women than men in the total population; this relationship is reversed in low-income countries, and it is especially pronounced in the region of South Asia.

As this section has shown, women and men face unique health challenges and, on average, experience divergent health outcomes. Thus, we can clearly say that a gender gap in global health exists. However, the health inequities between women and men do not just operate in one direction. Both men and women are negatively affected, in different ways, by inequitable health status and outcomes.

THE ROOTS OF THE GENDER GAP IN GLOBAL HEALTH

The gender gap in global health has roots in both biological and social causes. Some health disparities between men and women are rooted in biology, including health issues associated with male and female sex organs as well as genetic and hormonal variations between males and females. Ovarian cancer for women and testicular cancer for men are obvious examples of health differentials rooted in biology. In other cases, divergent health outcomes for men and women result from underlying cultural, social, and political factors that shape health behaviors, treatment, and access to health care.

Gender norms—the culturally prevailing constructs of presumed "normal," "appropriate," or "ideal" behavior and identities of men (masculinity) and women (femininity)—are among the most influential social causes of the differential health status of men and women. Dowry violence and female infanticide are prominent examples of health disadvantages for women and girl children that are rooted in gender. The higher rates of injury and mortality in occupations, like mining or construction, and the fact that men are more likely to be injured or die as combatants in war provide examples of gendered health disadvantages faced by men.

Notably, both biology and gender often work together to contribute to the gender gap in global health. For example, maternal conditions are sex-specific health challenges rooted in biology. Yet, the extent to which maternal conditions contribute to burden of disease depends very much on socially constructed gender norms that partially determine women's access to perinatal and postnatal care as well as the general social and economic determinants that shape women's health status around the globe. As the example of maternal health suggests, divergent health outcomes in some areas reflect legal and political biases, including the fact that men in most societies have dominated political decision-making over health care policy and budgets (Buvinic et al. 2006: 197). Male biases in medical research also are pertinent, as reflected in the practice of conducting research with only male subjects but developing medical practices based on this research on the presumption that the findings also will be applicable to women.

Gender biases may also play a fundamental role in shaping the data that suggests the existence of a gender gap in global health. As indicated in the previous section, global data suggest a male disadvantage on several health indicators. Such a finding appears to be counterintuitive and is in tension with the reality that many men, especially elite men, enjoy economic, social, and political advantages due to the privileged status of masculinity in most societies. On the one hand, the health disadvantages faced by men signal that the presumption of the uniformly positive benefits of "male privilege" oversimplifies reality. Other variables, including economic, ethnic, and religious status, shape the health behavior and outcomes of men as well as women. On the other hand, the data suggesting a multidirectional gender gap in global health may be distorted by underlying gender biases. Incomplete health statistics, cultural norms that contribute to underreporting of certain diseases for women (including stigma associated with sexual diseases), and the fact that women are less likely to seek health care in many societies likely results in an underestimation of women's global burden of disease (Buvinic et al. 2006: 198). In short, although the health disadvantages faced by men are real, this component of the gender gap in global health may be exaggerated by gender norms which make it less likely that the health disadvantages faced by women are captured by the prevailing indicators used to measure the health status of populations.

Indeed, leading health indicators may not capture burdens faced by women globally that undermine the quality of their lives without necessarily constituting disease or disability or without being categorized as health challenges. For instance, women in the developing world, especially in rural areas, commonly have primary responsibility for running households. Women often are responsible for child-rearing, growing and cooking food for the family, obtaining water for the household, which often involves walking significant distances, caring for frequently-sick children, and facing high mortality rates among their children. These burdens are especially pronounced in high-fertility countries where women are often pregnant and raising several young children at the same time. These sorts of socio-economic burdens may negatively affect the quality of women's lives without necessarily resulting in diseases or disabilities that show up in general health indicators. This caveat suggests that there are limitations to treating health as a discrete variable independent of its social and economic context. Thus, feminist scholars of international relations interested in the gender gap in global health will be well-served by placing the analysis of global health into the larger context of economic and social development.

Methodological and data collection/reporting practices by international organizations and scholarship in global health also raise questions about the comprehensiveness of global data on men's health. Unfortunately, international organizations do not consistently gather or report data on men's burden of disease, complicating efforts to provide a comprehensive overview of sex differentials in the global health status of men and women. Notably, the World Health Organization did not provide break-out data for the male burden of disease in its 2004 update report on the global burden of disease, though it did include a section on illnesses contributing to women's burden of disease. In a similar vein, most global health texts provide specialized chapters on women's health but do not include comparable chapters on men's health. The lack of attention to men's health seems especially problematic given that men have a health disadvantage on important health indicators, including life expectancy and health-adjusted life expectancy. The failure to provide comprehensive data on men's global health also complicates efforts to ascertain the extent to which there are biologically-rooted and gender-based inequities between men and women's health because of the lack of data for the purposes of comparison.

THE EVOLUTION OF INTERNATIONAL RESPONSES TO WOMEN, GENDER, AND GLOBAL HEALTH WITHIN THE UNITED NATIONS SYSTEM

The United Nations and its affiliated agencies play a critical role in norm creation and dissemination on a range of global issues. Global health initiatives led by UN organs and affiliated agencies have evolved from a narrow focus on women's fertility and maternal health to a much broader formulation of women's health rights. It is important to note that the United Nations is not a monolithic institution, and different agencies within the UN system have responded to women's health in a different and frequently highly competitive manner (Miller and Roseman 2011). An in-depth consideration of the intra-UN contestations over how to frame and conceptualize women's health goes beyond the scope of this chapter. Instead, this chapter will focus on the general evolution of the framing of women's health in major UN conferences and declarations. In this regard, the UN's overarching approach to global health initiatives has remained rooted in an outlook that conflates gender with biological sex and remains focused almost exclusively on women's issues alone. As a result, the UN fails to consider the gender constraints that shape women's health-seeking behavior and health outcomes and, at the same time, neglects health challenges that disproportionately affect men.

UN efforts to address global health disparities between men and women began, in the 1960s and 1970s, with a narrow focus on only a few issues related to women's health. During this period, international women's health initiatives emphasized efforts to curb population growth through a focus on women's fertility behavior. Global health funding and programming during this era also was directed towards maternal and child health, though the primary emphasis was on children rather than mothers (Buvinic et al. 2006: 196). During the 1980s, global health programming remained focused on maternal and child health. However, the UN focused to a greater extent on the health needs of mothers and considered ways in which gender norms affected maternal and child health (Buvinic et al. 2006: 196). For example, the UN Women's Conference in Nairobi identified health as a key theme for achieving broader goals of peace, equality, and development. The report identifies women as intermediaries between the natural environment and society and asserts their central role in providing safe water, fuel supplies, and sanitation. To this end, the Nairobi report (par. 28) asserts that improving the situation of women could help reduce mortality, morbidity, and population growth in ways that will benefit the environment. The report (par. 29) notes that efforts to control fertility rates and population growth must be done in ways that protect basic reproductive rights (United Nations 1986).

When it placed reproductive health and rights on the women's health agenda during the 1990s, the UN broadened its focus yet further. UN agencies also started to draw attention to gender violence during this period (Buvinic et al. 2006: 208). The Vienna Declaration, adopted by the World Conference on Human Rights in 1993, condemns all forms of gender-based violence. Article 37 calls for the United Nations to integrate the equal status and human rights of women into the mainstream of its activities, bodies, and mechanisms, a process that has come to be known as "gender-mainstreaming."

The report of the 1994 UN Conference on Population and Development calls for the full participation of men and women in productive and reproductive life, "including shared responsibilities for the care and nurturing of children and maintenance of the household." (Article 4.1) The report calls for such shared responsibilities, in part, as a means for reducing work burdens and power inequities that undermine women's health. The report also prioritizes basic reproductive rights and the reproductive health needs of women. Furthermore, the report draws attention to the social and economic risks that make women especially vulnerable to HIV/AIDS. The conference report also calls for equal relationships between men and women as a means for promoting sexual and reproductive health. Finally, it identifies violence against women, including domestic violence and rape, as threats to women's health and also names FGM as a harmful traditional practice that undermines women's rights and women's health.

The Platform of Action of the Fourth World Conference on Women in Beijing (1995) contains a similarly broad formulation of women's health rights. This report asserts the right of women to the highest attainable standard of physical and mental health, echoing the norms articulated in international human rights treaties to be discussed in the subsequent section of the chapter. Paragraph 89 of the report asserts that the fundamental right to health has not been achieved by the majority of women. Paragraph 90 notes that women have different and unequal access to basic health resources, including primary health care. It highlights gender biases in national health policies and health systems. Paragraph 91 contends that decreases in public health spending disproportionately harm women. In paragraph 93, the report draws attention to discrimination against girls, including son preference, access to nutrition, and access to health services, as practices that undermine the health of female children. The Platform of Action reiterates the calls in the 1994 UN Conference on Population and Development for sexual and reproductive health and rights for women. It also echoes the calls in previous UN reports for attention to gender-based violence as a threat to women's health. The Platform of Action goes beyond previous UN reports in identifying armed conflict as a fundamental threat to women's health and well-being.

The Millennium Development Goals, originating in the 2000 Millennium Devlopment Summitm, also prioritize women's issues that are pertinent to female health status and outcomes. Goal 3 calls for the promotion of gender equality and the empowerment of women, specifically targeting the elimination of gender disparities in primary and secondary education as an objective. Goal 5 calls for the improvement of maternal health, with the specific goal of reducing the maternal mortality ratio by three-quarters. To this end, the MDGs call for an increase in the proportion of births attended by skilled health personnel. Specific women's health issues addressed in the MDGs are not as broad as some of the global health initiatives coming out of UN-affiliated agencies in the 1990s. That said, the MDGs also prioritize a number of health-related goals, including the eradication of extreme poverty and hunger and combating HIV/AIDs, malaria, and other diseases, which create disproportionate health burdens for women.

These international efforts to bring women's health issues into focus, from the 1960s to the present, represent important progress towards recognizing inequities in the global health status of women and men. At the same time, these global health initiatives and programs share some of the same limitations of efforts to reduce gender inequities in other issue areas. For instance, the UN and its affiliated agencies have pursued a gender-mainstreaming approach in their efforts to promote peace building and post-conflict justice in war-torn societies. However, the UN has often conflated the concepts of gender and biological sex and, in doing so, has limited its ability to effectively ameliorate gender inequities in peace building and post-conflict justice processes. In particular, the UN and its affiliated agencies have typically used the term gender to denote women and children. In accordance with the equation of gender with women and children, the UN has made the mistake of assuming that international organizations can simply "add women and stir" in order to combat gender inequities (DeLaet 2008: 323-324).

In a similar vein, gender mainstreaming approaches to global health that simply incorporate attention to women's issues without seriously engaging with the gender constraints that shape women's health-seeking behavior and health outcomes will not lead to appropriate or adequate responses to global health challenges faced by women. At the same time, a gender mainstreaming approach that equates "gender" with women's issues will fail to consider health disparities, including occupational injuries and war-related violence, which present particular challenges for men.

WOMEN, GENDER, AND GLOBAL HEALTH IN INTERNATIONAL HUMAN RIGHTS LAW

A wide variety of international treaties contain provisions relevant to a human right to health. The 1951 Genocide Convention prohibits acts, including killing and causing serious bodily or mental harm, that are committed with the intent to destroy, in whole or in part, members of particular national, ethnic, racial, or religious groups. These prohibited acts have obvious health implications for members of targeted groups. The International Covenant on Economic, Social, and Cultural Rights (ICESCR), which entered into force in 1976, codifies a human right to health in Article 12. The International Covenant on Civil and Political Rights (ICCPR), which also entered into force in 1976, contains a number of articles that indirectly suggest basic health rights for human beings, including prohibitions against the arbitrary deprivation of life, torture, slavery, and arbitrary detention. Even though the ICCPR does not specify the health implications of these rights, all of these fundamental civil rights are relevant to bodily integrity, which has obvious connections to physical and mental health. The 1979 *Convention on the Elimination of Discrimination Against Women* (CEDAW) also contains provisions relevant to a human right to health. The 1984 *Torture Convention* prohibits torture and other cruel and degrading treatment. In doing so, it further elaborates on the bodily integrity rights codified in the ICCPR. The *Torture Convention* does not explicitly discuss the health implications of these bodily integrity rights, though they have obvious connections to physical and mental health. Finally, the 1989 *Convention on the Rights of the Child* (CRC) contains provisions relevant to children's health rights.

The International Covenant on Economic, Social, and Cultural Rights (ICESCR) is the core international legal document establishing a human right to health under international law. Article 12 of the ICESCR asserts "the right of everyone to the highest attainable standard of physical and mental health." As the language in Article 12 indicates, this right to health is articulated in gender-neutral and universalist language. All human beings have a right to health. They have a right to the highest attainable standards of health, not merely to minimal health standards. The right to health is framed broadly to encompass mental as well as physical health. The ICESCR also specifically recognizes the right to a decent standard of living, food, and housing, all basic needs that are essential to fulfilling a human right to health. Although the core rights claims asserted in the ICESCR are made in gender-neutral language, the treaty also underscores particular health needs of women and children. In identifying specific steps that state parties should take to realize the human right to health, Article 12 calls for reductions in still-birth rates and infant mortality and affirms the importance of promoting the healthy development of the child. Article 10 calls for special protection for mothers before and after childbirth and indicates that the employment of children in work that could be harmful to their health should be punishable by law.

In addition to the ICESCR, the 1979 Convention on the *Elimination of Discrimination Against Women* (CEDAW) is the other key international treaty that contains provisions explicitly relevant to a human right to health. CEDAW goes further than the ICESCR in outlining provisions that specifically relate to particular health challenges and needs of women. For example,

CEDAW contains provisions asserting that women have a right to equal access to family planning information and services, to basic prenatal care, and to maternity leave with pay. Article 4 notes that special measures aimed at accelerating de facto equality between men and women shall not be considered discriminatory. Article 5 calls for modifications in the social and cultural patterns of conduct of men and women with a view towards eliminating prejudices and practices based on the idea of the inferiority or superiority of either sex. Article 11 calls for state parties to eliminate discrimination in the right to protection of health and safety in working conditions. Article 11 also calls for measures that would prevent discrimination or dismissal due to pregnancy or maternity leave, calls for states to offer maternity leave with pay or comparable social benefits and to provide special protections to women during pregnancy working in harmful conditions. Article 12 calls upon state parties to eliminate discrimination in health care in order to ensure equal access to health care services, including family planning. It calls for state parties to ensure women access to appropriate health services for pregnancy, birth, and post-natal health needs. Article 14 calls upon state parties to pay particular attention to the needs of rural women, including health care needs.

This brief overview of international human rights law indicates that the human right to health is codified in largely gender-neutral language. To the extent that international human rights law contains provisions that are not formally gender-neutral, most deviations from gender-neutrality involve language that calls for attention to the particular health needs of women. Both the ICESCR and CEDAW contain provisions calling for special protections for women before and after childbirth. CEDAW contains provisions calling for state parties to provide maternity leave with pay or comparable social benefits. It also calls upon states to take steps to prevent discrimination or dismissal due to pregnancy or maternity. These deviations from pure gender-neutrality in favor of women may be logical given women's biological role in pregnancy and child-bearing. On the other hand, the provision calling for maternity leave (without parallel language requiring paternity leave) reinforces assumptions that women do (and should have) primary responsibility for child-rearing and, in doing so, may reinforce gender structures that are disadvantageous to women.

In addition to these special protections related to particular health needs of women, CEDAW also contains a provision that calls for gender equity for both men and women. As mentioned previously, Article 5 deals perhaps most directly with the concept of gender as socially constructed ideals about the proper roles, behaviors, and identities of men and women. It calls for modifications in the social and cultural patterns of conduct for men and women, with a view towards eliminating prejudices and practices based on the idea of the inferiority or superiority of either sex. Article 5 stands out from other provisions in international human rights law in relation to the concept of gender. Most provisions of international human rights law are gender-neutral in the sense that they merely call for equal treatment for women and men. Other provisions of international human rights law call for special attention to the particular needs of women. In contrast to both of these approaches, Article 5 highlights the importance of paying attention to socially constructed gender norms in any efforts to promote fundamental human rights. Moreover, it does so in a way that acknowledges that men as well as women might be harmed by prejudices or practices based on the idea that either men or women are inferior or superior. In this way, Article 5 might be seen as "gender-proscriptive" rather than gender-neutral.

This overview of provisions codifying a human right to health suggests that global health norms embedded in international human rights law are largely gender-neutral with a few provisions that might be considered "biased" in favor of women. However, this bias does not in any way suggest that international human rights law creates health advantages for women or health disadvantages for men. To the contrary, the provisions of international human rights law that single out the specific health needs of women presume women and children as a vulnerable category and, in doing so, may cast women as victims rather than agents in international relations. In this way, international human rights law may reinforce rather than challenge gender norms and structures that (re)produce women's subordination. For example, provisions that call for maternity leave but not paternity leave reinforce the presumption that women have primary responsibility for child-rearing, an assumption that limits the range of economic and social options available to both women and men. Notably, gendered assumptions about women's responsibility for childrearing can have a significant impact on women's health status, for example, by limiting the likelihood that they will engage in income-generating work or have access to employer-provided health care.

Moreover, the state-centric nature of international human rights law suggests that it will have, at best, minimal effects on actual state behavior. International human rights law contains ambivalent language in terms of creating concrete state responsibilities, loopholes that ultimately defer to state sovereignty, and weak enforcement mechanisms. As a result, international human rights law primarily functions as a political tool that can be used to advance specific rights-based causes. In this regard, the emphasis on women's particular health needs in international human rights law might provide women's health advocacy organizations with a potential political instrument for advancing arguments intended to improve the health and well-being of women around the globe that is not available to proponents of men's health. Because rights-based instruments governing health norms do not include enforceable, concrete obligations on the part of states, it cannot be said that international human rights law creates any specific health benefits or advantages for women. Instead, it is essential to look beyond norm creation and international human rights law to global health initiatives and programming as an indication of the extent to which global norms contribute to or exacerbate the gender gap in global health.

IS GLOBAL HEALTH GENDER-NEUTRAL?

Global health indicators suggest that global health disparities between women and men work in both directions, with particular health disadvantages for men as well as women. UN declarations and policy initiatives related to global health and international human rights law appear to suggest a mix of gender neutrality along with some norms that might appear to slightly favor women. However, any apparent gender gap in global norms on paper is meaningless if it does not translate into actual effects in practice. Indeed, an examination of the available data on global health aid indicates that, whereas UN initiatives and international human rights law formally prioritize women's health issues in some respects, global health aid itself tends to deemphasize health challenges that pose significant threats to women, including maternal/reproductive health and poverty-related health problems. In this regard, the evidence suggests a gender gap in global health aid that may work to the disadvantage of women.

At the outset, it must be noted that available data on global health aid is limited. Unfortunately, governments, international agencies, and nongovernmental organizations involved with global health initiatives do not maintain comprehensive records of spending on all global health funding initiatives. Where such records exist, they do not fully disaggregate global health aid by spending category. The Organization of Economic Cooperation and Development (OECD) gathers statistics on health spending by specific countries and on bilateral aid programs. It also collects data on international spending on various development programs, including health initiatives. However, these OECD statistics do not include consistent data on public health spending that corresponds to sex and gender differentiated health conditions and illnesses. Any effort to evaluate the nature of any gender gap in global health aid is further complicated by the fact that a complicated array of actors—including non-governmental organizations, states, and international organizations—finance a variety of global health initiatives. The quality of reporting by various donors varies, adding further complexity to efforts to utilize available health funding data to evaluate any gender gap in global health aid (The Institute for Health Metrics and Evaluation 2009: 52-53).

Because comprehensive and disaggregated data is unavailable, this chapter relies on more general information on funding of global health initiatives in order to draw preliminary if tentative conclusions about the nature of any gender gap in global health aid. A 2009 report by the Institute for Health Metrics and Evaluations shows that development assistance for health (DAH), which refers to external aid directed towards health-related development projects in low- and middle-income countries (The Institute for Health Metrics and Evaluation 2009: 15), has increased dramatically in recent decades, from $5.6 billion in 1990 to $21.8 billion in 2007. Publicly financed health aid constituted a majority of this money, and contributions from nongovernmental organizations also increased during this period. The report also concludes that DAH provided to low- and middle-income countries correlates positively with the burden of disease in these countries (The Institute for Health Metrics and Evaluation 2009: 8). Unfortunately, although this report disaggregates data by country and disease category, it is not compiled in a way that enables ready analysis of the question of whether DAH is distributed in a gender equitable manner.

A comparison of funding for HIV/AIDS programs with funding of other global health initiatives sheds some light on the question of whether a gender gap in global health aid exists. In recent years, HIV/AIDS funding has increased significantly in comparison to other important global health funding categories. Global funding for HIV/AIDS initiatives increased from approximately six percent of all global health aid in 1998 to roughly half of total global health funding in 2007. This dramatic increase in funding was paralleled by a major decrease in funding for other prominent global health issues. For instance, funding for health systems declined from roughly 62 percent to 26 percent of total health aid during this period. Similarly, funding for population and reproductive health declined from 26 percent to 12 percent of total health aid between 1998 and 2007 (Shiffman et al. 2009). At the same time, funding for other categories increased significantly in parallel with HIV/AIDS funding. Most pertinent to the analysis here, global health aid for maternal and child health increased by 105 percent from 2003 to 2008 (Pitt et al. 2010: 1485-96).

In terms of absolute numbers, the gulf between spending on HIV/AIDS and other global health initiatives is vast. Global health aid directed towards HIV/AIDS rose from $300 million in 1996 to $15.6 billion in 2008 (UNAIDS & The Henry J. Kaiser Foundation 2009). This figure includes aid from national governments, multilateral funding organizations, most prominently the Global Fund to Fight AIDS, TB, and Malaria, and the private sector. Development funds for health initiatives to fight tuberculosis and malaria were smaller but still significant. In 2007, global donors spent $0.6 billion on tuberculosis programs and $0.7 billion on malaria programs (The Institute for Health Metrics and Evaluation 2009: 25). Notably, HIV/AIDS received much higher levels of funding than either tuberculosis or malaria despite the fact that both of these diseases account for a higher percentage of the burden of disease in low- and middle-income countries.

As this data indicates, a clear disparity has emerged in global health aid between HIV/AIDS and other funding categories in recent decades. The fundamental question that must be addressed is whether this disparity is warranted. HIV/AIDS is the major cause of both male and female mortality in major recipient countries of Global Fund monies. In Africa, HIV/AIDS is responsible for both the largest proportion of burden of disease and is also the major cause of mortality among both males and females. In this regard, one might argue that the prioritization of HIV/AIDS in global health aid to Africa is not only gender neutral but also represents an appropriate response to one of the most vexing and devastating global health challenges in history.

Indeed, although HIV/AIDS receives a disproportionate amount of development assistance for health in both relative and absolute terms, it does not necessarily hold that this spending gap hinders progress on other global health challenges. No consensus exists among scholars or practitioners on the question of whether HIV/AIDS funding has spill-over effects that benefit general health systems or other specific health challenges in developing countries or, instead, diverts global health aid in ways that undermine the development of national health systems and programs targeting other diseases (Poku and Whitman 2012: 146-161). Proponents of the prioritization of HIV/AIDS in global health funding argue that this funding has positive spill-over effects that improve health outcomes in other areas as well and may contribute positively to the development of health systems within recipient countries (Shiffman et al. 2009). HIV/AIDS funding may benefit national health systems by raising the profile of public health as a policy priority, strengthening public health infrastructure, and expanding access to primary health care services as vulnerable populations participate in HIV treatment programs (Yu et. al 2008). Further, some scholars argue that regardless of the effects on general health care, the significant demographic and social effects of HIV/AIDS in "hyper-endemic" countries, particularly in Southern Africa and Eastern Europe, warrants disproportionate amounts of attention and funding in global health programs (Smith et al. 2011: 345-356).

Critics, however, charge that HIV/AIDS funding has hindered the development of strong national health systems by crowding out funding for general health care and other critical health priorities (Lordan et. al 2011 351-355; Shiffman et. al 2009). According to critics, the billions of dollars spent on HIV/AIDS not only inappropriately divert funding from other health priorities but also draw critical health care personnel away from work in key sectors of the health care system for more lucrative positions with HIV/AIDS programs (Yu et al. 2008).

For the purposes of this chapter, the question of whether or not global health aid directed towards HIV/AIDS enhances or hinders efforts to promote maternal health is particularly relevant. Notably, HIV prevalence is especially high among women in many developing regions. Women also constitute a majority of the HIV positive population in Sub-Saharan Africa. Thus, women in countries with high HIV prevalence are among the primary beneficiaries of the increase in global health aid for HIV/AIDS. Further, as noted previously, funding for maternal and child health has actually increased in parallel with the growth in HIV/AIDS funding. Between 2003 and 2008, a time period characterized by dramatic growth in global aid for HIV/ AIDS, development assistance for maternal and child health increased by 105 percent (Pitt et al. 2010: 1485-96). Thus, it seems apparent that women have benefitted from increased global funding for HIV/AIDS.

Nevertheless, the question of whether women benefit *more* from funding for HIV/AIDS than they would if the same level of funds were directed towards other health challenges faced by women is pertinent. In this regard, a consideration of global funding for maternal and child health in comparison with HIV/AIDS is instructive. Global funding relative to burden of disease from each of these health conditions indicates disproportionate emphasis on HIV/AIDS. Together, HIV/AIDS, tuberculosis, and malaria are responsible for 23.5 percent of the burden of disease in Africa. In comparison, neonatal infections, birth asphyxia and trauma, and prematurity/low birth weight cause 9.2 percent of the burden of disease. If you add diarrheal diseases to this figure, then newborn and child health issues constitute almost eighteen percent of the burden of disease. Thus, the percentage of DALY losses attributed to HIV/AIDS is just over five percent higher than DALY losses caused by child health conditions alone; this figure does not even include specific maternal health conditions.

The discrepancy between HIV/AIDS funding and development assistance for maternal/child health is striking. Global assistance to maternal, newborn and child health is significantly lower than funding for HIV/AIDS as well as tuberculosis and malaria. In 2006, just under $3.5 billion was directed to maternal/child health initiatives. That figure rose to $4.7 billion in 2007 and $5.4 billion in 2008. Even though funding for maternal/child health has increased in recent years, it is notable that it is significantly lower in absolute terms than global health aid for HIV/AIDS (Pitt et al. 2010: 1485-96).

Notably, a significant portion of global health aid for maternal/child health is channeled through HIV/AIDS initiatives, raising questions about whether maternal/child health funding is primarily a vehicle for targeting health challenges associated with HIV/AIDS or whether this funding emphasizes maternal/child health as a distinct and important health category in its own right.

Of course, as noted previously, HIV-infected women are among the primary beneficiaries of HIV/AIDS funding. Nevertheless, despite the fact that women constitute a majority of the HIV-infected population in many countries with high HIV prevalence, maternal/child health problems constitute a large proportion of the burden of disease for women in countries with high

HIV prevalence rates that is significantly disproportionate to the amount of aid directed towards these problems. Arguably, the devastating social and demographic consequences of HIV/AIDS warrant what has been called AIDS exceptionalism. (Smith et al. 2011: 345-356) One can argue, however, that maternal/child health challenges have equally pernicious demographic and social consequences that are not sufficiently considered by scholars and researchers. Female literacy and women's access to education are positively correlated with higher levels of economic development (Sen 2001). To the extent that persistent challenges related to maternal and reproductive health limit women's ability to pursue education, the failure to adequately fund maternal health initiatives has far-reaching social and economic consequences. In addition to the criticism that that global funding priorities do not reflect the burden of disease in recipient countries, other scholars have pointed out that global HIV/AIDS initiatives have not been integrated with existing health programs and structures to the same degree as reproductive or maternal health programs. As a result, it might be argued that increased funding for reproductive and maternal health would be more likely to generate spill-over benefits than HIV/AIDS initiatives that typically have been implemented as vertical, crisis-driven programs (Windisch et. al 2011)

A particularly egregious example of the ways in which global HIV/AIDS initiatives might actively work to the disadvantage of women involves the emergence of male circumcision as one of the primary global strategies for combating HIV/AIDS in developing regions. The results of three randomized, controlled clinical trials carried out in three separate locations in South Africa, Kenya, and Uganda indicated that male circumcision reduced the risk of HIV transmission by 50 to 60 percent. The strength of these findings led many scientists, practitioners, and public health officials to endorse male circumcision as a strategy for fighting AIDS in regions with high prevalence rates. Athough this policy has been widely embraced by key actors involved in framing the global health agenda, including the WHO and the Gates Foundation, critics argue that a range of methodological issues limit the validity of these findings. In particular, critics charge that it will be difficult to reproduce the same results in complicated social, cultural, and political settings in comparison with controlled clinical settings and that the resources required to scale up voluntary male circumcision programs would be better spent on other initiatives (Fox and Thomson 2010).

A detailed consideration of these criticisms goes beyond this scope of the chapter, however, one criticism is particularly relevant. The results from the clinical trial underlying the global push to adopt male circumcision as an HIV preventive strategy indicated that male circumcision reduced the risk of the transmission of HIV *for circumcised men via active penetrative sex in these controlled settings*. These studies did *not* indicate a reduced risk of transmission among the receptive sexual partners of circumcised men. To the contrary, evidence that male circumcision might actually increase the risk of infection among women exists. Previous studies have identified male circumcision as a risk factor for HIV infection in women (Chao et. al 1994). One of the concerns is that circumcision may increase the risk of infection among women who have sexual intercourse with recently circumcised men whose wound has not yet healed. Economic modeling provides indirect evidence that women will eventually benefit from male circumcision that reduces the risk of infection among infected men (Katz and Wright 2008). However, the reliance on projected future benefits seems a cavalier dismissal of immediate risks of increased infection among women and does not adequately consider the ways in which gender dynamics, the problem of sexual violence, and inequitable power structures often limit women's autonomy in sexual relationships (Baeten, Clum, and Coates 2007).

A number of challenges complicate efforts to draw further conclusions about the nature of the gender gap in global health aid. For one thing, the WHO classifies data by region, country income grouping, and age cohorts for the purpose of analyzing the burden of disease for women. When classified in this way, HIV/AIDS, tuberculosis, and malaria constitute the most important cause of burden of disease for women aged 15–59 in Africa. Maternal conditions constitute the second largest cause of burden of disease for African women in this age cohort. However, the causes of burden of disease would shift if the WHO categorized the data in a different way. For instance, if WHO looked simply at the burden of disease for women/girls without breaking out data for age cohorts, then maternal conditions and related childhood illnesses, rather than HIV/AIDS, likely would constitute a greater cause of burden of disease for women and girls in the developing world. Such a shift would have implications for funding priorities and programming directed at addressing causes of women's burden of disease in developing countries.

Furthermore, to explore the nature of the gap in global health aid, this chapter relies on data from the African region. At one level, it makes sense to look at the African region as a proxy for other developing areas because African countries are major targets for development aid due to extensive poverty and the concomitant poverty-related health challenges in the region. At the same time, Africa has unique patterns of morbidity and mortality in comparison with other developing areas. In Africa, the primary causes of DALY losses are HIV/AIDs, lower respiratory infections, diarrheal diseases, malaria, neonatal infections, birth asphyxia and trauma, prematurity/low birth weight, tuberculosis, road traffic accidents, and protein-energy malnutrition (WHO 2008: 45). Africa, especially southern Africa, is distinguished by especially high rates of HIV prevalence. Thus, global health aid directed largely at HIV/AIDS may be more appropriate in Africa than other regions.

In the region of the Americas, the top five causes of DALY losses are unipolar depressive disorders, violence, heart disease, alcohol use disorders, and road traffic accidents. In South-East Asia, lower respiratory infections, diarrheal diseases, heart disease, depression, and prematurity/low birth weight are the primary causes of DALY losses. Lower respiratory infections, diarrheal diseases, heart disease, neonatal infections and other child health conditions are major causes of DALY losses in the Eastern Mediterranean region (WHO 2008: 45). A similar pattern emerges in regards to causes of death across these regions. In the Americas, injuries are the major cause of death among adults, followed by cardiovascular diseases, communicable illnesses (not including HIV/AIDS), and cancers. In South-East Asia, the leading causes of adult mortality are injuries, infectious and parasitic diseases, cardiovascular disease, and other communicable illnesses (not including HIV/AIDS). The Eastern Mediterranean region follows a similar pattern (WHO 2008: 17). The WHO does not consistently disaggregate morbidity and mortality data by sex across regions. However, it is notable that a number of the major causes of morbidity and mortality in these regions, including depression, lower respiratory illnesses, and maternal and child health conditions, disproportionately harm women's health. At the same time, other major causes of illness and death in these regions, including injuries, alcohol use disorders, and road traffic accidents, have gendered dimensions that are more likely to have negative effects on men's health.

The regional differences in burden of disease data actually strengthen rather than limit the utility of the analysis being put forth here. Even in the African region, where HIV prevalence rights are the highest in the world, data suggest that HIV/AIDS is receiving a proportion of global health aid that does not reflect the actual burden of disease in the region and that this disparity has gendered implications to the extent that funding for maternal and child health conditions, reproductive health, and other women's health issues is not proportionate to the burden of disease in this category. This disparity is likely even more pronounced in other regions where HIV/AIDS does not have prevalence rates as high as those in the African region.

The extent to which funding gaps in global health aid exacerbate health disparities between men and women requires further investigation. However, maternal/child health, reproductive health, and health systems funding (which is essential to addressing basic health needs in countries with serious poverty-related health challenges) preliminarily suggests a gender gap in global health aid that works to the disadvantage of women. Additional questions remain. The preliminary analysis in this chapter assumes that examining the extent to which global health aid is directed towards the major causes of morbidity and mortality in the developing world will help shed light on the gender gap in global health. However, this assumption does not address questions of cost-effectiveness or efficacy of global health initiatives. The potential effectiveness of public health interventions also depends on health system capacity in targeted countries (Jamison et al. 2006: xiv). In addition, the analysis in this section has focused primarily on global health aid, rather than total health spending. When total health spending (including national expenditures on health) is taken into consideration, it is noteworthy that a small portion of total global health monies is spent in low- and middle-income countries, despite the fact that these countries carry most of the global burden of disease (The Institute for Health Metrics and Evaluation 2009: 3). This reality reminds us that some of the most significant disparities in global health are rooted in economics rather than gender or biological sex.

CONCLUSIONS

This chapter has described a gender gap in global health. This gender gap is a messy one that works in multiple directions, with gender inequities in health status and outcomes sometimes working to the disadvantage of women and in other cases to the disadvantage of men. Global health initiatives within the UN system have beneficially moved beyond a narrow focus on women's fertility to a broader focus on women's health rights. In doing so, global norms generated within the UN system have helped to raise the profile of women's health issues and have helped to generate funding and programming directed at women's health. The prioritization of women's health issues in the Millennium Development Goals is a prominent case in point.

Despite broadening its approach to women's health, the UN has not engaged the concept of gender in a meaningful way that would lead it to focus on the gender constraints that shape the health of both women and men. Health-related provisions in international human rights law are largely gender-neutral, with some provisions that appear to favor women. However, international human rights law has not produced concrete, enforceable health benefits for women and, by conceptualizing women as a vulnerable category in need of special protection, may reinforce gender norms that rationalize the subordination of women. Moreover, the need to take an expansive look at global health challenges for women comes out in the chapter by Marinova and James on human trafficking.

Similarly, the chapter also suggests that health challenges that pose significant threats to women, including maternal/reproductive health and poverty-related health problems, are under-funded. Although the UN and its affiliated agencies have given women's health issues an apparently prominent place on the international agenda, the visibility of rhetoric on women's health issues has not been effectively translated into policy by either international organizations or states. (This point parallels the citations of U.S. policy in the chapter by Baird, which draws attention to the uneven performance of the

United States, as well, regarding women's global health.) Indeed, the evidence explored here suggests a gap in global health aid that works to the disadvantage of women's health. For example, the significant growth in global health aid directed towards HIV/AIDS has been accompanied by a diminishing proportion of funds directed towards maternal/child health programs.

Moving forward, additional research is necessary to determine the extent and nature of the gender gap in global health. The agenda needs to encompass even legal issues, as the chapter by Sjoberg reveals. Numerous questions remain. How do global norms shape sex and gender differentials in global health? Are current patterns in global health aid appropriate for addressing gender inequities in global health? Specifically, are HIV/AIDS programs the best way to advance women's health in developing countries, or would money be better spent on poverty-related health challenges, including child and maternal mortality and the lack of access to adequate nutrition and clean water? Similarly, is the emphasis on HIV/AIDS in global health initiatives the most beneficial for men's health? Would funding of health programs designed to reduce occupational hazards for men be more beneficial? Should more international funding be directed towards reducing wartime violence in an effort to reduce war-related deaths among men? Should the international community prioritize development projects that will build up public health infrastructure in developing countries as a means to reducing poverty-related health challenges that affect both men and women in an effort to improve global health? All of these questions represent fruitful avenues for future research on the gender gap in global health.

REFERENCES

2010. "The Worldwide War on Baby Girls," *The Economist*, March 4.

Baeten, J.M., C. Clum, and T.J. Coates. 2007. "Male Circumcision and HIV Benefits and Risk for Women." *Lancet* 374: 182-184.

"Burden of Disease: DALYs." 2008. The Global Burden of Disease: 2004 Update. Geneva: World Health Organization.

Buvinic, M., A. Médici, E. Fernández, and A.C. Torres. 2006. "Gender Differentials in Health." Pp. 197 in *Disease Control Priorities in Developing Countries*, 2d. Ed., edited by D.T. Jamison, J.G. Breman, A.R. Measham, G. Alleyne, M. Claeson, D.P. Evans, P. Jha, A. Mills, P. Musgrove, Eds. New York: Oxford University Press; Washington, D.C.: The World Bank.

Chao, A. et. al. 1994. "Risk Factors Associated with Prevalent HIV-1 Infection Among Pregnant Women in Rwanda." *International Journal of Epidemiology* 23: 371-380.

DeLaet, Debra L. 2008. "Gender, Sexual Violence, and Justice in War-Torn Societies." *Global Change, Peace & Security* 20(3): 323-24.

Financing the Response to AIDS in Low and Middle Income Countries: International Assistance from the G8, European Commission and Other Donor Governments in 2008. 2009. New York: UNAIDS/The Henry J. Kaiser Foundation.

Fox, M. and M. Thomson. 2010. "HIV/AIDS and Circumcision: Lost in Translation." *Journal of Medical Ethics* 36: 798-801.

Human Development Report. 2009. United Nations Development Programme. Available online at http://hdr.undp.org/en/statistics/ .

The Institute for Health Metrics and Evaluation. 2009. Financing Global Health 2009: Tracking Development Assistance for Health. Seattle, Washington: The University of Washington. Available online at http://www.healthmetricsandevaluation.org/print/reports/2009/financing/financing_global_health_report_full_IHME_070.pdf.

Jamison, D.T., J.G. Breman, A.R. Measham, G. Alleyne, M. Claeson, D.B. Evans, P. Jha, A. Mills, and P. Musgrove, eds. 2006. *Disease Control Priorities in Developing Countries* 2d. Ed. New York: Oxford University Press; Washington, D.C.: The World Bank.

Katz, I. T. and A. A. Wright. 2008. "Circumcision—A Surgical Strategy for HIV Prevention in Africa." *New England Journal of Medicine* 359 (23): 2412-2415.

Lordan, Grace, Kam Ki Tang, and Fabrizio Carmignani. 2011. "Short Report: Has HIV/AIDS Displaced other Health Funding Priorities? Evidence from a New Dataset of Development Aid for Health," *Social Science & Medicine* 73: 3: 351-355.

Mathers, C.D., C.J.L. Murray, and J.A. Salomon. 2003. "Methods for Measuring Healthy Life Expectancy." *Health Systems Performance Assessment: Debates, Methods, and Empiricism*, edited by C.J.L. Murray and D.B. Evans. Geneva: World Health Organization.

"Millennium Development Goals: A Compact Among Nations to End Human Poverty." Human Development Report. 2003. New York: United Nations Development Program. Available at http://www.undp.org/hdr2003 .

Miller, Alice M. and Mindy J. Roseman. 2011. "Sexual and Reproductive Rights at the United Nations: Frustration or Fulfillment?" *Reproductive Health Matters* 19 (38): 102-118.

Pitt, Catherine, G. Greco, T. Powell-Jackson, and A. Mills. 2010. "Countdown to 2015: Assessment of Official Development Assistance to Maternal, Newborn, and Child Health between 2003-2008." *The Lancet* 376(9751): 1485-96.

Poku, N. and J. Whitman. 2012. "Developing Country Health Systems and the Governance of International HIV/AIDS Funding," *International Journal of Health Planning and Management* 27 (2): 146-161.

Report of the World Conference to Review and Appraise the Achievements of the United Nations Decade for Women: Equality, Development, and Peace. 1986. New York: United Nations. Available online at http://www.un.org/womenwatch/confer/nfls/Nairobi1985report.txt .

Sen, Amartya. 2001. "The Many Face of Gender Inequality," *The New Republic* September 17, 2001: 35-40.

Shiffman, Jeremy, D. Berlan, and T. Hafner. 2009. "Has Aid for AIDS Raised All Funding Boats?" *Journal of Acquired Immune Deficiency Syndromes* 52(1): S45.

Smith, Julia, Khaled Ahmed, and Alan Whiteside. 2011. "Why HIV/AIDS Should be Treated as Exceptional: Arguments from Sub-Saharan Africa and Eastern Europe." *African Journal of AIDS Research* 10 (Supplement 1): 345-356.

United Nations. *Report of the World Conference to Review and Appraise the Achievements of the United Nations Decade for Women: Equality, Development and Peace* (Nairobi, 15–26 July 1985). Available online at: http://www.un.org/womenwatch/daw/beijing/otherconferences/Nairobi/Nairobi%20Full%20Optimized.pdf.

United Nations. *Report of the International Conference on Population and Development* (Cairo, 5-13 September 1994). Available online at: http://www.un.org/popin/icpd/conference/offeng/poa.html.

United Nations. *The United Nations Fourth World Conference on Women: Platform for Action* (Beijing, September 1995): Available online at: http://www.un.org/womenwatch/daw/beijing/platform/plat1.htm.

Windisch R., D. de Savigny, G. Onadia, A. Somda, K. Wyss, A. Sié, and B. Kouyaté. 2011. "HIV Treatment and Reproductive Health in the Health System in Burkina Faso: Resource Allocation and the Need for Integration." *Reproductive Health Matters* 19 (38): 163-175.

World Health Statistics 2009. 2009. Washington D.C.: World Health Organization.

The Global Burden of Disease: 2004 Update. 2008. Geneva: World Health Organization.

Yu, Dongbao, Y. Souteyrand, M.A. Banda, J. Kaufman, and J.H. Perriens. 2008. "Investment in HIV/AIDS Programs: Does it Help Strengthen Health Systems in Developing Countries?"

Globalization and Health 4(8). Available at http://www.ncbi.nlm.nih.gov/pmc/articles/PMC2556650/.

Chapter Three

Social Norms and Policies on Prostitution and Trafficking

Nadejda Marinova and Patrick James

INTRODUCTION: A DEFINITION OF TRAFFICKING AND SCOPE OF THE PROBLEM

Human trafficking is a grave modern-day problem, and one of global dimensions. It represents one of the darkest chapters in the unfolding story of globalization. The United Nations estimates that at any given time, 2.5 million persons, the vast majority of whom are women and girls, are trafficked from 127 and exploited in 137 countries worldwide (UNODC 2007; UNODC 2009b). According to UN reports, approximately four-fifths of the people trafficked internationally are moved for purposes of sexual exploitation. The element of exploitation is inherent in the definition of trafficking, as stipulated in the 2000 *United Nations Convention against Transnational Organized Crime and its Protocols,* in particular the *Protocol to Prevent, Suppress and Punish Trafficking in Persons, Especially Women and Children.* In contrast to human smuggling, trafficking involves use of coercion or deception and, in instances of trafficking, transportation of the person must be for the very purpose of exploitation, without consent on the part of the individual (UN 2006).

States enact different policies towards prostitution and trafficking of persons. In this chapter, we primarily seek to examine the rationale for why three seemingly similar European countries have adopted different policies towards these problems. At this point, one might ask "what does this have to do with women's global health?" Given the inclusive mandate of this volume, it makes a great deal of sense to study human trafficking. State policies in this area have important implications for risks to women's health that result from human trafficking and the prostitution associated with it; sexually transmitted diseases, violence and drug addiction are only the most obvious examples. Thus the current chapter may be seen as the volume's most visible departure from a narrow construction of women's global health in terms of reproductive issues and the like. The chapter is deliberately inclusive in probing the effects of state policy in an area that needs more attention in general.

We begin the analysis by elaborating on the link between trafficking of women and prostitution. The next section draws on the theoretical contribution of International Studies (IS) feminists regarding the importance of norms in creating and reinforcing a specific social context. With regard to case selection, we compare characteristics of Sweden, Germany and the Netherlands (including the trend of trafficked women who originate mainly in the post-communist states of Eastern and Central Europe and in several African states) (Marinova and James 2012). The three countries' rationales for adopting different policy approaches to the problem then are reviewed. We further incorporate the scholarly literature to present an overview of the countries' diverse social norms. The final section of the chapter contains the conclusions.

LINKAGE BETWEEN TRAFFICKING AND PROSTITUTION

Trafficking and prostitution inherently are linked. This interconnection is acknowledged within the main theoretical approaches to the subject, which include: the prohibitionist and repressive viewpoints (both opposed to the legalization of prostitution); the abolitionist perspective (whose proponents believe in outlawing prostitution, but placing the penalty on the consumer of sexual services); and the laborist/sex-worker approach (whose supporters maintain that prostitution should be a legal form of work).[1] When applied as state practice, the last approach is sometimes known as "regulationist," as it involves the monitoring of legalized prostitution activities by governmental agencies.

While the theoretical prisms differ in their interpretation of the problematiques of trafficking and prostitution, they all envision a connection between the two (Marinova and James 2012). Analysts and activists who favor the prohibitionist and repressive approaches hold that prostitution should be unlawful, and consider that state actions against prostitution simultaneously address trafficking (Anderson and O'Connell Davidson 2002 in Jakobsson and Kotsadam 2010:6). In contrast, supporters of the laborist approach, who argue that prostitution should be regarded as work, oppose its criminalization, yet also denounce human trafficking (Jakobsson and Kotsadam 2010). These theorists consider that the solution lies in the placing of prostitution within the law, which would eliminate the exploitation implicit in its non-legality, including trafficking for sexual purposes. Finally, supporters of the abolitionist approach also envision prostitution and trafficking as inter-related. They maintain that outlawing prostitution and placing penalties on the buyer also will undercut trafficking. This combination of policies, from an abolitionist point of view, will contribute to the long-term goal of abolition of both trafficking and prostitution (Jakobsson and Kotsadam 2010).

GENDER DIMENSIONS OF THE ISSUE AND FEMINIST THEORIZING ON SOCIAL NORMS

We draw on the work of IS feminists, in light of the pronounced gender dimensions of prostitution and human trafficking.[2] Women are particularly susceptible to becoming victims of these interrelated crimes. UNODC data indicate that, among the 61 countries globally for which gender and age information is available, 79 percent of trafficking victims are female. This figure includes 66 percent women and 13 percent girls (UNODC 2009a; 2009: 11). Furthermore, an approximate 79 percent of trafficking worldwide, according to the United Nations Office of Drugs and Crime, is for the purposes of sexual exploitation (UNODC 2009b).

Studies on human trafficking reveal at least a partial explanation for the normative fabric underlying the existence of trafficking: the perpetuation of social norms that exclude and treat "the other" as inferior (Mohanty 1991: 23-24). A multi-country pilot study by the IOM on trafficking of women reveals the extent to which this phenomenon is demand-driven (Anderson and O'Connell-Davidson 2003). Based on numerous interviews with consumers of sexual services, the pilot study underlines that demand is socially constructed, generally among average citizens: "people are not born with the demand for paid sexual services any more than being born with the demand to drink Coca-Cola and play the lottery" (Anderson and O'Connell-Davidson 2003: 41-43). Even with awareness that the worker may be an "unfree" prostitute, users of sexual services predominantly view foreign trafficked sex workers as unworthy of the treatment that another woman or even a prostitute of the same country ought to be accorded. Therefore, the attitude towards exploitation often is rationalized with the notion that these women are from "backward" and "uncivilized" countries and thus are not entitled to the same rights as a fellow citizen (Mohanty 1991: 23-24). Mohanty (1991), whose conceptualization we apply to human trafficking, examines how citizenship laws incorporate norms and conceptions of the "other," not treating him/her as equal.

Research also reveals that the distinction between middle class/white/ European and poor/non-white/Third World identities intensifies suffering in the developing world. Enloe (2001) describes the impact on the international political system through the prototype of a white European woman on vacation in Jamaica. The actions of this white woman, when she employs a Jamaican maid, legitimate the job of the maid and, in the presence of other factors, reveal how self-esteem is damaged in the process (2001:1). In other words, Jamaicans in this process of employment begin to internalize a sense of inferiority, especially among the women (Enloe 2001). Such effects, if anything, are more pronounced regarding prostitution and human trafficking, which in the European context is also from less developed to wealthier states.

An IOM (2001) study illustrates attitudes towards trafficked women that bear a resemblance to what Moon (2000) describes for South Korea in particular. American servicemen have often regarded Korean prostitutes in military camps as "Orientals" who, by virtue of their origin and background, became justifiable targets of sexual objectification and exploitation (Moon 2000). Among the countries surveyed, IOM (2001) observes that the majority of men involved become aware that women are entered forcibly into prostitution. In spite of this involuntary aspect, the consumers of services offered by prostitutes view them as self-marketing commodities. In no instance among respondents for five countries does the percentage of those aware of trafficking into prostitution drop below three-quarters.[3]

IOM's report emphasizes that social attitudes are significant not only in the approach towards an unfree prostitute, but also in terms of the norms that prompt a man to seek sexual services. Consider Thailand, for instance. Men are more likely to seek prostitutes in order to maintain a "masculine" image within a fraternal group. By contrast, norms in a country such as Denmark are against soliciting the services of prostitutes (Anderson and O'Connell-Davidson 2003: 17-18). Over fifty percent of the interviewees in the survey, moreover, said they would report to the police a case of an unfree prostitute (Anderson and O'Connell-Davidson 2003: 24).

Actions of individuals are specifically influenced by the institutional, social, and cultural context (Anderson and O'Connell-Davidson 2003: 41-42): "These variations are unlikely to reflect individual differences of personality, and are more readily explained by the very different sets of socially agreed standards regarding the right and proper way to act in the commercial sex market (ideas that are reinforced by the state's response—or lack of it)" (2003: 42). Numerous feminist scholars from IS argue (Hooper 2001; Meyer and Prügl 1999, among others) that the conception of what is deemed acceptable in a society largely derives from norms that can perpetuate social settings detrimental to women. Societal traditions influence institutions and are important in reinforcing and delineating what is acceptable. Inequality thus can be traced to the more basic cultural setting. State and society then reinforce each other in perpetuating the norm that an inferior position for women is acceptable.

In terms of upholding the standard for maintaining gendered norms and paradigms, the role of the state is by no means novel. Ill treatment of trafficked women (i.e., regarding trafficking merely as a migration problem) by European governments parallels that of empires in reinforcing racist and gendered stereotypes over previous centuries (Sinha 1987, quoted in Hooper 2001: 71). By not addressing the issue of trafficking, modern European states effectively sanction and reinforce attitudes that victims are material objects and deemed unworthy of human rights (or even those rights accorded to prostitutes from the home country), due to their status of origin in less economically developed states. The basic idea put forward here in terms of a center and periphery in world politics, complete with relations of exploitation, is well-established in IF (Galtung 1980).

Detrimental gender approaches exist on the international level as well. These flawed dispositions, based on a sense of superior center versus inferior periphery, find expression in the security policies that states adopt. Such policies rarely include a concern for trafficking victims across international borders. A more convincing version of global security must be inclusive: "the achievement of peace, economic justice, and ecological sustainability is inseparable from overcoming social relations of domination and subordination; genuine security requires not only the absence of war, but also the elimination of unjust social relations, including unequal gender relations" (Tickner 1992: 128). Thus state security is just the surface issue; human security lies beneath it and components such as trafficking especially are neglected.

Norms in a society, in summary, impact upon public policy. To the extent that an issue resonates in the public sphere, egalitarian and/or non-egalitarian societal conventions held by citizens can explain a great deal of the guidelines that become enshrined into law and enacted within policy programs.

CASE SELECTION AND PURPOSE

We address divergent policies and underlying social norms, in the instances of Germany, the Netherlands and Sweden. The Netherlands and Germany legalized prostitution and adopted the laborist/regulationist stance approximately a decade ago, the former by lifting the ban on brothels in October 2000, and the latter by passing a law recognizing prostitution as a legal profession, effective January 2002. In contrast, abolitionist Sweden has outlawed prostitution since 1999 and punishes the buyer, not the prostitute.

The three states have been selected for a comparative inquiry due to their parallel characteristics, which include (in the period 1999–2010): shared

membership in the European Union, as well as adherence to the preponder-
ance of the same UN, OSCE and Council of Europe agreements. All three are
high-income economies located in Northern/Central Europe and are destina-
tion countries for trafficking (US State Department 2001, 2009). In all three
states, the basic data confirms that the trafficking trend is largely from the
post-communist democracies of Eastern Europe (some of them EU members), as well as from several countries in Africa, into the developed democracies of the EU.

Data on gender and age of victims, as well as on suspects in the three
cases, shows that trafficking is a crime generally organized and perpetrated
by men against young women between sixteen and thirty to thirty-five
years,[4] the majority of whom are under twenty-four years old. With regard to
characteristics of the perpetrators of trafficking crimes, they are primarily
men; in no country is the percentage of male trafficking suspects lower than
75 percent in any given year. Gender dimensions of human trafficking are
underlined by the fact, as former Dutch National Rapporteur on Trafficking
in Human Beings Anna Korvinus points out, that, as generally assumed (Van
Gelder 1998 in Korvinus 2003), men and boys are much less often victims of
trafficking in human beings than women and girls (Korvinus 2003: 63).
Wijers and Lap-Chew (1997, in Derks 2000: 14) also argue that trafficking is
not gender-neutral, since it concerns mostly women.

With the gender dimension in mind, we examine the normative context
underpinning the three states' adoption of dissimilar approaches to addressing trafficking and prostitution. The purpose of this chapter is hypothesis
generation rather than testing. With a focus on three states with a high
standard of living, membership in most of the same elite intergovernmental
organizations and location in the same region, the current research design
facilitates the search for causal mechanisms that differ from one case to the
next. Moreover, with so many *material* similarities among the states included
for study, intuition points toward a focus on *ideational* factors. In terms of
the volume's overall mission, this chapter looks at state policy as impacted
upon by societal norms in a relatively neglected domain of women's global
health. The end product of this approach, if intuition is confirmed, will be a
norm-based general hypothesis about state-level policy differences with regard to prostitution and associated human trafficking.

WHY A DIFFERENCE IN APPROACHES? NORMS IN GERMANY, SWEDEN AND THE NETHERLANDS

Divergence in policies is explained by the fact that fundamentally, Sweden,
Germany, and the Netherlands exhibit a different social construction of (a)
what a person's position in society should be; and (b) which values are

significant. Essentially, three distinct models are at work: the Dutch case reflects a pragmatism regarding social issues on which there is no consensus, and a "live and let live" attitude towards the matter, hand in hand with a focus on individual rights. In Germany, the overriding factor is conservative social values, which envision the woman's rightful place as a mother and protector of the home. Thus, the adoption of the regulationist (sex-work) approach in Germany reflects the reluctance of the majority to adopt any discourse on patriarchy. Outlawing of prostitution would translate into accepting the possibility of interpreting the discourse on prostitution as a form of patriarchy, perpetrated by men against women and their bodies. Alternatively, in Sweden, the 1999 legislation to ban the purchase of sexual services, which enjoys widespread support among the public, reflects the traditional Swedish values of equality and tolerance.[5]

Pragmatism prevails in the Netherlands. Prostitution is seen as inevitable and the question becomes "What is the best way to regulate it?" (Kavemann et al. 2007: 37-38; Outshoorn 2001; Vincenten 2008). In January 2010, a member of the City Council of Amsterdam remarked that the red light district was part of Amsterdam's status as a metropolis (RNW 2010). Prior to 1999, the Netherlands on paper had an abolitionist regime (Outshoorn 2001: 473). The Dutch Directorate for the Coordination of Equality Policy, the women's policy agency, beginning in the 1980s and into the 1990s, gradually accepted that prostitution can be a form of violence against women – but also a choice by a woman as work (Outshoorn 1998, 2000 in Outshoorn 2001). This distinction was eventually codified in the Penal Code (Outshoorn 2001: 474-475).

When the Dutch parliament debated the issue of prostitution prior to the passage of the 2000 law, the dialogue reflected two different visions about the fate of women. The distinction between voluntary and forced prostitution was incorporated in the position of the political Left (Outshoorn 2001: 477). As Outshoorn (2001: 476-477) observes: The potential conflict between prostitution as the exercise of male power and the right to sexual self-determination in the Left's discourse was solved by adopting the distinction between 'forced' and 'voluntary' prostitution. This allowed it to develop a position permitting both legalization and regulation. Reserving the sexual domination discourse for forced prostitution (later linked with trafficking of women from abroad, turning them into victims of trafficking), the Left drew on the sex-work frame when discussing voluntary prostitution, the third discourse used in parliament.

Dutch Christian Democrats, by contrast, decided to be pragmatic, maintaining that prostitution is an ill that cannot be eliminated in society, and one that does not fit with their beliefs. Thus, in order to protect the prostitute, this political party had to accept the existence of prostitution. The resulting passage of the law reflected the consensus of views expounded across the political spectrum in the Netherlands.

In Germany, prior to the Act Regulating the Legal Situation of Prostitutes (Prostitution Act), which came into force on January 1, 2002, no specific legislation pertained to prostitution. Before 2002, prostitution had not been forbidden completely, but restricted by a host of different legal regulations that left it in a grey area, with a number of related activities being illegal and unregulated (Kavemann et al. 2007: 3-4). The opinion that drove the change in the German decision to pass the new prostitution law is expressed in the words of Social Democrat Anni Brandt-Elsweiler in the Bundestag: "Norms aren't permanent values, but exposed to constant changes. Today a large part of the German population does no longer consider prostitution being immoral [sittenwidrig]" (Cited in Dodillet 2004: 6). Sittenwidrigkeit (immorality) is a term used in the German judicial system, according to which an act is defined as sittenwidrig (immoral) when it is in opposition to the social consensus. This interpretation became crucial in the debate. In the German parliament, ideas that are in sync with the traditional social system have a higher chance of being accepted. In this case, the rationale was that, as prostitution becomes increasingly a part of society and accepted, it no longer contravenes convention and cannot be forbidden (Dodillet 2004: 6).

The German policy reflects conservative norms to a great extent. These values find expression not only in the Christian Democratic view of prostitution as something immoral (sittenwidrig), but also in the notion of the family as the foundation of society that is dominant in Germany. During the times of Bismarck, in the 1880s, German social laws were based on the idea of the family as a central unit of society. The constitution in West Germany after WWII only strengthened that position; until 1976, a law required a wife to have the permission of her husband to work outside the house (Dodillet 2004:10; Bennhold 2010). In general, even feminist movements that have emerged in Germany tend to center on the role of a woman as mother. Positions that reflect on mechanisms of patriarchy are marginalized in German debates (Dodillet 2004: 13).

This marginalization was combined with a somewhat pragmatic view, shared by all politicians who took part in the debate in the German Bundestag, that prostitution cannot be abolished. An interpretation of prostitution as an expression of a patriarchal society can be found only in a legislative proposal of the Green Party from 1990. Nonetheless, subsequent debate saw that reference to patriarchy toned down by all parties. Instead of arguments on patriarchy, it was underscored that not only women but also men are affected by legal discrimination (Dodillet 2004: 9). Overall, during the parliamentary debates, lobbying of prostitution projects had an important impact on German legislators (Outshoorn 2001). In Germany, a one-page law was passed stating an intention to regulate the market and help improve the position of prostitutes (Kavemann et al. 2007).

Nonetheless, an analysis of the distribution of power in the society, which incorporates a strong gender dimension and references to patriarchy, could not gain ground in the German setting (Dodillet 2004:9). In October 2001 the prostitution law passed with the votes of the Social Democrats, the Green Party, the Liberals and the Socialist Party. The Christian Democrats voted against this law to recognize prostitution as a legitimate profession. They were driven by their view of prostitution as immoral and did not share in the shift in social consensus.

Traditional values of equality and concern with overall social welfare are reflected in Swedish legislation against prostitution and trafficking. The argument that attitudes towards prostitution reflect societal norms in this instance is advanced by Palmer (2000), who argues that socially engaged Swedes strive to uphold egalitarian values and institutions. In terms of collective constraints on everyday life regarding prostitution and pornography, among other issues, Palmer points out that those limitations reveal the social construction of consciousness. Swedes, Palmer holds, articulate and practice an ethic of solidarity, treating others as if already equal. This is corroborated by statements from the Swedish government, according to which "a gender equality perspective will inform throughout" a government inquiry into the effectiveness of the prostitution ban and its effect on trafficking for sexual purposes (Ministry of Integration and Gender Equality 2009: 15).

This outcome reflects the influence of the women's movement. In the case of Sweden the dominant belief is that "prostitution . . . gives rise to suffering, degradation, spreading of sexually transmitted diseases, compulsion and danger of outrage," as the Social Democratic Party described it in a bill from 1991 (Dodillet 2004: 1-2). In terms of the linkage between trafficking and prostitution, the view is that one cannot be separated from the other. "If we have no prostitution, or if there is no market for it, there is no trafficking," Ulla-Britt Hagström, a member of the conservative Christian Democratic Party, explained (Dodillet 2004: 1-2). Overall, in the case of Swedish citizens, the prevailing view is that prostitutes are victims. In the words of a legislator from the Swedish Liberal Party: "We know that the majority of the women who are prostitutes have been subject to sexual abuse of some kind during their childhood, or experienced drug abuse in the form of tobacco, alcohol or narcotics" (Dodillet 2004: 3).

Therefore, the distinction between forced and voluntary prostitution, which exists in the case of Germany and the Netherlands, is in fact regarded as absurd by Swedes (Dodillet 2004: 5). In the Swedish case, there is no such thing as a woman choosing to prostitute herself. Thus, the Swedish case incorporates a feminist understanding of prostitution as inherently unequal and patriarchal (Dodillet 2004). Essentially, feminist organizations such as

ROKS and Fredrika Bremerförbundet initiated the debate on prostitution and influenced the Swedish parliament, which incorporated a gender perspective into its analysis and subsequent vote (Dodillet 2004: 9-13). In the Swedish case, the legislation banning prostitution was a part of a more comprehensive package to advance gender equity, also targeting rape and assault, which came into force July 1, 1998 (Lazaruk 2005; Vincenten 2008). The Act Banning the Purchase of Sexual Services also enjoyed wide domestic support after its passage (Lazaruk 2005, Kavemann et al. 2007: 36, 39-41). The Swedish view is summarized by Social Democrat Ulla Pettersson: "By accepting prostitution society tolerates a humiliating perception of women. The view that women can be bought for money expresses a disdain for women as human beings" (cited in Dodillet 2004:4).

Additionally, an explanation for the divergent approaches can be found in an interpretation that sees the outcomes as being rooted in different political cultural assumptions, for example in the Netherlands and Sweden: different beliefs about the role of the state vary among those three societies, as well as their emphasis on collective versus individual rights (Vincenten 2008). On the one hand, in Sweden, the main question is how an issue will impact upon the view of an equal society (Dodillet 2004). This is linked both to a stronger state and a stronger focus on collective rights. On the other hand, in the Netherlands, there is a liberal view, in which the state is not to interfere with private lives of the individuals, but is more responsible for the preservation of social order in what Vincenten terms "conservative toleration" (2008: 43). Since the beginning of the 20th century, Swedish politicians have defined prostitution as a problem that needs to be eliminated, whereas Dutch politicians tend to see prostitution as a given and they merely seek to reduce the harm of the sex sector to society (Vincenten 2008: 21).

Sweden is characterized by a normatively "optimistic view on humanity," originating from the Enlightenment. The idea that human beings can be reformed and developed in such a way that they will be more inclined to do what is right has underpinned a combination of liberty with central control that characterizes state-society relations in Sweden since the 16th century (Rojas 2005: 7 cited in Vincenten 2008: 39-40). The role of the state in the case of Sweden in seeking to abolish prostitution can be attributed largely to a combination of (1) a weak liberal tradition; and (2) belief that the Swedish state has the prime responsibility for the establishment of the norms and values of society and legislation, signaling what is right and wrong (Dodillet 2005: 5 in Vincenten 2008: 37).

Alternatively, the Netherlands represents historically a more liberal tradition and a more heterogeneous society. In the Calvinist portrayal of mankind, humans are bound to sin and it is thought to be impossible to reform human nature (Vincenten 2008: 38). As Michael Wintle writes, "Dutch tolerance . . . has on the whole been a rather grudging acceptance that, although many people are wrong headed, they are unlikely to go away, and therefore should be incorporated and confined in the socio-political system as an exercise in damage limitation" (2000: 144, cited in Vincenten 2008: 38).

CONCLUSIONS

Why do countries that share a number of common economic and geo-political characteristics adopt contrasting approaches to prostitution and human trafficking? To assess more comprehensively the link between prostitution and trafficking, it is necessary to investigate the moral underpinnings behind the legality of certain procedures. Feminist theorists from IS have argued that equality or inequality prescribed by gender relations norms underpin the social and political decision-making context. These principles, when codified into law, determine state policies and may perpetuate unjust, or alternatively, more egalitarian gender relations.

The role of social norms in creation of law provides an explanation for the dissimilar country approaches on trafficking of persons and on prostitution in the German, Dutch, and Swedish cases. Conservative social norms and an emphasis on the family in society made acceptance of a feminist position unlikely and explain the German legalization of prostitution; a strong tradition of individual rights, toleration, and state non-interference in private affairs accounts for the Dutch legalization, and a focus on equality and the welfare of society at large underpins the Swedish abolitionist model.

From the standpoint of hypothesis generation, the study of norms and state policies carried out here produces encouraging results: Variation in social norms affects state policies with regard to prostitution and human trafficking for Germany, the Netherlands, and Sweden. Since the three states included in the present study vary only a little in terms of material conditions, it becomes a priority to include a wider range of cases in future research.

Further research is needed to investigate more closely the linkage between social norms and trafficking of women, particularly in countries that have differential socio-economic characteristics, as well as in those that serve as states of origin for trafficked persons, in order to more fully understand the normative context of some of the root causes of the problem. The exercise in hypothesis generation carried out here has occurred under the rubric of a highly inclusive sense of women's global health and, it is hoped, the results lend further support to that perspective on the subject.

REFERENCES

Anderson, B., and J. O'Connell-Davidson (2002) *Trafficking: A Demand Led Problem?* Save the Children Sweden, Stockholm.

Anderson, B. and J. O'Connell-Davidson (2003) *Is Trafficking in Human Beings Demand Driven? A Multi-Country Pilot Study*, International Organization for Migration (IOM), IOM Migration Research Series, No 15, Switzerland.

Bennhold, K. 2010. "In Germany, A Tradition Falls and Women Rise." 17 January. *New York Times*. http://www.nytimes.com/2010/01/18/world/europe/18iht-women.html.

Derks, A. (2000) "From White Slaves to Trafficking Survivors," Working Paper # 00-02m. The Center for Migration and Development, Princeton University, Princeton, NJ.

Dodillet, S (2004). "Cultural Clash on Prostitution: Debates on Prostitution in Germany and Sweden in the 1990's." Paper presented at the 1st Global Conference on Sex and Sexuality in Salzburg, 14th October 2004.http://www.inter-disciplinary.net/ci/transformations/sexualities/s1/Dodillet%20paper.pdf

Dodillet, S. (2005) "Cultural Clash on Prostitution: Debates on Prostitution in Germany and Sweden in 1990s." In: Sonser Breen, Margaret and Fiona Peters (eds.) *Genealogies of Identity: Interdisciplinary Readings on Sex and Sexuality* (Amsterdam: Editions Rodopi), pp. 39-56.

Enloe, C. (2001) *Bananas, Beaches and Bases: Making Feminist Sense of International Politics* (updated edition), Berkeley: University of California Press.

Galtung, Johan. (1980) "'A Structural Theory of Imperialism'—Ten Years Later." *Millennium* 9: 181-196.

Gelder, P. van (1998). *Kwetsbaar, kleurig en schaduwrijk. Jongens in de prostitutie: een verschijnsel in meervoud*. Amsterdam: Thela Thesis.

Hooper, C. (2001) *Manly States: Masculinities, International Relations and Gender Politics*, New York: Columbia University Press.

IOM (2001) *IOM Counter Trafficking Strategy for The Balkans and Neighboring Countries*, Geneva: International Organization for Migration. http://www.iom.int/en/PDF_Files/other/Balkan_strategy.pdf

Jakobsson, N. and A. Kotsadam. (2010) "The Law and Economics of International Sex Slavery: Prostitution Laws and Trafficking for Sexual Exploitation." Working Papers in Economics, No. 458. (June). Department of Economics, University of Gothenburg, Sweden. http://andreaskotsadam.files.wordpress.com/2010/06/trafficking.pdf

Kavemann, B, Rabe, H., and Claudia Fischer (2007) *Findings of a Study on the Impact of the German Prostitution Act*. September. Berlin: SoFFI K.

Kelly, L. and Regan, L. (2000) *Rhetorics and Realities: Sexual Exploitation of Children in Europe*, London Metropolitan University, Child and Women Abuse Study Unit (CWASU), London. http://www.cwasu.org

Korvinus, A.G. (2003) *Trafficking in Human Beings: Supplementary Figures. Second Report of the Dutch National Rapporteur*. Bureau NRM: The Hague, The Netherlands.

Lazaruk. N. (2005) *Assessing the Implications of the Swedish Prostitution and Trafficking Model*. MA Thesis. University of Victoria, Canada. http://dspace.library.uvic.ca:8080/dspace/bitstream/1828/847/1/lazaruk_2005.pdf

Marinova, N. K. and P. James (2012) "The Tragedy of Human Trafficking: Competing Theories and European Evidence." *Foreign Policy Analysis* 8: 1-22.

Meyer, M.K. and E. Prügl (1999) "Gender Politics in Global Governance." In M.K. Meyer and E. Prügl (eds.), *Gender Politics in Global Governance*, pp. 3-16. Lanham, MD: Rowman and Littlefield.

Ministry of Industry, Employment and Communications of Sweden (2004) "Prostitution and Trafficking in Women: Factsheet." Stockholm: Government Offices of Sweden. http://www.sweden.gov.se/content/1/c6/01/87/74/6bc6c972.pdf

Ministry of Integration and Gender Equality (2009) "Against Prostitution and Human Trafficking for Sexual Purposes." 15 October. Stockholm.http://www.sweden.gov.se/sb/d/11503/a/133671"

Mohanty, C. T. (1991) "Cartographies of Struggle: Third World Women and the Politics of Feminism," in Mohanty, C., Russo, A. and Torres, L. (eds), *Third World Women and the Politics of Feminism*, Bloomington: Indiana University Press.

Moon, K. (2000) *Sex Among Allies: Military Prostitution in US-Korean Relations*. New York: Columbia University Press.

Outshoorn, J. (1998) "Sexuality and International Commerce: The Traffic in Women and Prostitution Policy in the Netherlands," pp. 190–200 in T. Carver and V. Mottier (eds.). *Politics of Sexuality: Identity, Gender and Citizenship.* London and New York: Routledge.

Outshoorn, J. (2000) "Legalizing Prostitution as Sexual Service: The Case of the Netherlands," paper presented at the European Consortium for Political Research, Joint Sessions of Workshops, Copenhagen, 14–19 April.

Outshoorn, J. (2001) "Debating Prostitution in Parliament: A Feminist Analysis," *European Journal of Women's Studies*, Vol. 8, pp. 472-90.

Palmer, B. (2000) *Wolves at the Door: Existential Solidarity in a Globalizing Sweden*, Ph.D. Dissertation, Harvard University.

Rojas, M. (2005) *Sweden after the Swedish Model: From Tutorial State to Enabling State.* Stockholm: Timbro.

RNW (2010) "Restricting Amsterdam Red Light District." 19 January. Radio Netherlands Worldwide.http://www.rnw.nl/english/article/restricting-amsterdam-red-light-district

Sinha, M. (1987) "Gender and Imperialism: Colonial Policy and the Ideology of Moral Imperialism in Late Nineteenth-Century Bengal," in Kimmel, M. (ed.), *Changing Men: New Directions in Research on Men and Masculinity*, Newbury Park and Beverly Hills: Sage Publications.

State Department (2001) *Victims of Trafficking and Violence Protection Act of 2000: Trafficking in Persons Report*, Washington, D.C. http://www.state.gov/documents/organization/4107.pdf

State Department (2009) *Trafficking in Persons Report*, Washington, D.C. http://www.state.gov/g/tip/rls/tiprpt/2009/index.htm

Tickner, J.A. 1992. *Gender in International Relations: Feminist Perspectives on Achieving Global Security.* New York: Columbia University Press.

UN (2006) *The United Nations Convention against Transnational Organized Crime, the Protocol to Prevent, Suppress and Punish Trafficking in Persons, especially Women and Children, supplementing the United Nations Convention against Transnational Organized Crime*; Document A/55/383, United Nations. http://www.unodc.org/unodc/crime_cicp_signatures_trafficking.html

UNODC (2007) "UNODC launches Global Initiative to Fight Human Trafficking." 26 March. United Nations Office on Drugs and Crime. httphttp://www.unodc.org/unodc/en/press/releases/2007-03-26.html

UNODC (2009) *Global Report on Trafficking in Persons*, Vienna: United Nations Office on Drugs and Crime. http://www.unodc.org/documents/Global_Report_on_TIP.pdf

UNODC (2009a) *Global Report on Trafficking in Persons: Executive Summary*, Vienna: United Nations Office on Drugs and Crime. http://www.unodc.org/documents/human-trafficking/Executive_summary_english.pdf

UNODC (2009b) "UNODC report on human trafficking exposes modern form of slavery." 12 February. http://www.unodc.org/unodc/en/frontpage/unodc-report-on-human-trafficking-exposes-modern-form-of-slavery-.html

Vincenten, P. (2008) "Realism versus Idealism: A Historical Institutionalist Explanation of the Current Prostitution Policy of Sweden and the Netherlands," MA Thesis, Department of Political Science, Leiden, June 2008 http://www.iiav.nl/epublications//2008/Realism_versus_Idealism.pdf

Wijers, M. and Lap-Chew, L. (1997) *Trafficking in Women, Forced Labour and Slavery-like Practices in Marriage, Domestic Labour and Prostitution*, Utrecht: Foundation Against Trafficking in Women.

Wintle, M. (2000) "Pillarisation, Consociation and Vertical Pluralism in the Netherlands Revisited: A European view," *West European Politics* 23(3): 139-152.

NOTES

1. For an overview of the theoretical and policy outlooks that define state policies on prostitution, please see Marinova and James (2012).

2. The scope of theorizing in this chapter does not extend as far as world systems theory. With its emphasis on material conditions, notably class conflict and exploitation at a global level, world systems theory lies beyond the scope of this study, which draws more directly from IS-based feminism for its theorizing about norms.

3. The percentages are Japan (77), India (86), Thailand (89), Italy (96) and Sweden (100).

4. For Germany and the Netherlands, the majority are under 30. For Sweden, the reported information is that most victims are aged between 16 and 35, hence the 30/35 figure.

5. The legislation, passed in 1998 and effective January 1999, is very popular among Swedes. A poll in June 1999 reported that 76 percent of respondents favored the new law. By October 2002, its popularity had increased, with 81 percent of surveyed respondents in favor (Ministry of Industry, 2004:1).

Chapter Four

Morality, Legality, and Health

Laura Sjoberg

"Some women who want abortions trigger them by inserting sticks, knitting needles or spoons, for example, into their uteruses. Others may go to tradition-al healers or people with some medical knowledge, but who know little about abortions. The result can be infection and sterility or even death" (De Capua 2006).

Stories about the dangers of illegal abortions are incredibly common—so much so that a substantial literature concludes that, globally, when abortion is illegal, women's health suffers both directly (from illegal abortions and pregnancy) and indirectly (from the impacts of poverty). This literature seems, however, to "stop at the door" of the legality of abortion—assuming that it is a first step to correcting these problems. Crossing research interests between gender and global politics and discrimination law, this chapter ex-plores whether the positive effects for women's health are the same across abortion-legalizing countries. Particularly (controlling for poverty), this chapter explores the argument that both the degree of legality and the grounds on which abortion was legalized impacts upon the health results of legalization. Specifically, the project uses a comparative case study from Mozambique and Tanzania to argue that women in states that use justifica-tions which retain the taboo on abortion (such as privacy, health, rape, and third-party decision-making) get fewer health benefits from legalization than states which legalize abortion on grounds that transgress the prohibition (women's rights, labor issues). The chapter concludes with theoretical in-sights about the problem.

Before proceeding, however, it is important to note that nothing in this chapter is meant to espouse the belief that legalization is a catch-all answer to the health problems caused by unsafe abortions. First, (as argued below), legalization does not always lead to comfort when seeking legal abortions in health care facilities, and, certainly, the grounds of legalization are not the only influence on that willingness. Second, (of course) the availability of safe abortions in health care facilities depends not only on the level of legality, but also on the general quality of the health care system. This is in part a function of the level of economic prosperity, but in part a function of the overall quality of the health care system in a particular country. The engagement in this chapter with the grounds of legalization is undertaken because there is a (statistical and policy) consensus that legalization does have an impact decreasing the health risks of abortion, controlling for these other factors. This work is meant to explore the utility of going deeper into the question of whether all legalization has a similar effect, or whether legalization needs to be unpacked to be best understood.

THE HEALTH RISKS OF ILLEGAL ABORTION

When abortion is illegal, abortions still take place frequently (WHO 2003). The complication rate for illegal abortions is much higher than for legal abortion, where fully one percent of people who have illegal abortions die from complications and almost five percent have permanent health complications (WHO 2008). Legal abortion, by contrast, is actually less likely to cause fatalities than childbirth (Planned Parenthood 2002). Worldwide, between 50,000 and 80,000 women die every year from complications from illegal abortions (WHO 2008), and abortion-related deaths drop around ninety percent in the first five years of legality (Grimes et al 2006).

Scholarship in the fields of medicine, politics, economics, and the law establishes that unplanned and unwanted pregnancies (and illegal or unsafe abortions often used to end them) pose very serious challenges to public health, especially in the developing world and especially where abortion is illegal (e.g., Crane and Smith 2006). The issue of deaths from unsafe abortions was first placed on the agenda of the International Conference on Population and Development (ICPD) in 1994, and since then experts estimate that three quarters of a million women have died either during or directly because of the administration of unsafe abortions (Crane and Smith 2006). Increasingly, international attention has become focused on the health consequences of the illegality of abortion, especially in terms of its relationship to other goals concerning development and health care (e.g., Bloom et al 2009).

Crane and Smith (2006: 4) write about the relationship between the illegality of abortion and the United Nations Millennium Development Goals (MDGs), arguing that "the persistence of unsafe abortion in many countries is a key obstacle to meeting the MDGs." While a majority of the population of the globe now lives in states where there is at least some legal access to abortion, "thirty-six percent of the world's population lives in countries where laws permit abortion only to save the woman's life or to protect her physical health" (Crane and Smith 2006: 4, citing CRR 2005). Crane and Smith explain that this is a problem which ends up compounding itself in terms of health consequences and maldevelopment:

> Restrictive national laws, particularly in developing countries, result in inequitable access to safe abortion, large numbers of maternal deaths and injuries, and violations of women's sexual and reproductive rights. The women most harmed by restrictive laws and policies are usually those without financial means or social connections: women who are poor, adolescents, survivors of sexual violence, victims of racial or ethnic discrimination, or others in vulnerable circumstances. (Crane and Smith 2006: 4)

It is estimated that 46 million abortions take place each year, and 19 million of those are classifiable by the World Health Organization as unsafe—either by persons lacking the necessary skills to perform an abortion or in an environment that does not meet minimum medical standards (WHO 2004). Over their lifetimes, on average, nearly one unsafe abortion will take place for every woman in the developing world (Crane and Smith 2006: 5, citing Shah and Ahman 2009). It is estimated that deaths from unsafe abortion currently constitute about thirteen percent of all maternal deaths (WHO 2008). Of those, ninety-seven percent are in the developing world (WHO 2004). Some scholars see these estimates as conservative, and believe that, with unreported deaths, it is likely that between 115,000 and 125,000 women die every year from complications related to unsafe abortions (Machungo, Zanconato, and Bergstrom 1997: 1607).

This is where the analysis of the Millennium Development Goals is most potent—the target of the fifth MDG is to reduce maternal mortality seventy-five percent by 2015—a goal that it would be hard to imagine accomplishing without reducing deaths due to unsafe abortion. Still, according to a number of experts, these deaths "could be virtually eliminated by the provision of appropriate health information and services and through law reform efforts to allow such information and services to reach the women who need them" (Ernst and Diachok 2002: 7). In other words, a combination of legality and the provision of services might make the fifth MDG realizable, while the continued illegality of abortion unless a woman's life is in danger for many places around the world is a threat not only to women, but to health care and development.

Even when unsafe abortions do not kill women, they often cause very serious health problems. These harmful effects are documented less well, and paid less attention, than deaths from unsafe abortions. Side effects of unsafe abortions include "sepsis, hemorrhage, cervical trauma, uterine perforations, as well as chronic and permanent conditions" and are suffered by between ten and fifty percent of women who have unsafe abortions (AbouZahr and Ahman 1988). In this situation, "the probability of complications may be greater for a poor woman than for a nonpoor woman." The reason, in part, is that a nonpoor woman is likely to seek and pay a legitimate medical provider; but "even when the provider is the same, e.g., a medical doctor," because poor women are likely to have less information about the availability of abortions (and therefore have them later) and less likely to understand and/or be able to follow advice about how to care for themselves afterwards, their outcomes are worse (Prada et al. 2005: 25). Additionally, "poor women may not have the economic resources to buy antibiotics . . .[and] may have poorer overall health and nutrition" (Prada et al. 2005: 25). In a study on Uganda, half of women who induce their own abortions suffer serious health consequences; between one third and one half who seek out some sort of practitioner who is not a physician experience such consequences; and almost one third of rural poor women who have abortions from physicians still suffer serious consequences (Prada et al. 2005: 26).

These unfortunate outcomes occur partly because of the covert nature of illegal abortions. While other factors matter (in addition to poverty, there are influences from overall quality of the health care system, overall level of gender equality and reproductive rights for women, and religious influences, among others), research shows a negative impact of illegality—abortions are more unsafe when there are laws against them than they are when they are legal (Shah and Ahman 2009). When there are restrictive national laws, "the procedure is performed in secrecy and often under dangerous conditions" (Prada et al. 2005: 1). In these situations, "because of economic, geographic, and social disadvantages . . .poor women, especially those in rural areas, are most at risk" (Prada et al. 2005: 1). It is also partly because of the methods used when abortions are illegal that women suffer unduly. For example, while medical and vacuum abortions are the safest, in the case of illegal abortions, "about thirty-seven percent of facilities used dilatation and curettage only, which is known to contribute to a higher rate of complications and requires longer hospital stays" (Gallo et al. 2004: 223). As such, it is almost universally agreed that "prohibition of induced abortion does not lead to a reduction in the number of abortions, but the complication rate is markedly increased" (Justesen, Kapiga, and van Asten 1992: 328). Given that fully half of abortions that take place every year are illegal and most of those take place in places where abortion is illegal, advocates strongly urge legalizing abortion to benefit the health of women seeking abortions (Myers and Seif 2010).

THE CONVENTIONAL WISDOM: LEGALIZED ABORTION HELPS WOMEN'S HEALTH

Conventional wisdom is that legalizing (or lightening the laws against) abortion makes it safer for a number of reasons. One is pure access. Women are more likely to have safe abortions when safe abortions are an option for them (WHO 2008). Another is availability of technology to practitioners. When abortion is legal, appropriate technology to perform the procedure is more likely to be available (Robertson 2011). A third is the methods practitioners use—in the Western/developed world, where abortion is now almost universally legal, a vacuum method is usually used (Salhan and Kaul 2012). Yet, for example, in Uganda, where abortion remains illegal in all circumstances, "nearly all (ninety-six percent) of [practitioner] respondents reported that dilation and curettage is used" (Prada et al. 2005: 8). In this sense, the legality of abortion is likely to provide women with not only access and technology, but the availability of reliable methods as well.

Legal abortion, as the argument goes, saves the lives of women with heart disease, kidney disease, anemia, and severe diabetes who would have serious medical complications with pregnancy (e.g., Drenthen, et al 2010). It decreases the rate of "children having children," where those parents and children are most likely to die of starvation and preventable disease (Regushevskaya 2009). As Crane and Smith (2006: 16) argue, "safe abortion is clearly an issue of economic and social justice."

A number of studies have demonstrated that legality matters. In places where abortion is illegal, "the dire health consequences of illegal abortion are obvious primarily from the fact that 3% of the women suffered a maternal death" (Machungo, Zanconato, and Bargstrom 1997: 1611). In addition, "about one fourth of them suffered severe and potentially life-threatening sequelae necessitation blood transfusions, parenteral antibiotics, and prolonged hospital stay" (Machundo, Zanconato, and Bargstrom 1997: 1611). On the other hand, legality is likely to change those tragic statistics. As Crane and Smith point out, "evidence points to a strong correlation between liberal abortion laws and policy, safer abortion, and lower maternal mortality" (Crane and Smith 2006: 7, citing Berer 2004). As Bernstein and Rosenfield explain:

> Women who do not want to be pregnant will go to extraordinary means to end the pregnancy. The concern, therefore, really should be whether abortion is safe or unsafe which, in most cases, equates with its legal status. But even where abortion is legal, access to safe abortion procedures is also essential (Bernstein and Rosenfield 1998: S116).

Bernstein and Rosenfield (1998: S118) use the case of the United States as an example, where abortion case-fatality rate was almost one percent previous to the legalization of abortion, and is now less that 0.3 per 100,000 abortions. When abortion is legalized, they argue, "the number of deaths due to abortion complications drops significantly" (Bernstein and Rosenfield 1998: S119).

COMPLICATING THE CONVENTIONAL WISDOM

Looking deeper into some of the cases of legalization of abortion, this chapter argues that, while legalizing abortions is likely necessary to decreasing the death rate from unsafe abortions, it is not sufficient. A number of sources in the literature acknowledge this point already. For example, Crane and Smith note that "among those countries where abortion is allowed by law only to save the woman's life or in the case of rape, safe public sector services are commonly not available even for eligible women" (Crane and Smith 2006: 4). This implies (though it does not assert) that the degree of legality matters. Likewise, Agadijanian (1998: 114) implies that the maintenance of a taboo against abortion seems to matter as much if not more than the technical legalization, explaining that "the more serious opposition to abortion stems from deeply entrenched pronatalist attitudes and the enduring perception of the high economic and social value of children."

Abortion is legal for some reason in most countries in the world (WHO 2008 reports 98 percent), yet most countries in the world also maintain constraints on the situations in which abortions may be obtained (WHO 2008 reports forty-five percent, though that does not control for timing restrictions, which make it closer to ninety percent). Given this, it is worth asking whether (and if so, how) conditions on the availability of abortion to women interact with the health-beneficial impacts of the legalization of abortion. As Agadijanian notes in reference to sub-Saharan Africa, "although the post-colonial era has seen a gradual liberalization of abortion legislation in many young nations, almost all Sub-Saharan countries continue to ban abortion on request, and clandestine abortion is rampant" (Agadijanian 1998: 111). Likewise, according to a study:

> As the Zambian experience has shown, legalization of abortion on request does not necessarily eliminate the problem of clandestine abortion, because of insufficient information and outreach and limited technical capacity of legal abortion services (Agadijanian 1998: 115, citing Castle, Likwa, and Wittaker 1990).

As such, it may be important to think about the intervening variables between the legalization of abortion and the widespread availability of safe abortions to women who would otherwise avail themselves of illegal and usually unsafe abortions. The existing literature that does deal with this, like the discussions cited above, focuses mostly on questions of capacity. These questions of capacity address both the ability of (1) medical providers in the state with legal abortions to obtain the equipment and expertise to perform abortions safely and (2) those providers and governments to team up to educate women who might be seeking abortions. While both of these factors are undoubtedly important, data suggests (e.g., Machungo, Zanconato, and Bergstrom 1997) that a significant number of women who avail themselves of illegal and often unsafe abortions have both knowledge of and technical access to safer abortions than they ultimately experience. In other words, sometimes abortion is legal, and safe access could be found manageably and affordably, yet women choose unsafe abortions anyway.

This suggests that there may be some other factor than those acknowledged by the conventional wisdom standing between the legalization of abortion and the health benefits that legalization could potentially provide to women. As implied by several studies (e.g., Crane and Smith 2006; Agadijanian 1998), part of that difference can and should be accounted for by the degree of legalization of abortion. This chapter, however, contends that there is more to it than the simple linear degree of legalization. Instead, it argues that the degree of legalization interacts with the grounds on which abortion is legal(ized) in a given state.

THE GROUNDS OF THE LEGALITY OF ABORTION

Whether abortion is made legal by a court case (as in the United States) or by legislative process, a "grounds" on which abortion is legal almost always accompanies the jurisprudence or legislation. For example, in the United States, privacy is the grounds for abortion legality. In other places, involuntariness of the pregnancy, out-of-wedlock pregnancy, "maternal" health, and other grounds maintain the general taboo against abortion but make exceptions for certain circumstances understood as extreme. Other grounds for the legality of abortion eschew the taboo, characterizing abortion as generally acceptable behavior rather than permissible only in extreme circumstances. These grounds include women's rights and women's labor arguments.

Some advocates of abortion legalization suggest that the grounds of legalization are irrelevant to the provision of abortion services (and therefore the resulting health benefits of that legalization). Others' work suggests that there are a number of reasons why the degree or grounds of legalization might matter. For example, as Crane and Smith (2006: 4) note, "among those countries where abortion is allowed by law only to save the woman's life or in the case of rape, safe public sector services are commonly not available even for eligible women." I contend that this might be because the degree of legalization is limited and the grounds on which it is legalized maintain a general moral taboo against abortion. On the other hand, as advocates, Crane and Smith suggest a rights-based approach to thinking about the legalization and provision of abortion:

> A "rights-based framework" is one that bases laws and policies on the princi-
> ples and norms defined by the international human rights system . . . Govern-
> ments that embrace abortion laws and policies grounded in human rights prin-
> ciples would: support a woman's autonomy in deciding whether to continue or
> terminate a pregnancy . . . minimize procedural and administrative barriers . . .
> ensure that 'conscience' clauses, if enacted, do not impede women's access to
> care . . . consider rescinding all criminal laws specific to abortion. (Crane and
> Smith 2006: 17-19)

In other words, why states take on the responsibility to ensure access to legal abortion, and how much access they guarantee provision of both may matter in determining whether or not the citizens of that state actually come to have access to legal abortion. While it might be easy to look at a general trend of health benefits from the legalization of abortion and read that as a message that the grounds of legalization do not matter, the case studies in this chapter suggest that the general upward curve, while it applies to all legalizers, is more dramatic for some legalizers than for others.

This chapter looks to get at one slice of the differential distribution of the health benefits from legalization of abortion. It contends that grounds matter in two important ways. First, grounds matter materially: they dictate who is entitled to the legal provision of abortion and when. For example, grounds of the legalization of abortion for women's health require some demonstration of health impact of pregnancy and/or birth in order to deem a woman eligible for an abortion. Grounds that legalize abortion for the purpose of stopping women's suffering (and childbirth) as a result of rape require a proffer of the occurrence of rape. Second, and perhaps more interestingly, the grounds of legalization may tell us about (and co-constitutively shape) the degree to which the taboo on abortion in a particular society is (or is not) maintained despite the liberalization of abortion legislation. This chapter argues that the formal maintenance of a moral taboo on abortion embedded within the grounds of legalization may temper the health benefits of legalization. Partic-ularly, it suggests that there are (broadly speaking) two sorts of grounds for the legalization of abortion: taboo-maintaining and taboo-deconstructing.

THE ABORTION TABOO

A survey of South African high school students suggest that a taboo on abortion is strong there, despite the legalization of abortion (Madu, Kropiunigg, and Weckenmann 2002: 68). A taboo makes something difficult if not impossible to talk about, and information difficult to transmit. Madu, Kropiunigg, and Weckenmann document some impacts of that taboo in their survey population:

> The abortion taboo, similar to that of homosexuality, and of sexuality in general (Kisekka 1990), can also lead to stress, fear, and anxiety (Koberle 1974) and to misconceptions about abortion. The abortion taboo can also force a young girl to give birth to an unwanted child, which may in turn lead to child abandonment, child maltreatment, an increase in the number of street children, and many other social evils. Some young girls, because of fear of what their parents would do if they knew about their pregnancy, resort to unsafe methods of abortion, thereby endangering their health or their lives.

Even recognizing "a global trend toward liberalization of abortion laws [that] has been observed during the past two decades" (Kulczycki 2011, citing Kulczycki 1999 and Boland and Katzive 2008), Kulczycki particularly is concerned about the negative impacts of the maintenance of abortion taboos. Doing empirical work on different abortion laws (and resulting differences in availability of safe abortions), Kulczycki (2011) suggests that the abortion taboo can not only drive abortion-seekers underground but actually keeps the number of abortions in total higher than those places in which there is less taboo on it. In addition to these material impacts, Eve Kushner notes that there are important social impacts of the maintenance of taboos on abortions as well, explaining that "a taboo on abortion prevents us from discussing it on a personal level. There seems to be no socially acceptable way to come forward and share our stories" (Kushner 1997: xviii).

In these terms, "ethnographic accounts of abortion experiences often mention stigma as a dimension of women's experience," but there is little understanding of the material and/or psychological impact of that stigma (Kumar, Hessini, and Mitchell 2009: 2). At the same time, that it has an impact is almost undeniable. Kumar, Hessini, and Mitchell (2009: 4) identify the abortion stigma as "a social phenomenon that is constructed and reproduced locally through various pathways" and this has different severity and impact:

> In the Netherlands, Norway and other Scandinavian countries, where abortion is less legally restricted, public attempts to control pregnant women's actions through guilt or shame are cast as deviant, patronising and inappropriate . . . yet women who terminate their pregnancies are expected to be contrite or

vaguely apologetic when exercising their rights . . . [on the other hand] Zambia has one of the more liberal abortion laws in Africa, but access to safe services remains limited due to a variety of factors including policy restrictions, distance to health facilities, cost, lack of trained providers and stigma. Koster-Oyekan (1998) describes the secrecy, shame, fear of ridicule and taboos associated with abortion. She also reports a high level of unsuccessful abortions that resulted in health complications. Girls who abort are considered infectious, with the ability to harm others ... The potential contagion also extends to providers, hospitals, medical or nursing schools, pharmacies, family members and others. (Kumar, Hessini, and Mitchell 2009: 4, 3)

These concerns lead one to disaggregate the expected effects of legalization of abortion where abortion taboos are (1) maintained and (2) actively deconstructed. In such a framework, grounds for the legality of abortion that remove it from the private sphere and argue that it is a gender-based right, either in terms of equal protection of the laws or in terms of inequities in labor performed or the labor market, are taboo-deconstructing. In countries where these are the grounds for legalization, the interconnections in women's inequality between forced sex, economic deprivation, and reproduction are recognized as a matter of law. Any existing taboo against abortion does not automatically disappear upon the enactment of the taboo-deconstructing law, but the law explicitly rejects the maintenance of the taboo. I suggest that legalization with taboo-deconstructing grounds has the greatest health benefits for women who would have otherwise resorted to illegal abortions.

By contrast, taboo-maintaining grounds do not focus on women's rights, women's economic subordination, or deconstructing the public-private divide particularly as it relates to women's bodies. Instead, they often focus on either violations of or risks to women's bodies or women's privacy. More often than not, the "taboo-maintaining" grounds for legalizing abortion relegate women's abortions specifically and their bodies generally to the private sphere of social and political life, a reification of the personal/political divide that feminists have always found both insidious and materially harmful to women. The division of the political and social world into "public" and "private" marginalizes those interests which are in private places, like inside the home, or inside their bodies. When issues fall on the "private" side of the public/private dichotomy, public law and public policy either support or fail to intervene in taboos related to it (Sjoberg 2011). Also, "privacy rights" are often treated as negative rights and even more often subject to situational enforcement (Sjoberg 2011). These grounds both privatize and stigmatize the decision to seek, and have, an abortion. They also often limit the women to whom abortions are available. I suggest that legalization with taboo-maintaining grounds has fewer and less immediate health benefits than legalization with taboo-deconstructing grounds.

EVIDENCE THAT GROUNDS MAY MATTER

Cross-national anecdotal evidence suggests that there is some reason to believe that there are differential impacts of different grounds for legalization. Statistically, it is clear that legalizing abortion significantly reduces abortion-related deaths and injuries, regardless of economic status in the country or grounds for the legalization of abortion. However, there is not clear and collectable data on the degree of the health benefit, largely because collection of data on the health impacts of unsafe abortion only began systematically in 1995, post-legalization in many places around the world (see discussion in WHO 2004). As such, the "pre-legalization" health situation in many countries is not available (WHO 2008). Even now, when the World Health Organization (WHO) tries to collect data on the health impacts of both legal and illegal abortion, many studies suggest that the data remains unreliable (WHO 2004).

At the same time, there is a consensus in the community that the legalization of abortion is not itself sufficient to end deaths from illegal or unsafe abortion, and that there is more to disparate results than economics or information (e.g., Agadijanian 1998, citing Castle, Likwa, and Wittaker 1990). For example, a study on the use of legal and illegal abortion providers in Mexico notes that, despite the legalization of abortion in some situations, "the procedure remains a taboo topic" (de Weiss and David 1990: 716). The situations in which abortion is legal are the result of rape, incest, or a threat to the life of the mother—simply put, things perceived to be worse than abortion. This is a taboo-maintaining ground for legalization. As a result, even women to whom abortion might be legally available resort to clandestine abortions, which, at the time of writing, constituted "the fifth largest cause of maternal mortality and the third highest reason for admission to gynecological services in the metropolitan hospitals of the Mexican Social Security System" (de Weiss and David 1990: 715). Citing security and anonymity, women chose non-physician providers in non-clinical settings frequently, resulting in more than two times the number of complications as women who chose physicians and clinical settings (de Weiss and David 1990: 715-16). When abortion is legal but culturally taboo and restricted in its legality and social status, this research suggests that the health benefit of legalization is lower since abortion consumers may still choose illegal or clandestine abortions to avoid the taboo.

A similar story can be found across the world in Ghana, where abortion is legal in some situations and remains illegal in others. Abortion laws in Ghana are slightly more permissive than those in Mexico—abortion is allowed when the pregnancy might cause "injury to [the pregnant woman's] physical or mental health; or where there is a substantial risk that if the child were born may suffer from a serious abnormality or disease" as well (Lithur 2004:

71). Still, "it is accepted that there is a stigma attached to abortion and those who perform abortions in Ghana" (Lithur 2004: 71). As such, despite its legality, abortion is not either provided or sought out in the public sphere even by women who would qualify, because "abortion stigmatization permeates officialdom and is a silent and ignored contributor to statistics on maternal mortality in Ghana" (Lithur 2004: 71). Therefore, "as a result of stigmatization . . . unsafe abortion is being silently performed underground within the communities in Ghana and outside the formal health service structures" (Lithur 2004: 72, citing Clement 2001, 108). As Lithur recounts, "destigmatisation" is a complicated process that does not correspond one-to-one with legalization (Lithur 2004: 73).

Again this is not to say that taboo-deconstructing laws automatically rid states of abortion taboos. For example, Canada has a taboo-deconstructing law, where the courts rejected all restrictions on abortion on women's rights grounds (see Tatalovich 1997). While, as a result, Canada is one of the safest places in the world to procure abortion services, the Canadian government still struggles with questions of whether to "consider barring protests outside abortion clinics . . . [or] outlawing the stalking of abortion doctors" (Tatalovich 1997: 141). Though the taboo is weak in Canada and legal abortion services are available and taken advantage of, all taboo on abortion has not disappeared. While taboo-deconstructing laws, then, are not a magic solution to taboos on abortion, there is evidence that taboo-maintaining laws sustain taboos and taboo-deconstructing laws contribute to their dissolution. The next section of this chapter explores cases that might give some insight on this relationship: Mozambique and Tanzania. Because this is a theory-building exercise, those cases are selected not for some comparative-case or hypothesis-testing logic, but instead because each has some internal comparability that might help explore whether or not the grounds for legalization had something to do with the health results of legalization. Each case also has the potential to show the overlap (and independent effect) of the degree of legalization.

ABORTION LEGALIZATION, GROUNDS, AND HEALTH IN MOZAMBIQUE AND TANZANIA

Mozambique is a country with a long history of legal restrictions on abortion. Writing in 1997, Machungo, Zanconato, and Bergstrom characterize abortion as unofficially legal in Mozambique:

> In Mozambique, the actual policy, though not officially recognised, is oriented towards the legalisation of abortion. In this setting the confidentiality assured to the women in the target group having alleged miscarriage gave us access to

a significant proportion of those actually having had an IA (illegal abortion). (Machungo, Zanconato, and Bergstrom 1997: 1610).

Noting that "legislation has long been against abortion," the authors are also aware that "interpretation of existing law has gradually become less restrictive" (Machungo, Zanconato, and Bergstrom 1997: 1607). Gallo et al. detail:

> Induced abortion in Mozambique currently has a quasi-legal status. Although the criminal code calls for imprisonment for the provision or procurement of abortion unless the woman's health or life is at risk, a 1981 Ministry of Health (MOH) decree supported a broad interpretation of this risk, and abortion has been available upon request in several public hospitals ever since. (Gallo et al. 2004: 219)

As such, "Mozambique [is] one of the few African countries where comparative studies on illegal and legal abortion can be carried out" (Machundo, Zanconato, and Bergstrom 1997: 1607).

In fact, one of the most comprehensive studies comparing legal and illegal abortion in the same place was done in Mozambique, where, over the time of the study, ninety-three percent of patients at clinics that provided abortion services were interviewed (Gallo et al. 2004: 223). Many of these patients, however, came to clinics only after having tried to perform abortions themselves or seeking the services of someone who was not a medical professional. Despite the availability of abortion on demand in many hospitals, clandestine abortion remained rampant through this era of quasi-legalization (Agadijanian 1998: 111). As a result, as recently as a couple of years ago, "approximately one in seven women [in Mozambique] dies during pregnancy," one of the highest rates in the world, where "maternal mortality and morbidity are often the result of unsafe abortion" (Gallo et al. 2004: 218).

Evidence suggests that this had something to do with the grounds on which abortion was legalized and the official state position towards its morality. While abortion has been available on demand for a long time, the availability is juxtaposed with both official government statements and cultural taboos that stem "from deeply entrenched pronatalist attitudes and the enduring perception of the high economic and social value of children" (Agadijanian 1998: 114). As a result, Agadijanian (1998: 115) notes that "the future of abortion on request in Mozambique depends to a considerable degree on the evolution of its legal status. The paradox of de jure prohibition and de facto availability is not likely to be ignored much longer."

In fact, after twenty-six years of de facto legality, a debate started in 2007 on de jure legalization for the purpose of decreasing the number of illegal abortions obtained as the de facto legalization kept the taboo in place. While abortion-related deaths decreased after the 1981 choice to make abortions available in a wide enough selection of situations to make them de facto legal, fatalities did not disappear. In fact, in 2007:

> Botched abortions accounted for an estimated eleven percent of maternal fatalities registered at the central hospital in Maputo, the nation's capital, in the 1990s. More than forty percent of cases of serious pregnancy complications treated at the hospital's maternity clinic are said to be the result of clandestine abortions. "These are only the cases of people who went to the central hospital," said Graca Samo, executive director of the Women's Forum, an umbrella organization for women's rights' nongovernmental organizations. "It does not count the people who don't come in, who die in rural clinics. And often when someone dies, the family will never say what really happened." (IRIN 2007).

There is evidence that the health benefits of de facto legalization are being erased by stringent opposition to de jure legalization, which has revived the sometimes-dormant taboo to argue that abortion is a "sin," a "crime against life," an "act contrary to this nation," and contend that it should not just be de jure but de facto illegal (Katerere 2007). There has been, over the last four years, a contentious debate about abortion policy in Mozambique that had largely been avoided in the 1981 de facto legalization. The history of abortion law and practice in Mozambique suggests that there were indeed health benefits from the taboo-maintaining legalization, but that they are both vulnerable to the taboo and incomplete because of its maintenance. The health benefits are vulnerable to the taboo because the taboo could become more salient at any point in time, forcing legal abortions underground and increasing the number of clandestine abortions and (as a result) the number of complications and deaths from those illegal abortions. The health benefits are incomplete as well. In Mozambique, legal abortions were fairly readily available in hospitals to women who signed a statement desiring one, yet illegal abortions continued rampantly during de facto legalization because of the taboo on abortion. While deaths from abortion did decrease, the level of deaths remained high (even controlling for poverty and education levels) compared to states that use taboo-deconstructing grounds for legalization.

Tanzania, on the other hand, is a place where abortion is not available on demand at all. While the law explicitly decriminalized abortion in certain situations in 1973, it increased the punishment and the threat of legal enforcement for abortions that did not meet the narrow criteria of legality under the law, related only to the health of the woman who was pregnant. In other words, abortion is legal in Tanzania, but only for the health of the mother, and remains clearly morally condemned. As such, abortions for health reasons became (in theory) acceptable, publically available, and cost-covered by the state public health system, while abortions for other reasons (and on demand) were classified as criminal offenses.

According to recent studies, "the exact magnitude of the problem of induced abortion [in Tanzania] is unknown" (Rasch, Muhammad, Urassa, and Bergstrom 2001: 496). There is evidence that illegal (and unsafe) abortions are common, even among women who might have access to an abortion legally (Rasch et al. 2001, citing Justesen et al. 1992). In several places around Tanzania, unsafe induced abortions account for up to 15 percent of maternal deaths (Rasch et al. 2001, 497, citing Urassa et al. 1996). Unlike in Mexico or even in Ghana, the partial legalization of abortion is accompanied both by official and unofficial maintenance of the taboo; abortion is, in fact, discouraged even when it is technically legally available.

As a result, though abortion has been legal for almost four decades in the cases where the health of the mother is at risk, there has been very little decrease in the level of death or health complications from the administration of illegal abortions. While there has been some change, it has not even been proportional to those women who would have justifiable grounds to obtain legal abortions. Instead, most abortions in Tanzania remain illegal and most illegal abortions remain unsafe. Given the strength of the taboo,

> women and girls turn to amateurs, who may dose them with herbs or other concoctions, pummel their bellies or insert objects vaginally. Infections, bleeding, and punctures of the uterus or bowel can result, and can be fatal. . . . Maternal mortality is high in Tanzania: for every 100,000 births, 950 women die. . . . On a Friday in January, six of twenty patients in the women's ward were recovering from attempted abortions. . . . One, a twenty-five-year-old schoolteacher . . . had scraped the inside of her womb with a curet, a small metal instrument. It was a vigorous, bloody procedure . . . [she] lay in bed moaning and writhing (Grady 2009).

The history and trajectory of abortion law and practice in Tanzania suggests that the legalization of abortion had limited health benefits for a number of reasons. These reasons include that the legalization was limited in scope, that problems with access to health care generally compound problems with access to abortion, and that education levels about the availability of abortion specifically and contraception generally remain low. Still, there is evidence that the taboo-maintaining grounds of the legalization also cause women to seek illegal and unsafe abortions even when legal, safer abortions might be available to them, given the stigma placed on the procedure even in cases where it is legal and the limited understanding of its acceptability as a process. The case of Tanzania, like the case of Mozambique, suggest that there is more to getting the health benefits from the legalization of abortion than just legalization—that it is wrapped up instead in how the law interacts with abortion taboos.

WHAT IF THE GROUNDS MATTER?

There may be a number of things going on in the examples of Mozambique and Tanzania, as well as in any number of other cases where the anecdotal evidence about the relationship between abortion legalization grounds and health benefits appears to be influential. One causal story that could be told would hold the grounds of legalization primarily responsible for the level of health benefit provided, after controlling for levels of education and levels of poverty. While this story is plausible, leaving it there it would neglect the question of the relationship between law and sociopolitical interaction.

Particularly, the grounds of the legalization might be a signifier for and/or representative of already-held beliefs and norms in a society, such that societies where the abortion taboo is strong tend to legalize on taboo-maintaining grounds, and societies where the taboo is weak tend to legalize on grounds that deconstruct the taboo. Issues like religion, culture, and sexual ethics certainly interact with the question of why (if at all) abortions should be legal to obtain in a given state. If the grounds of legalization were purely representative of already-held beliefs and norms in a society, then the question of a state's prevalent beliefs and norms about abortion would be the correct one to ask rather than the question of the legal status of abortion and the grounds on which any legalization took place.

This chapter, though, suggests that a middle ground between these two accounts forms the most plausible way to understand the role of the grounds of legalization on the health results of that legalization. It seems intuitive that the grounds of legalization (in part or in whole) are signifying and responding to the social and political predispositions towards abortion in any given state. Still, like other areas of law, there is evidence that the content and status of the law affects the social and political norms in a society about matters that engage moral controversy (e.g., Tyler 2006). Particularly, there is evidence that abortion taboo-maintaining grounds for legalization make taboos stickier, where abortion taboo-deconstructing grounds for legalization loosen taboos (Kushner 1997). That evidence, along with the empirical exploration in this chapter, suggests that it is worthwhile to consider the grounds of legalization as among the factors accounting for whether or not legalization is successful in providing the health benefits associated with ending clandestine abortions and providing free access to safe abortion.

If the grounds matter, looking at the question of the grounds for the legalization of abortion through feminist lenses suggests a way forward. Particularly, feminist lenses may suggest taking a critical look at the role that the public/private dichotomy plays in constructing and sustaining taboo-maintaining grounds for the legalization of abortion. As feminists have noted, men (and their rights) are often described as a part of the public sphere, where women (and any rights they might have) are often relegated to the private sphere (Okin 1998). The private sphere is then often characterized as something the law cannot interfere with (or even outside of the law) rather than something that the law can provide rights and guarantees within (Sjoberg 2011). Sometimes, taboo-maintaining abortion laws grant women the right to abortion for reasons that involve protecting a woman's privacy specifically or the private sphere more generally.

Still, "even when the private sphere is protected, the protection is not to inquire what goes on there, rather than regulating it to protect women" (Sjoberg 2011, citing Okin 1998: 50). The consequences have been observed by feminist theorists in a number of situations for years. As Catherine MacKinnon explains, women's rights are relegated to the private sphere, and women are "distinctively unequal" in private in part for the self-fulfilling and circular reason that they are "defined as second-class citizens by virtue of their being identified with the private" (MacKinnon 2001: 1411). Feminist analysis has suggested that

> [w]hile the private has been a refuge for some, it has been a hellhole for others, often at the same time. In a gendered light, the law's privacy is a sphere of sanctified isolation, impunity, and unaccountability. . . . Everyone is implicitly equal in there. If the woman needs something—say, equality to make these assumptions real, privacy law does nothing for her (MacKinnon 1991: 1311).

The feminist literature has suggested that women's rights be thought of as public-sphere, rather than private-sphere rights, and that the feminist movement go further to deconstruct the separation of the dichotomy between the public and private spheres (e.g., Baldez, Epstein, and Martin 2006). Many feminist criticisms of the public/private divide generally and of the relegation of abortion to the private sphere specifically suggests that they serve to "force women to assume the role and perform the work that has traditionally defined their secondary social status" and to (unjustly) treat a sex-oppressive social order as "natural, just, and pre-political" (Siegel 1992: 350-1; Sunstein 1992: 31-2). By pointing out the relationship between taboo-maintaining grounds for the legalization of abortion, the maintenance of the public/private dichotomy, and sex discrimination, feminist theory can make legal and policy prescriptions that might push forward the potential health benefits from legalizing abortion further and faster than legalization alone.

Particularly, thinking of abortion law in terms of labor rather than in terms of sex might provide a strong taboo-deconstructing grounds for legalization even in states where the taboo is strong (Sjoberg 2011). There is indeed a reason that we call "labor" by that name, both in English and mirrored in a number of other languages around the world. This is because there is work and commitment involved in pregnancy, often frequently and unexpectedly. In addition to the work of carrying the fetus to term, pregnancies often involve particular vitamins, particular diets, particular activity pre-scriptions, need for access to specialized medical care, awareness of certain stages of pregnancy and their effects on the body, and bouts of sickness and discomfort. In other words, for a woman carrying a fetus, pregnancy is (vol-untary or involuntary) work, employment, or service. Yet in almost every society one can find, we assume that women perform the labor of childbear-ing (not to mention childrearing) joyfully and without compensation. While that assumption is doubtless true sometimes and in some cases, forcing wom-en to remain pregnant when they do not want to be not only deprives them of their liberty, it also deprives them of their work and labor.

Thinking about abortion as an issue of labor rather than an issue of sex removes it from the taboo-maintaining moral debates that abortion law is often mired in now. For example, in the discussion of Mexican abortion law above, the litmus test for legality is something approximating when abortion is the lesser of evils. In Mozambique, abortion's permissibility relies on a cloak of silence where it is almost always allowed but almost never accept-able given a strong social norm that having children is not only good but necessary. In Tanzania, opposition to making abortion available more widely exists for religious grounds—the argument holds that abortion is wrong and the law should limit citizens' access to the ability to do things that are wrong. Yet none of these states would explicitly legalize the forced appropriation of labor, even if some of them would deny the productivity of a separate and equal sphere for women's rights. In short, a feminist labor economics ap-proach to legalization grounds may be a way to transition many taboo-main-taining legalizers into taboo-deconstructing legalizers without battling the social and religious factors that keep them in the taboo-maintaining category. Such an approach might provide quicker results than generational change in norms and taboos if the goal is to obtain the maximum amount of health benefits available from the legalization of abortion.

REFERENCES

AbouZahr, C. and E. Ahman. 1988. "Unsafe Abortion and Ectopic Pregnancy." In *Health Dimensions of Sex and Reproduction*, edited by C.J.L. Murray and A.D. Lopez. Geneva: World Health Organization.

Agadijanian, V. 1998. "Quasi-legal Abortion Services in a Sub-Saharan Setting: Users' Profiles and Motivations." *International Family Planning Perspectives* 24:111-16.

Baldez, Lisa, L. Epstein, and A.D. Martin. 2006. "Does the U. S. Constitution Need an Equal Rights Amendment?" *Journal of Legal Studies* 35(2).

Berer, Marge. 2004. "National Laws and Unsafe Abortion: The Parameters of Change." *Reproductive Health Matters* 12(24 Supplement): 3-8.

Bernstein, P. S. and A. Rosenfield. 1998. "Abortion and Maternal Health." *International Journal of Gynecology & Obstetrics* 63(S1):S115-S122.

Bloom, David E., David Canning, Gunther Fink, and Jocely E. Finlay. 2009. "Fertility, Female Labor Force Participation, and the Demographic Dividend," *Journal of Economic Growth* 14(1):79-101.

Boland, Reed and Laura Katzive. 2008. "Developments in Laws on Induced Abortion: 1998–2007." *International Family Planning Perspectives* 34(3): 110–120.

Castle, M.A., R. Likwa, and M. Wittaker. 1990. "Observations on Abortion in Zambia." *Studies in Family Planning* 21(4): 231-35.

Clement, A. 2001. "Incidence of Induced Abortion in Southern Ghana." *International Family Planning Perspectives* 27(2): 96-108.

Crane, Barbara B. and C.E.H. Smith. 2006. Access to Safe Abortion: An Essential Strategy for Achieving the Millennium Development Goals to Improve Maternal Health, Promote Gender Equality, and Reduce Poverty. Background paper to the *Report of the UN Millennium Project to Contribute to Public Choices, Private Decisions: Sexual and Reproductive Health and the Millennium Development Goals.* United Nations Millennium Project.

Center for Reproductive Rights (CRR) 2005. Abortion and the Law: Ten Years of Reform. Available online athttp://www.reprorights.org/pdf/pub_bp_abortionlaws10.pdf.

De Capua, Joe. 2009. "Illegal Abortions Kill and Maim Kenyan Women and Girls." *Voice of America* October 31, accessed November 17, 2013 at http://www.voanews.com/content/a-13-2006-08-31-voa23/318311.html.

Drenthen, Willem, Eric Boersma, Ali Balci, Philip Moons, Jolien W. Roos-Hesselink, Barbara J. M. Mulder, Hubert W. Wliegen, Arie P. J. van Dijk, Adriaan A. Voors, Sing C. Yap, Dirk J. vanVeldhuisen, Petronella G. Pieper, and On behalf of the ZAHARA Investigators. 2010. "Predictors of Pregnancy Complications in Women with Congenital Heart Diseaese," *European Heart Journal* 31(17):2124-2132.

Ernst, Julia L. and Molly Diachok. 2002. "The Global Gag Rule: A Primer." *Women Lawyers' Journal* 87(2): 7-10.

Gallo, Maria F., H. Gebreselassie, M.T.A. Victorino, M. Dgedge, L. Jamisse, and C. Bisque. 2004. "An Assessment of Abortion Services in Public Health Facilities in Mozambique: Women's and Providers' Perspectives." *Reproductive Health Matters* 2004:12(24 Supplement): 218-226.

Grady, Denise. 2009. "The Deadly Toll of Abortion by Amateurs." *New York Times.* 1 June.

Grimes, David A., Janie Benson, Sushella Singh, Mariana Romera, Bela Ganatra, Friday E. Okonolua, and Iqbal H. Shah. 2006. "Unsafe Abortion: The Preventable Pandemic," *The Lancet* Sexual and Reproductive Health Series (#4).

IRIN Humanitarian News and Analysis. 2007. "Mozambique: Government Considers Legalising Abortion to Stem Maternal Deaths." 29 May, accessed November 17, 2013 at http://www.irinnews.org/printreport.aspx?reportid=72421.

Justesen, Aafke, S.H. Kapiga, and H.A.G.A. van Asten. 1992. "Abortions in a Hospital Setting: Hidden Realities in Dar es Salaam, Tanzania." *Studies in Family Planning* 23(5): 325-329.

Katerere, Fred. 2007. "Safe Abortions May Soon be Legal in Mozambique." *Afrol News* 11 June, accessed November 17, 2014 at http://www.afrol.com/articles/25706.

Kisekka, M.N. 1990. "Gender and Mental Health in Africa." *Women and Therapy* 10:1-13.

Koberle, A. 1974. "Cause and healing of ellesioge nic neuroses." *Analytische Psychologie* 5:55-61.

Koster-Oyekan, W. 1998. "Why Resort to Illegal Abortion in Zambia? Findings of a Community-Based Study in the Western Province." *Social Science and Medicine* 46 (10):1303-12.

Kulczycki, Andrzej. 2011. "Abortion in Latin America: Changes in Practice, Growing Conflict, and Recent Policy Developments." *Studies in Family Planning* 42(3): 199-221.

Kulczycki, Andrzej. 1999. *The Abortion Debate in the World Arena.* London: Macmillan; New York: Routledge.

Kumar, Anunradha, Leila Hessini, and Ellen M. H. Mitchelll. 2009. "Conceptualizing the Abortion Stigma." *Culture, Health, and Sexuality* 2009, DOI:10.1080/13691050902842741, p.1-15.

Kushner, Eve. 1997. *Experiencing Abortion: A Weaving of Women's Words.* New York: Psychology Press.

Lithur, Nana Oye. 2004. "Destigmatizing Abortion: Expanding Community Awareness of Abortion as a Reproductive Health Issue in Ghana." *African Journal of Reproductive Health* 8(1): 70-74.

Machungo, Fernanda, G. Zanconato, and S. Bergstrom. 1997. "Reproductive Characteristics and Post-Abortion Health Consequences in Women Undergoing Illegal and Legal Abortion in Maputo." *Social Science Medicine* 45(11): 1607-1613.

MacKinnon, Catherine. 2001. *Sex Equality*. New York: Thomson-West.

MacKinnon, Catherine. 1991. "Reflections on Sex Equality under the Law." *Yale Law Journal* 100(1): 1281-1315.

Madu, S.N., U. Kropiunigg, and M. Weckenmann. 2002. "Health Complaints of High School Students in the Northern Province and Taboo Themes in their Family." *South African Journal of Education* 22(1): 65-69.

Myers, Jenny E. and Mourad W. Seif. 2010. "Global Perspective of Legal Abortion—Trend Analysis and Accessibility." *Best Practice and Research Clinical Obstetrics and Gynaecology* 24: 457-66.

Okin, Susan Moeller. 1998. "Feminism, Women's Rights, and Cultural Differences." *Hypatia* 12(1).

Planned Parenthood. 2002. "Medical and Social Health Benefits Since Abortion Was Made Legal in the U.S." Pamphlet Circulated by the Planned Parenthood Federation of America.

Prada, Elena, F. Mirembe, F.H. Ahmed, R. Nalwadda, and C. Kiggundu. 2005. "Abortion and Postabortion Care in Uganda: A Report from Health Care Professionals and Health Facilities." *Occasional Report 17*. Alan Guttmacher Institute, New York.

Rasch, Vibeke, H. Muhammad, E. Urassa, and S. Bergtrom. 2001. "The Problem of Illegally Induced Abortion: Results from a Hospital-Based Study Conducted at District Level in Dar es Salaam." *Tropical Medicine and International Health* 5(7): 495-502.

Regushevskaya, Elena; Tatiana Dubikaytis, Made Laanpere, Minna Nikula, Olga Kuznetsova, Elina Haavio-Mannila, Hele Karro, and Elina Hemminki. 2009. "Risk Factors for Induced Abortions in St Petersburg, Estonia, and Finland." *The European Journal of Contraception and Reproductive Health Care* 14(3):176-86.

Robertson, John A. 2011. "Abortion and Technology: Sonograms, Fetal Pain, Viability, and Early Prenatal Diagnosis." *University of Pennsylvania Journal of Constitutional Law* 14: 327.

Salhan, Sudha and Sangeeta Kaul. 2012. "The Medical Termination of Pregnancy (MTP) and Safe Abortion," in *Textbook of Gynecology*, ed. Sudha Salhan. Delhi: JP Medical Ltd.

Shah, Iqbal and Elisabeth Ahman. 2009. "Unsafe Abortion: Global and Regional Incidence, Trends, Consequences, and Challenges." *Journal of Obstetrics and Gynaecology Canada* December: 1149-58.

Siegel, Reva. 1992. "Reasoning from the Body: A Historical Perspective on Abortion Regulation and Questions of Equal Protection." *Stanford Law Review* 44(1): 261-351.

Sjoberg, Laura. 2011. "What are the Grounds for the Legality of Abortion? The 13th Amendment Argument." *Cardozo Journal of Law and Gender* 17(3): 527-550.

Sunstein, Cass. 1992. "Neutrality in Constitutional Law." *Columbia Law Review* 92(1): 1-47.

Tatalovich, Raymond. 1997. *The Politics of Abortion in the United States and Canada: A Comparative Study*. London: M.E. Sharpe.

Tyler, Tom R. 2006. *Why People Obey the Law*. Princeton, NJ: Princeton University Press.

Urassa E., S. Massawe, G. Lindmark, and L. Nystrom. 1996. "Maternal Mortality in Tanzania—Medical Causes are Interrelated with Socio-economic and Cultural Factors." *South African Medical Journal* 86, 436-444.

de Weiss, S. Pick, and H.P. David. 1990. "Illegal Abortion in Mexico: Client Perceptions." *American Journal of Public Health* 80(6): 715-716.

World Health Organization. 2008. *Unsafe Abortion: Global and Regional Estimates of the Incidence of Unsafe Abortion and Associated Mortality in 2008*. Sixth Edition. Geneva: World Health Organization.

World Health Organization. 2004. *Unsafe Abortion: Global and Regional Estimates of the Incidence of Unsafe Abortion and Associated Mortality in 2004*. Fourth Edition. Geneva: World Health Organization.

World Health Organization. 2003. "International Policy and Practice: Responding to Unsafe Abortion," informational pamphlet distributed with Ipas (a women's health NGO).

Chapter Five

U.S. International Family Planning Policy and Domestic Divisions

Karen L. Baird

U.S. leadership in international family planning produces positive and negative consequences. On the positive side, the United States is the principal funder for many programs through the United States Agency for International Development (USAID) and United Nations Population Fund (UNFPA). On the negative side, the United States exerts great control over many aspects of family planning around the world. And U.S. rules and regulations dramatically change with each new presidential administration, as the conflictive, internal politics of the country lead to ideologically different administrations. What, then, is the result? The domestic politics of one country, the United States, greatly influence women's lives and access to family planning around the globe.[1] Specifically, women's bodies around the world are the venue on which the internal political divisions of the United States are played out.

This tension will be examined through the lens of the "Global Gag Rule," (GGR) and how it is enacted and rescinded as presidents come and go in the United States. Most recently, President George W. Bush imposed the GGR and President Barack Obama rescinded it. Even though much evidence shows the rule's harmful effects on family planning, its enactment is continually debated. The framing of issues related to the funding of family planning services and the GGR—how the rule's imposition was rationalized and how its repeal was justified—will be discussed. With regard to President G.W. Bush, the imposition of the GGR was part of a larger pattern of policy-making. This pattern is highlighted because it is important in developing solutions to the "ping-pong" effect of the imposition and retraction of the rule.

Even though President Obama lifted the order, history and domestic disputes over abortion show that its enactment is likely to be attempted again. Potential solutions for capitalizing on the lifting of the GGR are explored. How might unrestricted and comprehensive funding be sustained? How strategically, and on what basis? How might such a commitment be framed as to engender broad-based support? Possible solutions include passage of a Congressional law; clarifying issues that are about federal funding of abortion and ones that are not; restoring the role of science and evidence-based policy-making; and establishing new global health programs that combine various health and family planning programs.

In this chapter, the history of the GGR will be presented. Next, the importance of family planning for women's health, and thus how the GGR impacts women's health, will be discussed. In the section that follows, patterns of policy-making in the G.W. Bush Administration are presented, and the last section discusses options to combat such policymaking processes and to enact more permanent and sustainable funding for family planning.

HISTORY OF THE "GLOBAL GAG RULE"[2]

Various U.S. presidents have issued and then retracted the GGR throughout its twenty-five year history. The policy, an executive order, disqualifies foreign non-governmental organizations (NGOs) from receiving U.S. family planning funds if they provide counseling on abortion, discuss the availability of abortion, or participate in political debate on abortion with the intent of making it more widely available, even if achieved with non-U.S. funds.

The Helms Amendment, a Congressional law, already prohibits U.S. funds from being used to pay for abortion services in foreign NGOS. This law was first passed in 1973 and has continuously been in effect since that time. In 1984, the administration of President Ronald Reagan announced at the International Conference on Population in Mexico City *further* restrictions regarding foreign NGOs that accept U.S. funds (the "Mexico City Policy"); this policy is what has been labeled the GGR because it limits what NGOs can *say* about abortion.

Reagan's 1984 policy remained in effect until 1993. When President Bill Clinton entered office in January 1993, he promptly rescinded the GGR. But after the Congressional elections of 1994 in which the U.S. Congress returned to Republican control, abortion opponents sought to reinstate funding restrictions through legislative bills. Such members of Congress forced the withholding of payments to the United Nations (UN) in protest by attaching to such appropriation bills language that would reinstate the rule. President

Clinton vetoed the first version of such an attempt in 1998, but in 1999 was forced to sign the bill in order to preclude the United States from losing its voting rights in the General Assembly. At that point, the United States owed almost $1 billion in unpaid dues to the UN (Cohen 2000). Clinton vowed that the restrictive policy would only be in effect for one year (Fiscal Year 2000 appropriations). Indeed the promise was kept, but the fiscal year 2001 appropriations for USAID family planning funds were delayed in their release until February 2001 to allow the newly elected president to institute new restrictions (CRLP 2001).

On January 22, 2001, President George W. Bush issued an executive order reinstating the GGR. This latest version of the executive order forbids foreign NGOs from receiving USAID funds if they "perform or actively promote abortion as a method of family planning in USAID-receipt countries or provide financial support to any other foreign nongovernmental organization that conducts such activities."[3] This includes providing counseling that includes information about abortion (except when the woman's life is endangered, or in cases of rape and incest) and lobbying a foreign government to legalize or to continue the legalization of abortion (CRLP 2001; CRS 2001; U.S. White House Memorandum 2001).[4] NGOs cannot use U.S. funds to engage in such activities, but they are also prohibited from using *any* funds to engage in such enterprises. It is also important to note that such activities only include organizations that advocate *for* the availability or legalization of abortion; organizations that choose to engage in anti-abortion activities are not barred. NGOs may use funds to treat injuries and illnesses caused by legal or illegal abortions (PAI 2006a; U.S. White House Memorandum 2001).

NGOs that wish to accept USAID funds have to sign a statement agreeing to the restrictions. The restrictions only apply to foreign NGOs and do not apply to foreign governments, for diplomatic reasons. If a foreign government engages in the prohibited activities, it must keep the U.S. monies separate and be able to show that the U.S. funds are not being used for the restricted activities.

The latest change in the restrictions came on January 23, 2009, when newly elected President Barack Obama repealed the GGR. "These excessively broad conditions on grants and assistance awards are unwarranted. Moreover, they have undermined efforts to promote safe and effective voluntary family planning programs in foreign nations" (Obama 2009).[5] President Obama's lifting of the GGR was only one of many efforts by the new administration; he also lifted the ban on embryonic stem cell research, initiated efforts to restore the role of science in federal-level policy-making, and announced a new Global Health Initiative. These are discussed later below.

But first, in order to understand the consequences of the GGR for women, an overview of family planning and women's health in developing countries is provided.

FAMILY PLANNING AND WOMEN'S HEALTH[6]

Reproductive health issues are the leading cause of ill health and death for women worldwide, but in developing countries, being a woman is particularly perilous. Maternal mortality and morbidity, including risky pregnancies, dangerous deliveries, and unsafe abortions, are the main contributors to women's poor reproductive health.

It is estimated that a woman in a developing country runs a one in 150 lifetime risk of dying from maternally related causes. This number has greatly improved as 539,000 women died from maternal causes in developing countries in 1990 and only 284,000 died in 2010 (WHO 2012). Put another way, the maternal mortality ratio (MMR) for developing countries in the world is estimated to be 240 per 100,000 live births. By region, the MMR is the highest in Sub-Saharan Africa at 500 maternal deaths per 100,000 live births, followed by Southern Asia (220), Oceania (200), South-eastern Asia (150), Latin America and the Caribbean (eighty), Northern Africa (seventy-eight), Western Asia (seventy-one), the Caucasus and Central Asia (forty-six), and Eastern Asia (thirty-seven) (WHO 2012).

Abortion, hemorrhage, obstructed labor, sepsis, and pre-eclampsia/eclampsia are the medical causes of maternal death and disability. But why do these conditions or procedures cause death and disability? It is primarily lack of access to quality health care, and with regard to abortion, illegality or unavailability of safe abortion services. For example, severe hemorrhage is estimated to occur in ten percent of live births (AbouZahr 2003). It rarely occurs in the developed world where childbirth primarily takes place in hospitals or other medical settings; it occurs principally in developing countries. The vast amount of complications arising from abortion occurs when the procedure is performed in nonmedical settings and/or by unskilled personnel (AbouZahr 2003, 9).

The causes of death and disability are also more likely to occur when pregnancies are repeated and closely spaced, when pregnancies occur in younger women or girls, when pregnancies are unintended, and when women's health is already compromised by other conditions. In addition:

> It is most often the poor and illiterate who pay the highest price for inadequate reproductive services; they do so with their lives, broken families, poverty, social isolation and chronic ill health. The human toll exacted from unintended and unwanted pregnancies is typically a hidden one, buried under often age-old social norms governing the roles of women in society. Economic marginal-

ization, poor education, and geographical isolation contribute further to inconsistent reportage, but are by no means the only indicators of high maternal mortality rates (Global Health Council 2002, 23).

Early marriage, gender inequality, lack of control over sexual decision-making, and violence against women also exacerbate the factors that contribute to death and disability.

Abortion, when performed in a safe medical setting by trained personnel, is very safe and women suffer few complications; in fact, in the United States, the procedure carries less risk than carrying a baby to term and giving birth. Many women live in countries in which abortion is illegal or legal only under certain circumstances. For example, in sixty-eight countries, abortion is prohibited or is only legal to save the life of the woman; this is the law for twenty-six percent of the world's population (Center for Reproductive Rights 2011).

Sadly, if women cannot get legal and safe abortions, they are forced to resort to unsafe ones. One study estimated that from 1995 to 2000, three-fourths of unintended pregnancies in the world were ended by abortion (Global Health Council 2002). Many complications and sometimes death result from unsafe abortions (Ahman and Shah 2004; Global Health Council 2002). Complications include hemorrhage, perforated uterus, poisoning, and secondary complications such as gangrene or acute renal failure; long-term complications include chronic pelvic pain, pelvic inflammatory disease, and infertility. For every woman who dies as a result of unsafe abortion, it is estimated that thirty more will suffer chronic disability (Global Health Council 2002: 30). An estimated fourteen percent of maternal deaths can be attributed to abortion complications, and these deaths are the highest in Africa and South Asia where services are limited (Global Health Council 2002).

Family planning plays a large role in reproductive health. Singh and others (2003) report that more than half of women in developing countries are at risk for unintended pregnancy; many of these women are using either no method of birth control or traditional methods that have very high failure rates. Unmet need for contraception is fairly high in developing countries: seventeen percent of women of reproductive age (1–49 years old) have an unmet need for contraception, and twenty-four percent of married women in Sub-Saharan Africa have an unmet need for contraception (Sedgh et al. 2007; Seltzer (2002). The most common reason women have unmet need is difficulty in accessing supplies and services, but also concerns about side effects, health effects, and the inconvenience of specific methods play a role (Sedgh et al. 2007).

Meeting contraceptive need is very cost-effective, increases women's equality and economic empowerment, and improves their health; in addition, HIV transmission can be reduced. For example, according to the Guttmacher

Institute, the $615 million spent for international family planning and repro-
ductive health programs in FY2011 provided contraceptive services and supplies to 37.4 million couples, *averting* 11.7 million unintended pregnancies,
5.1 million unplanned births, 5.1 million induced abortions (about 3.7 million
of them unsafe), and 32,000 maternal deaths (PAI 2012). Providing contraception to all who desire it is an easy, inexpensive, and effective way to
improve women's lives and women's health, and reduce the need for abortions.

FAMILY PLANNING, WOMEN'S HEALTH, AND EFFECTS OF THE GLOBAL GAG RULE[7]

Loss of family planning funds and services when the GGR is in place has
been well-documented.[8] The policy has said to cause "more unintended pregnancies, more unsafe abortions, and more maternal and child deaths" and has
been labeled a "cruel, extremist policy" ("IPAS declines to sign Global Gag
Rule," 206). Crane and Dusenberry (2004) state, "The Gag Rule has neither
broad-based political support nor a compelling public health or development
rationale" (134). During the tenure of G.W. Bush, many organizations refused to abide by the restrictions and refused the USAID funds, which se-
verely curtailed their ability to provide services. In Kenya, Marie Stopes
International Kenya and the Family Planning Association of Kenya closed
clinics, laid off staff, and raised prices to fill the gap after they refused to
accept U.S. funds (PAI 2006b). In Nepal, Family Planning Association of
Nepal (FPAN) lost its thirty-two-year partnership with USAID because of its
refusal to abide by the GGR. Consequently, EngenderHealth, a partner of
FPAN, withdrew $100,000 that supported three reproductive health clinics
that served more than 20,000 clients (PAI 2006c). Even after larger contributions were made by other donors to help make up the loss, FPAN had to
terminate sixty staff members, lay off doctors, and was forced to introduce a
fee for services. FPAN also lost $400,000 in USAID-funded contraceptives,
the major contributor to its contraceptive program (PAI 2006c).[9]
      In country after country, if organizations refused to adhere to the GGR,
family planning services were cut when funding from USAID came to an
end. Unfortunately, reduction in contraceptive services only *increases* the
rate of unintended pregnancies and thus the need for abortion services. This
is, of course, in direct opposition to the intended goal of the GGR: to reduce
the provision of abortion services.

THE G.W. BUSH ADMINISTRATION: SETBACKS FOR WOMEN'S HEALTH

The GGR is only one of many such agenda items that most conservative elected officials support. During the presidency of G. W. Bush, other such items include the banning of most embryonic stem cell research and promoting abstinence-only sex education as a method of HIV prevention. (Interesting to note, in that context, is the advocacy for such research among some conservative critics, most prominently Nancy Reagan.) With regard to abortion, his administration attempted and passed many pro-life regulations. Enacted policies include the Partial Birth Abortion Ban Act; the Born Alive Fetus Protection Act; the Teen Endangerment Act; declaration of the "Sanctity of Life" day; denial of abortions to women in the military; and withholding of funds to the UNFPA (Baird 2009). President G.W. Bush also supported a "Human Life Amendment" to the U.S. Constitution; such an amendment would overturn *Roe v. Wade*. Additionally, longstanding bans on federal funding of abortion services were continued (i.e., Helms Amendment, Hyde Amendment[10]).

Two patterns of policy-making in the G.W. Bush administration that the adoption of the GGR followed are the blurring of various issues around abortion and the lack of scientific and other evidence in policy-making.

Many policies that are not specifically about the funding or provision of abortion services, however, have been enacted. Some of these policies are contrary to scientific evidence. Additionally they represent attempts to enlarge the scope of agreed upon restrictions into other more controversial arenas. In other words, even though some policies are not about the provision of abortion *per se*, the ideology or reasoning behind the new initiatives—that is, policies that promote preservation of human "life" at the most minute level of cells, zygotes, and frozen embryos—if accepted, could be invoked in the abortion debate and used to make abortion illegal. In the words of one critic, this only resulted in "aborted thinking" (Holloway 2001). Consider the case of the ban on embryonic stem cell research.

Controversy over stem cell research goes back to the mid-1990s. The 1995 Dickey Amendment states that no federal funds may be used for "(1) the creation of a human embryo or embryos for research purposes; or (2) research in which a human embryo or embryos are destroyed, discarded, or knowingly subjected to risk of injury or death" (Kelly et al. 2004). In 2000, during the Clinton administration, new NIH guidelines came out that allowed federal researchers to use stem cells derived from *excess* embryos from fertility clinics if the patients gave informed consent. The NIH also established a committee to ensure that the regulations had been properly followed.

The election of George W. Bush drastically altered the path of stem cell research. In 2001, the new administration asked the NIH to review the previous recent policy. Its resulting policy recommendations were very unclear and the newly created NIH oversight committee was never convened (Kelly et al. 2004). But in August 2001, President G. W. Bush announced that research would only be permitted on the "more than sixty genetically diverse stem cell lines that already exist. They were created from embryos that have already been destroyed . . . where the life and death decision has already been made." The president continued, "Leading scientists tell me research on these sixty lines has great promise that could lead to breakthrough therapies and cures" (as quoted in Kelly et al. 2004, 22). (But in fact, there were not even sixty stem cell lines in existence; there were very few [Guttmacher 2001].) President Bush was ostensibly applying his "sanctity of life" and pro-life stance to stem cell research, assuring that only existing stem cell lines could be utilized. If new ones were created and used for research, potential life would be destroyed, he reasoned.

Stem cells can be obtained from tissue which has been removed during a pregnancy termination or from embryos produced during an in-vitro fertilization process. Once isolated, the cells can grow in the laboratory and be stored for future use; each cell can create what is called a cell line. Gathering tissue from destroyed embryos raises, for some, similar concerns as abortion. But scientific research on Parkinson's, Alzheimer's, and a host of other diseases could radically progress with research involving stem cells, and thus the controversy of destroying the "life" of embryos versus enabling medical progress to save lives is at stake.

But what happens to these unused embryos if they are not used for research? "Death or deep freeze is the fate of any embryo spared by the Bush policy from the indignity of contributing to medical progress" (Kinsley 2004).

With regard to the GGR, President Bush stated that "it is my conviction that taxpayer funds should not be used to pay for abortions or advocate or actively promote abortions" (as quoted in Cohen 2001). The Helms Amendment already forbids federal funds to pay for abortion services, and this is a fairly noncontroversial policy. The GGR additionally prohibits advocacy or even discussion of abortion. This shifting and enlarging of the line from accepted prohibitions against funding the procedure itself to controversial prohibitions against discussing or even mentioning the word "abortion" was a strategic choice. But talking about funding of abortions and discussing abortion rights as if they are all prohibited by the GGR creates confusion—desired confusion, I maintain.

A Gallup Poll assessed the public's support for numerous executive orders President Obama has issued. For the GGR the question was asked, "Would you say you approve or disapprove of . . . [a]llowing U.S. funding for overseas family planning organizations that provide abortions?" (Jones 2009). This wording is unclear as to what the GGR mandates. It is another obfuscation of funding, abortion services, and the GGR and is a result of the deliberately created confusion over the ruling.[11] The poll is then discussed in the media and by pro-life groups as evidence of the lack of support for President Obama's lifting of the GGR and support for its restrictions.

When President Obama proposed to lift the GGR, seventy-eight lawmakers sent him a letter urging him not to do so. The letter stated, "Not only is it inappropriate for the federal government to fund abortionists in the United States, but there is certainly no place for taxpayer-funded abortions overseas. Many Americans are not even aware that their hard-earned dollars are being exported to support this abhorrent practice. The exportation of abortions is change we do not want" (as cited in Norris 2009).

Many members of Congress are still muddying the issues.

G. W. BUSH: IDEOLOGY OVER EVIDENCE IN POLICY-MAKING

Another pattern present in the G.W. Bush administration is the "politicization of science" (Mooney 2005) or the use of "ideology over evidence." In abortion restrictions, stem cell research, anti-trafficking assistance, HIV/AIDS prevention, and clean needle programs, to name only a few, restrictions and regulations were instituted that ignored and even distorted scientific evidence.

President Bush noted that he was reinstating the GGR because "it will make abortion more rare" (as quoted in Cohen 2001). This is a goal that all could potentially agree upon. Most would desire fewer unwanted pregnancies and fewer abortions in the world. Unfortunately, there is no evidence to support the proposition that prohibiting family planning organizations from uttering the word "abortion" or prohibiting them from lobbying for its legality will lead to fewer abortions. In fact, it does not make logical sense. In fact, much evidence exists to the contrary—that imposing the GGR causes many major family planning organizations to reduce services or close clinics, thus reducing the provision of family planning services (PPI 2000a). Evidence shows that when women have unplanned and unwanted pregnancies, they commonly resort to abortion, whether it is safe and legal or unsafe and illegal (Baird 2004; Global Health Council 2002). For $100 million in family planning, 2.1 million unwanted pregnancies could be avoided and 825,000 abortions prevented (Speidel et al. 2009).

This ignoring of evidence and allowing ideology to drive policy formation was a pervasive pattern in the G.W. Bush administration. This has been well-documented (Kelly et al. 2004; Mooney 2005; UCS 2004a and 2004b), but a brief example of abstinence-only sex education will be covered.

The G. W. Bush administration first ignored and then distorted information on abstinence-only sex education and the efficacy of condoms in HIV prevention (UCS 2004a). Even when he was Governor Bush of Texas and was implementing abstinence-only sex education programs, such an approach was deemed ineffective in reducing teen pregnancy (UCS 2004a, 10). Most major health organizations, namely the American Medical Association, American Public Health Association, American Academy of Pediatrics, and the American College of Obstetrics and Gynecology, support comprehensive sex education. Additionally, after implementing abstinence-only sex education at the federal level, Congressional research documented its ineffectiveness and provision of incorrect information (GAO 2006; U.S. House 2004).

In addition to ignoring the evidence and developing policy at odds with the evidence, the Bush Administration also distorted information about the efficacy of abstinence-only programs. His administration changed the measures by which sex education programs were evaluated from performance-based measures such as the birth rates of abstinence-only program participants to only looking at program attendance and attitudes (UCS 2004a). Moreover, information on the efficacy of condoms in HIV prevention was altered and misinformation suggesting a link between abortion and breast cancer was published (UCS 2004a; Mooney 2005).

These two patterns of policy-making in the G.W. Bush administration— obfuscation of issues and employing ideology over evidence in policy-making—show how information can be manipulated and strategies to create confusion can be implemented. First, and perhaps to the great dismay of many pro-choice individuals, no federal funding for abortion services has become standard, accepted policy. President Obama, an ardent supporter of reproductive rights, recently reaffirmed this position in order to have major health care reform passed. It is now entrenched as the status quo (but see Lerner 2010 for an alternative view). We can and should fund ample (non-abortion) family planning services and comprehensive sex education for all so that the occurrence of unwanted pregnancies can be minimized. But because of the strongly divisive nature of abortion, no government funding for the service is a policy that pro-choice advocates have to accept, at least for now.

Other abortion-*related* matters, however, should not be confused with the funding of abortion services. The lifting of the GGR *only* removes the ban on discussing abortion or advocating for its legality. Pro-choice advocates need to make this distinction clear and be sure that support or lack of support for the GGR hinges on this aspect. Pro-choice advocates need to hold policy-makers accountable to this distinction and not let them conflate the two separate issues. I believe that if many people could clearly see that the GGR is about limiting what is considered in this country free speech, it would lose much support. Along with the ideas discussed below, these may provide fruitful paths to enacting long-term, institutional change with regard to U.S. funding of international family planning.

POTENTIAL SOLUTIONS FOR LONG-TERM CHANGE

Evidence-Based Policy-Making

One lucrative arena in which long-lasting institutional change can be made is evidence-based policy-making. Such strategies involve utilizing evaluation research to measure the effectiveness of programs and policies and basing future funding decisions on such evidence. President Obama has already taken steps to improve policy-making in his administration—"toward promoting a greater culture of evaluation in the modern regulatory state" (Coglianese 2011). "No president or budget director for a president have ever been so intent on using evidence to shape decisions about the funding of social programs as President Obama and former Budget Director Orszag" (Haskins and Baron 2011, 28).

Peter Orszag writes, "Rigorous ways to evaluate whether programs are working exist. But too often such evaluations don't happen" (Orszag 2009). The Obama administration has developed six pilot, evidence-based projects whose funding depends on showing efficacy. Though these projects were developed in conjunction with Congress, the continuance of them will depend not on Congressional approval but on them impacting the problems they are trying to solve (Haskins and Baron 2011). These have been called the largest effort by *any* presidential administration to utilize evidence in policy-making (Haskins and Baron 2011), and provide examples of how to rely on evidence and not "politics" to develop policy.

Even though no policy-maker can be forced to listen to or consider scientific evidence, institutional structures can be created that can greatly increase the chance of evidence-based policy-making. A different culture can be created, enabling diverse perspectives to be combined with scientific evidence about efficacy of various strategies—a culture in which goals and objectives are debated and developed in a democratic fashion, and then evidence-based strategies developed to meet these goals. Such a culture should reduce the chances of the GGR being reinstated as evidence has shown its detrimental effects on family planning.

Passing a Congressional Law

Since the initial inception of the GGR, numerous Congressional attempts to pass a law that would override the executive order have been made. A typical example is the Global Democracy Promotion Act introduced in many Congressional sessions by a bipartisan coalition of members of the House and Senate. Though a Republican president probably would veto such a bill, Obama would be much more likely to sign it. What, then, are the prospects for enacting a Congressional law?

In January 2009, after Obama rescinded the rule, a bill was introduced to restore the restrictions in the Senate; sixty senators voted "nay" and thirty-seven senators voted "yea" (U.S. Senate 2009). In December 2009, the Senate passed a measure to overturn the GGR but the conference committee rejected it. In the House, the Rules committee rejected an attempt to attach an amendment to a bill that would have put the restoration of the Mexico City Rule, President Reagan's first rendition of the GGR, to the House floor for a vote.

Rep. Nita Lowey (D-NY) and Senator Barbara Boxer (D-CA) introduced the Global Democracy Promotion Act of 2010; nearly 300 organizations supported the legislation. But then the 2010 mid-term elections occurred and the House returned to Republican control and the Senate's Democratic majority was reduced. Efforts to codify the Global Gag Rule have been attempted, as well as to permanently bar funding to the UNFPA. So far, these attempts have been unsuccessful.

Comprehensive Global Health Programs

The United States can provide funding for international programs in a variety of ways. It can provide bilateral funding which means it provides monies directly to a country or organization. Alternatively, it can provide multilateral funding whereby its monies are channeled through other international organizations, typically UN agencies, World Health Organization (WHO), World Bank, and so on. Bilateral aid gives the provider more control over the recipients and how the monies are spent; the funding USAID provides for family planning and which the GGR restricts is an example of bilateral aid. The funding the United States gives to the UNFPA is multilateral aid and the lack of control over who UNFPA funds is precisely the problem that many members of Congress and some presidents have with such allocations. But one possible solution to the GGR is to have the U.S. provide more family planning funds to and through UNFPA. The U.S. cannot impose the GGR on UNFPA recipients.

Another route that is being pursued by the Obama administration is to pool all global health programs into one package. This is called the Global Health Initiative. More than twenty U.S. government agencies work internationally with regard to health, but there has been little effort to coordinate efforts (IOM 2009). A central location for all international health programs would allow for a coordinated global health strategy as opposed to piecemeal and sometimes overlapping efforts. The initiative was created in 2009, and though it has had a slow start, it shows great promise.

Such comprehensive global health efforts would make it more difficult for restrictions such as the GGR to be applied to one agency's programs. Family planning would be housed with other "health" programs as opposed to "foreign aid" programs. Maternal and reproductive health, including family planning, would be linked, and it would be more difficult to enact a restriction on family planning programs that actually harms maternal and reproductive health when programs are viewed in such a comprehensive light.

CONCLUSION

The United States is the largest funder of family planning services around the world. The Global Gag Rule prohibits foreign NGOs from receiving U.S. family planning funds if they provide counseling on abortion, provide abortion services, or participate in political debate on abortion, even if achieved with non-U.S. funds. When in place, family planning services for women have been reduced, thus potentially increasing unplanned pregnancies and the need for abortions. Since the early 1980s, various U.S. presidents have ordered it and others have rescinded it, allowing women's lives and bodies around the world to be the site of struggle of the internal political disputes of the United States.

Potential solutions to this problem include passing a law that overrides executive orders, changing the culture of policy-making within the administration, and changing the way funding and policies are developed. Additionally a comprehensive approach to global health combined with evidence-based decision-making shows great promise for creating institutional change that makes it less likely that the GGR will be instituted again.

REFERENCES

AbouZahr, Carla. 2003. "Global burden of maternal death and disability." British Medical Bulletin 67: 1–11. http://bmb.oxfordjournals.org/cgi/reprint/67/1/1 (accessed August 18, 2012).

Baird, Karen L. 2004. "Globalizing Reproductive Control." In *Linking Visions: Feminist Bioethics, Human Rights, and the Developing World*, edited by Rosemarie Tong, Anne Donchin, and Susan Dodds, 133–45. New York: Rowman & Littlefield.

———. 2009. "Carrying the World on Her Back: Women's Health, Women's Lives, Women's Rights." In *Women and Politics around the World*, eds. Joyce Gelb and Marian Lief Palley, 115–128. Santa Barbara, CA: ABC–CLIO.

———. 2009. *Beyond Reproduction: Women's Health, Activism, and Public Policy*. With Dana–ain Davis and Kimberly Christensen. Madison, NJ: Fairleigh Dickinson University Press.

Center for Reproductive Law and Policy (CRLP). 2001. "The Bush Global Gag Rule: a Violation of International Human Rights and the U.S. Constitution." CRLP Publication, Item: B019, July.

Center for Reproductive Rights. 2011. "The World's Abortion Laws, 2011." http://reproductiverights.org/sites/crr.civicactions.net/files/documents/AbortionMap_2011.pdf (accessed August 18, 2012).

Cohen, Susan. 2000. "Abortion Politics and U.S. Population Aid: Coping with a Complex New Law." *International Family Planning Perspectives* 26 (3), September.

Coglianese, Cary. 2011. "The Administration's Regulatory Review Plans: Toward Evidence–Based Governance," May 26. http://www.law.upenn.edu/blogs/regblog/2011/05/the-obama-administrations-regulatory-reviews-plans-toward-evidence-based-governance.html [Accessed June 18, 2011].

Congressional Research Service (CRS). 2001. "International Family Planning: The 'Mexico City' Policy." (Updated April 2, 2001). http://www.policyalmanac.org/culture/archive/abortion_Mexico_City.pdf [Accessed March 28, 2010].

Crane, Barbara B. and Jennifer Dusenberry. 2004. "Power and Politics in International Funding for Reproductive Health: The US Global Gag Rule. " *Reproductive Health Matters* 12(24):128–137.

Global Health Council. 2002. *Promises to Keep: The Toll of Unintended Pregnancies on Women's Lives in the Developing World.* http://issuu.com/globalhealthcouncil/docs/promisestokeep/1 (accessed August 18, 2011).

Gold, Rachel Benson. 2004. "Embryonic Stem Cell Research—Old Controversy; New Debate." *Guttmacher Report on Public Policy* 7 (Oct., No. 4):4–6.

Government Accounting Office (GAO). 2006. *Abstinence Education: Efforts to Assess the Accuracy and Effectiveness of Federally Funded Programs.* GAO 07–87, October. http://www.gao.gov/new.items/d0787.pdf [Accessed March 24, 2010].

Guttmacher Institute. 2001. "Bush Okays Some Stem Cell Research Funding; Debate Continues." *Guttmacher Report on Public Policy* 4 (Aug., No.4). http://www.guttmacher.org/pubs/tgr/04/4/gr040412a.html [Accessed March 22, 2010].

Haskins, Ron and Jon Baro. 2011 (April). "The Obama Administration's evidence-based social policy initiatives: An overview," Part 6, in NESTA's *Evidence for Social Policy and Practice.* Washington, DC: NESTA.

Holloway, Marguerite. 2001. "Aborted Thinking: Reenacting the global gag rule threatens public health." *Scientific American* 284 (4, April):19–20.

Institute of Medicine (IOM), Committee on the U.S. Commitment to Global Health. 2009. *The U.S. Commitment to Global Health: Recommendations for the New Administration.* IOM: Washington, DC.

Jones, Jeffrey. 2009. "Americans Approve of Most Obama Actions to Date." A USA Today/Gallup Poll, February 2. http://www.gallup.com/poll/114091/Americans-Approve-Obama-Actions-Date.aspx?version=print [Accessed April 1, 2010].

Kelly, Henry, Ivan Oelrich, Steven Aftergood, and Benn H. Tannenbaum. 2004. "Flying Blind: the Rise, Fall, and Possible Resurrection of Science Policy Advice in the United States." Occasional Paper No. 2, December. http://www.fas.org/resource/12022004142618.pdf [Accessed March 28, 2010].

Lerner, Sharon. 2010. "Nowhere to Hyde." *The Nation*, April 19. http://www.thenation.com/doc/20100419/lerner[Accessed April 2, 2010].

Mooney, Chris. 2005. *The Republican War on Science.* New York: Basic Books.

Norris, Wendy. 2009. "Obama rescinds global gag rule despite Lamborn's efforts." *The Colorado Independent.* http://coloradoindependent.com/19978/obama-rescinds-global-gag-rule-despite-lamborns-efforts [Accessed March 28, 2010].

Obama, Barack. 2009, January 23. "Mexico City Policy—Voluntary Population Planning." Washington, DC: Office of the White House. http://www.whitehouse.gov/the_press_office/MexicoCityPolicy-VoluntaryPopulationPlanning/

Orszag, Peter. 2009. "Building Rigorous Evidence to Drive Policy." June 8, OMB Blog. http://www.whitehouse.gov/omb/blog/09/06/08/BuildingRigorousEvidencetoDrivePolicy/[Accessed June 15, 2011].

Population Action International (PAI). 2006a. "What You Need To Know About the Mexico City Policy Restrictions On U.S. Family Planning Assistance. *An Unofficial Guide.*" Washington, DC: Population Action International. http://www.populationaction.org/Publications/Reports/Global_Gag_Rule_Restrictions/GlobalGagRule.pdf [Accessed March 25, 2010].

———. 2006b. "Access Denied: the Impact of the Global Gag Rule in Kenya." Washington, DC: Population Action International. http://www.populationaction.org/PDFs/Kenya/GGRcase_kenya_2006.pdf [Accessed March 25, 2010].

————. 2006c. "Access Denied: the Impact of the Global Gag Rule in Nepal." Washington, DC: Population Action International." http://populationaction.org/wp–content/uploads/2012/01/Nepal.pdf [Accessed October 15, 2012].

————. 2012 (March). "Family Planning: The Smartest Investment We Can Make." Policy and Issue Brief. Washington, DC: Population Action International. http://populationaction.org/wp-content/uploads/2012/04/CostEffectiveness-2012.pdf [Accessed October 12, 2012].

Speidel, J. Joseph, et al. 2009. "Making the Case for U.S. International Family Planning Assistance," By Five Former Directors of the Population and Reproductive Health Program of the United States Agency for International Development (USAID). http://www.usaidalumni.org/docs/Making%20the%20Case.pdf [Accessed March 30, 2010].

Union of Concerned Scientists (UCS). 2004a. "Scientific Integrity In Policymaking: An Investigation into the Bush Administration's Misuse of Science." Cambridge, MA: Union of Concerned Scientists.

————. 2004b. "Scientific Integrity In Policymaking: Further Investigation of the Bush Administration's Misuse of Science," July. http://www.ucsusa.org/scientific_integrity/abuses_of_science/scientific-integrity-in.html [Accessed December 30, 2011].

U.S. House of Representatives, Committee on Government Reform–Minority Staff Special Investigation. 2004. "The Content of federally Funded Abstinence–Only Education Programs." Prepared for Rep. Henry A. Waxman. http://www.aac.org/site/DocServer/waxman_report.pdf?docID=3804 [Accessed March 25, 2010].

U.S. Senate. 2009. U.S. Senate Roll Call Votes 111th Congress—1st Session http://www.senate.gov/legislative/LIS/roll_call_lists/roll_call_vote_cfm.cfm?congress=111&session=1&vote=00019

U.S. White House Memorandum. 2001. "Memorandum of March 28, 2001—Restoration of the Mexico City Policy." March 29, 2001. *Federal Register* Vol. 66, No. 61, 17301–17313.

WHO (World Health Organization). 2012. *Trends in Maternal Mortality: 1990 to 2010.* Geneva Switzerland: WHO. Also at http://www.unfpa.org/webdav/site/global/shared/documents/publications/2012/Trends_in_maternal_mortality_A4–1.pdf (accessed Sept. 3, 2012).

NOTES

1. This same issue is played out in the regulations surrounding the provision of PEPFAR funds and antiretroviral drugs.

2. Some of this background information has appeared in Karen L. Baird, 2004, "Globalizing Reproductive Control." In *Linking Visions: Feminist Bioethics, Human Rights, and the Developing World*, edited by Rosemarie Tong, Anne Donchin, and Susan Dodds, 133-45. New York: Rowman & Littlefield.

3. U.S. President George W. Bush announced the new rule on January 22, 2001; it was issued as a memorandum to the administrator of USAID on March 28, 2001. It was codified in the Federal Register on March 29, 2001. *Federal Register* Vol. 66, No. 61, 17301-17313.

4. "Promoting abortion is defined as an organization committing resources 'in a substantial or continuing effort to increase the availability or use of abortion as a method of family planning.' Examples of what constitutes the promotion of abortion include: operating a family planning counseling service that includes information regarding the benefits and availability of abortion; providing advice that abortion is an available option or encouraging women to consider abortion; lobbying a foreign government to legalize or to continue the legality of abortion as a method of family planning; and conducting a public information campaign in a USAID-recipient country regarding the benefits and/or availability of abortion as a method of family planning" (CRS 2001, 2).

5. After the 2010 Republican takeover of the House, Republicans have unsuccessfully tried to pass a congressional law codifying the Global Gag Rule.

6. Much of this background information has appeared in Karen L. Baird, 2004, "Globalizing Reproductive Control." In *Linking Visions: Feminist Bioethics, Human Rights, and the Developing World*, edited by Rosemarie Tong, Anne Donchin, and Susan Dodds, 133-45. New York: Rowman & Littlefield, and Karen L. Baird, 2009. "Carrying the World on Her Back:

Women's Health, Women's Lives, Women's Rights." In *Women and Politics around the World*, eds. Joyce Gelb and Marian Lief Palley, 115-128. Santa Barbara, CA: ABC-CLIO.

7. Much of this background information has appeared in Karen L. Baird, 2004, "Globalizing Reproductive Control." In *Linking Visions: Feminist Bioethics, Human Rights, and the Developing World*, edited by Rosemarie Tong, Anne Donchin, and Susan Dodds, 133-45. New York: Rowman & Littlefield, and Karen L. Baird, 2009. "Carrying the World on Her Back: Women's Health, Women's Lives, Women's Rights." In *Women and Politics around the World*, eds. Joyce Gelb and Marian Lief Palley, 115-128. Santa Barbara, CA: ABC-CLIO

8. See http://www.populationaction.org/globalgagrule/Summary.shtml for some country-specific data.

9. Many organizations collaborated on a project documenting the consequences of the GGR called "Access Denied." Visit www.populationaction.org for extensive evidence of the consequences of the Global Gag Rule.

10. The Hyde Amendment was first passed in 1976 and has continuously been in effect since that time. It prohibits federal funds from being used to pay for abortion services. Various exceptions, such as to save the life of the mother, in cases of rape and incest, etc., have been debated, added, and deleted over the years.

11. Some thirty-five percent approved and fifty-eight percent disapproved.

Chapter Six

The Ethics of State Policies Restricting Access to Infant Formula and their Impact on Women's and Children's Health

Leah R. Perlman and Kathryn Roberts

INTRODUCTION

A governmental policy that protects and balances the health and rights of infants, as well as mothers, mobilizes the resources and support systems necessary to equip families to make the best decisions for mothers and their children. Legislating and criminalizing the actions of mothers who choose not to breastfeed runs contrary to such a policy. While many countries have become signatories to the Code of Marketing of Breast-milk Substitutes and others have progressed to creating and enforcing national laws about the availability of infant formula, Iran has defied this trend by making it illegal to purchase infant formula without a prescription from a healthcare provider. But has Iran gone too far? Is Iran promoting children's health through breast-feeding or infringing on a mother's right to determine how to feed her child?

At the intersection of a mother's and a child's rights, who prevails? This chapter will focus on the potential ethical, legal, and health ramifications of Iran's policy, arguing that criminalizing a woman's choice of infant feeding methods is the effective equivalent of forcing women to breastfeed. Iran's policy violates a mother's bodily autonomy and her right to self-determination. Iran's policy also isolates many mothers from economic, social, and political life. Neither infant nor mother benefit from a policy that does not balance the rights of infants and mothers.

Breast-milk is widely recognized as the best source of nutrition for infants; but it is not the only option available. Alternatives for infant feeding, beyond breastfeeding, include using commercially produced infant formula, locally made infant food, or a combination of the above. Mothers and their families most often choose whatever method is most complementary to their lifestyles, easily accessible, and economical. The way a woman and her family assess these factors depends heavily upon their health literacy and how much reliable and accessible information they have about the comparative benefits and drawbacks of breast-milk and infant formula.

Marketing strategies adopted by infant formula manufacturers have the potential to unduly influence this decision-making process. Barring any regulation, marketing and advertising provide much of the health information received by mothers, and their message may have broad reach and influence given extensive budgets and strong economic incentives to reach women before and after they give birth. However, the content of the information provided by infant-formula manufacturers usually touts the benefits of the product without mentioning the inadequacies and potential negative consequences of its use. In these marketing campaigns some companies claim, incorrectly, that infant formula is better for the child's nutritional needs and cognitive and physical development.

Infant-formula manufacturers rarely disclose the ways in which infant formula is inferior to breast-milk. In response to these deceptive marketing tactics, international breastfeeding advocates and the World Health Organization (WHO) collaborated to create the Code of Marketing of Breast-milk Substitutes (the Code). The Code outlines steps that states should take to regulate the conduct of manufacturers, distributors, and sellers of infant formula, as well as other products such as bottles, teats, and any nourishment specified as created for infants. While any country can choose to be party to the Code, it is not binding and carries no possibility of enforcement by the international community. States have the right to choose which, if any, of the provisions outlined in the Code they will adopt and implement after becoming signatories. The majority of party nations focus on regulating the actions of the infant formula industry: outlining manufacturing and marketing standards, as well as defining allowable interaction between companies, healthcare workers, and mothers.

BREASTFEEDING FOR HEALTHY CHILDREN

Before addressing the ethics of legislating access to infant formula, it is essential to explore why breastfeeding has garnered so much attention and why the Code is considered necessary by the WHO and the nations that follow its guidelines. An understanding of the value and importance of breast-milk to infant nutrition will facilitate an understanding of why the Iranian government has enacted legislation to mandate that all Iranian children are breastfed. However, even with this understanding, the justification for subverting women's rights to control their bodies remains to be seen.

The international community identifies breastfeeding as the most important, accessible, and economical way to decrease infant mortality globally. Breastfeeding is recognized as the best source of nutrition for the first six months of an infant's life, and should be given in combination with other nutritious foods after a child reaches six months. Breast-milk contributes to healthy growth of children's bodies, minds, and immune systems (WHO n.d.). The WHO, the United Nations Children's Fund (UNICEF), and other international organizations recommend that infants be breastfed exclusively from birth to six months. This means that a mother must be with her infant and able to breastfeed every day, every few hours, all day and night, or must have access to a breast pump and a method to keep the milk chilled until she can feed it to her child, or a milk maid, or a milk bank. It is recommended that children continue to breastfeed regularly between six months and two years and beyond, while parents simultaneously introduce appropriate complementary foods (WHO n.d.). In addition to providing the necessary calories and micronutrients necessary for growth, breastfeeding is associated with the development of a more robust immune system, leading to increased resistance to many illnesses including pneumonia, ear infections, urinary tract infections, allergies, asthma, various autoimmune and respiratory conditions, and obesity. Breastfeeding also promotes neurological development and higher IQ (WHO n.d.). In addition to health benefits for the child, breastfeeding is beneficial for mothers, delaying the early return of fertility, increasing spacing between children, reducing the risk of future miscarriage, postpartum hemorrhage, breast and ovarian cancer, obesity, helping a mother return to her pre-pregnancy weight, increasing bone re-mineralization postpartum, and promoting bonding between infant and mother (American Academy of Pediatrics. Work Group on Breastfeeding 1997).

If a mother decides not to or is unable to breastfeed, the best alternative is generally believed to be infant formula. Infant formula was developed to nourish infants; however, while nutritionally adequate, it does not promote growth and development as well as breast-milk. Infant formula lacks the antibodies present in breast-milk that enable infants to develop a stronger immune system and therefore decreases their risk of future acute and chronic diseases. Additionally, many of the vitamins and minerals that are present in infant formula, while similar in name and quantity to those present in breast-milk, are less bio-available to infants, resulting in comparatively fewer nutritional benefits.

Inferior nutrition and development of the immune system are among many potentially negative consequences of infant formula use. Globally, diarrhea is the leading cause of death of children under the age of five, with dehydration and malnutrition as the immediate causes of death (WHO n.d.). Water is necessary for mixing infant formula powder, as well as for washing bottles and nipples to prevent contamination. Potential negative consequences associated with choosing infant formula are increased considerably in places where potable water is not readily available. The use of non-potable or contaminated water to mix infant formula, coupled with a less robust immune system associated with formula use, increases the risk of childhood diarrhea, as many of the infectious and causal agents for diarrhea are found in water. Repeated or extended cases of diarrhea are associated with a significantly increased risk of illness, malnutrition, and death in children. Chronic diarrhea in infants can lead to malnourished and underweight children, which, in turn can lead to stunted growth, a condition that is impossible to correct through improved nutrition later in life. The malnourished and underweight child is then at greater risk for future infection and illness due to physical and immunological underdevelopment, causing a cycle of ill-health that can lead to impeded physical and mental development and even death, either from infection, or more often, from dehydration.

Additional, potentially harmful consequences of infant formula use are associated with incorrect preparation. When formula is not mixed to the appropriate strength, infants are at greater risk for malnutrition, including calorie, protein, and micronutrient deficiencies (WHO n.d.). Unlike breast-milk, which is usually readily available as long as the mother receives adequate nutrition and breastfeeds regularly after giving birth, infant formula is a costly, ongoing expense. If family finances are strained, caregivers may dilute the infant formula in order to make each tin last longer. The risk of malnutrition associated with the use of infant formula is compounded by low literacy rates in many parts of the developing world, particularly among women. Thus, even if families have clean water and enough money to buy an adequate supply of infant formula, parents may not be able to read and understand the instructions on infant formula tins, possibly leading them to give the wrong amount or concentration of formula to their child (Nathan 2008).

When neither breast-milk nor infant formula are feasible options, families may turn to locally available foods to meet an infant's dietary needs. Animal milks such as cow, buffalo, sheep, camel, and goat lack many of the essential vitamins, minerals, and antibodies necessary to optimal growth and development. Furthermore, an infant's delicate digestive tract is not able to digest many of the carbohydrates, fats, and proteins present in milk created for other mammals. Infants fed with animal milk during their first six months of life are more likely to develop diarrhea, gastroenteritis, dehydration, allergic reactions, intestinal bleeding, scurvy, and essential fatty acid deficiency, which can lead to dermatitis, stunted growth, and impaired cognitive development (WHO 2006). Moreover, there are issues of contamination of animal milk in communities where pasteurization and cold storage are unavailable. The WHO recommends adding supplements composed of fatty acids, minerals, and vitamins to animal milk in an effort to meet an infant's nutritional needs, if no other options are available (WHO 2006). However, the formula for these supplements, based on infant weight, age, and nutritional needs, are complex and may be unsafe if administered incorrectly. For example, iron deficiency leads to anemia, but iron supplements inappropriately provided to infants may lead to an increased incidence of malaria (WHO 2006 and UNICEF 2006).

Plant-based infant feeding supplements are perhaps the least preferable method for meeting infant nutritional needs. However, they are also often the most affordable and accessible. Gruels, cereals, rice, teas, and soy-based products may be appropriate as supplements for children over six months of age in conjunction with breast-milk, but are insufficient for infants under six months of age, especially when used as the primary source of nutrition. Plants do not meet an infant's need for calcium, riboflavin, iron, or zinc, as an infants' digestive tract is often not developed enough to process plant-based food (Gibson, Ferguson, and Lehrfeld 1998). Additionally, when infants are fed using supplements, they are not exposed to the antibodies in breast-milk and are at much higher risk for mortality from infectious diseases (Bahl et al. 2005).

The health of children is often used by international organizations as a yardstick by which to measure the health of a nation; for instance, the infant mortality rate and the mortality rate of children under five are both considered indicators of development. Another commonly recognized indicator of the health of a population is maternal mortality, which is based on the proportion of women who die while pregnant, during labor, or within a month of giving birth. The interconnectedness of the health of mothers and their children is embodied in both of these indicators, as healthy pregnancy, labor, and postpartum periods tend to lead to better outcomes for mothers and children. When the United Nations outlined the Millennium Development Goals, it looked at eight broad indicators of what the world hopes to achieve to serve the needs of all people. The health portion of the Millennium Development Goals prioritizes reduction of maternal and infant mortality, as well as universal access to reproductive health services. None of these goals is prioritized over another, as the ultimate goal is comprehensive healthcare for all, within the paradigm of sustainable and equitable development.

Iran's attempt to prioritize the reduction of infant mortality and improvement of infant nutrition is laudable. However, given the interconnectedness of maternal and child health, one cannot overlook the unintended consequences for both women and children of restricting access to infant formula. While the Iranian legislation does not explicitly force women to breastfeed, that is the de facto outcome when mothers are not offered support structures at work and in social realms to allow them to continue participation while breastfeeding. The legislative restriction of access to alternative acceptable choices for infant feeding essentially mandates that women use their bodies as the government decrees, rather than as women consider necessary and appropriate.

INFANT FORMULA NECESSITY AND PROMOTION

Respect for a woman's right to make informed decisions about how to feed her children is essential to maternal and child health. There is a large body of evidence demonstrating the protective nature of choosing to feed infants with breast-milk. The identification of influences on a mother's infant feeding decisions is a significant challenge to the goal of decreasing malnutrition and infant mortality. Corporate marketing strategies may not support the goal of decision-making based on accurate information; women may turn to health-care providers, friends, relatives, books, television, or magazines, or more recently, the Internet, to find information about how best to feed their children. Historically, some infant formula companies distributed information that was factually incorrect, leading mothers to believe that infant formula was preferable to breast-milk (Food and Nutrition Board 2004). In addition, infant formula companies promoted their products by supplying hospitals with free diaper bags filled with bottles, infant formula and other items, thereby increasing the mother's tendency to forego breastfeeding for the perceived convenience and ease of using infant formula. Receiving infant formula from a hospital or doctor sends a strong message to women about how they should feed their children and could even be interpreted as an endorsement, accompanied by a concomitant lack of support for breastfeeding from some medical providers. This is in addition to advertising strategies such as depiction of healthy babies on infant formula cans. Such representations tout the benefits of infant formula without addressing the risks and drawbacks of abandoning breastfeeding.

Breast-milk substitutes can be an enticing, and sometimes essential, option for a mother who experiences breastfeeding challenges. Breastfeeding is rarely easy for new mothers. Breast-milk is produced in response to suckling, so it usually takes three to five days after an infant is born for breast-milk to flow freely (U.S. Department of Health and Human Services' Office on Women's Health 2011: 16). During this time expressing milk and infant suckling can be painful. The mother must breastfeed every few hours, sometimes with frustrating results. Some infants have difficulty latching and suckling even weeks after birth, to which there is not an immediate resolution. Also, some mothers have health conditions, such as severe stress, postpartum hemorrhage, or diabetes that can delay the initial production of milk beyond the usual three to five days, thus further necessitating the use of nutritional substitutes (Thompson, Heal, and Roberts 2010).

For many mothers, breastfeeding is uncomfortable at first, but gradually becomes easier. However, for others breastfeeding is uncomfortable and even painful throughout, due to physical conditions such as low production of milk, latching difficulties, plugged milk ducts, or cracked or sore nipples (Lamontagne, Hamelin, and St-Pierre 2008). Most barriers are surmountable with the use of common home remedies, but some barriers, such as mastitis, may require medical intervention. Some fifteen to twenty percent of breast-feeding mothers suffer from mastitis, an inflammation of the breast that may be caused by stress, poor milk drainage, or infection (Scott, Robertson, Fitz-patrick, Knight, and Mulholland 2008). Treatment in the case of infection may be by antibiotics, but this would not be the appropriate treatment if the cause were stress. If improperly managed, mastitis can be painful and lead to early cessation of breastfeeding. Indeed, physical difficulties may lead to the cessation of breastfeeding, which is already challenging without additional complications. Even with proper support and medical treatment mothers may discontinue breastfeeding, as these frustrations are in addition to the often overwhelming experience of caring for a newborn. Without access to nutri-tionally adequate infant formula, mothers in these instances may resort to less desirable feeding choices.

In addition to physical barriers to breastfeeding, mothers may also face economic barriers. Mothers employed outside the home often cease breast-feeding in order to regain their full earning potential, especially in countries that do not have laws allowing breastfeeding mothers to take breaks during the day to pump or feed their infants, or in locations where refrigeration is not available for storing expressed breast-milk (Amin et al. 2011). Breast-milk substitutes offer women the freedom to return to work, allowing them to earn income that contributes to feeding all members of their family, as op-posed to just the infant they will be able to feed if they forego their jobs and remain at home. Indeed, women with the option not to breastfeed are freer to participate not just in economic realms of society, but in political and social realms as well.

In addition to instances when necessity dictates the use of infant formula, many mothers may choose to forgo breastfeeding as a result of the impact of marketing and promotion by infant formula manufacturers. The undue influ-ence of the marketing practices of infant formula producers has been recog-nized in the international arena. The full recognition of the power of this influence took many years, as did the growth in popularity of infant formula. Mothers have long utilized alternatives to breast-milk; commercial infant formula gained popularity in the United States during World War II, as more women began working outside of the home and needed an alternative to breastfeeding. During the 1960s, infant formula manufacturers began to expand their marketing efforts to include developing countries, distributing advertisements and infant formula tins portraying pictures of healthy, white babies, and implicitly touting the superiority of their products in comparison to breastfeeding. In developing countries consumers were generally less likely to be health literate or to have access to healthcare or other sources of information about infant nutrition. Infant formula manufacturers also distributed "educational" materials publicizing the product as superior to breastmilk and conveying the message that "good" mothers feed their infants formula.

The use of formula often results in a mother losing the option to breastfeed altogether and needing to rely on substitutes. A woman will eventually stop lactating if she relies on substitutes, usually after one to three weeks. Infant formula promotion in the developing world did not warn mothers of how quickly their breast-milk production would decrease, and eventually end, if they did not continue to breastfeed regularly. Though a mother may re-lactate, this often takes a few weeks. Even the partial introduction of breast-milk substitutes causes an infant to suckle less often and less vigorously, thus causing the mother to produce less milk and forcing her to turn to substitutes to satisfy her child's nutritional needs (WHO 1985: 7). Moreover, early introduction of a teat may condition an infant to suckle based on this artificial method, developing habits that can lead a child to refuse a breast or be unable to latch on (WHO 1998: 32).

The infant formula industry focused its efforts on early introduction of infant formula, targeting mothers in hospitals and encouraging use of formula from inception through the use of donations and free samples. If women immediately begin using formula rather than breastfeeding, infants miss the chance to receive colostrum, which women produce only during the first two weeks of the post partum period. Colostrum is different in content to mature milk (WHO 1985: 14). The content of antibodies, vitamins, and minerals is concentrated in this initial milk as compared to mature milk and is especially important for a child's healthy introduction to life in the external world. Additionally, research shows that women who receive free samples of formula in the hospital are significantly more likely to introduce artificial feeding and/or discontinue breastfeeding after four to six weeks (Frank, Wirtz, Sorenson, and Heeren 1987).

Marketing efforts of the infant formula industry and the lack of balanced information provided to mothers contributed to the decline of breastfeeding rates in developing countries as more and more families turned to breast-milk substitutes without realizing the consequences of this choice for the development of their children.

INTERNATIONAL AND STATE RESPONSE

During the 1970s, international organizations, the UN, and women's and breastfeeding advocates began to lobby against the infant formula industry's marketing and merchandising tactics. The controversy emerged in public discourse and, subsequently, the courts. In 1972, in response to growing concerns about mothers choosing infant formula without the information necessary to make an informed decision, the Protein Advisory Group of the United Nations released a statement affirming the superiority of breastfeeding, while acknowledging the need for substitutes and necessitating the need for education surrounding their use (Habicht, Davanzo, and Butz 1986). The statement declared, "It is clearly important to avoid actions that would accelerate the trend away from breast feeding. . . . At the same time, it is essential to make formulas, foods, and instructions for good nutrition of their infants available to mothers who do not breastfeed for various reasons" (Habicht et al. 1986). Here the goal is to promote breastfeeding as the best option, while also supporting mothers' access to infant formula if they wish to use it to nourish their children.

The statement made by the Protein Advisory Group of the United Nations did not deter the infant formula industry from promoting its products as optimal infant nutrition and preferable to breast-milk. Hence, nongovernmental organizations also tried to bring public attention to the unethical practices of the breast-milk substitute industry. In 1974, War on Want published a report entitled "The Baby Killer," which highlighted the effects of infant formula promotion on populations in the developing world. Later that year, the report was republished in Switzerland under the title "Nestlé Kills Babies," prompting Nestlé to file (and win) a libel suit against the publishers in UK courts and spawning an international Nestlé boycott, which continues to this day (Nestlé n.d.).

The infant formula industry attempted to placate its critics through self-regulation, creating the International Council of Infant Food Industries (ICIFI) in Zurich in 1975. This group developed a strategy in response to the growing international concern over infant formula manufacturers' marketing and promotion strategies in developing countries. Infant formula manufacturers developed a Code of Ethics and Professional Standards, whereby they affirmed the superiority of breastfeeding, while simultaneously acknowledging the need to educate mothers in the proper use of infant formula and the risks inherent in improper utilization (Post 1978). Although these guidelines showed a willingness to address concerns, corporate self-regulation was not sufficient or enforceable and public opinion of the industry was too deteriorated for this effort to satisfy the growing concerns of the UN, WHO and UNICEF. Trust in the infant formula industry's desire and ability to self-regulate was further weakened by its reaction to the Code, especially given

President of ICIFI Ernest Saunders' (also Vice President of Nestlé) description of the draft International Code of Marketing of Breast-milk Substitutes as unacceptable, restrictive, irrelevant, and unworkable (Baby Milk Action n.d.).

In 1979, the WHO and UNICEF co-hosted an international meeting to discuss the effect of infant formula marketing on global infant health. This meeting culminated in the call for the development of a code to set forth guidelines regarding the promotion of breastfeeding and proper limitations of infant formula advertisement and dissemination. The result was the WHO/ UNICEF International Code of Marketing of Breast-milk Substitutes, adopted by a Resolution of the World Health Assembly in 1981 (hereinafter "the Code") (Resolution World Health Assembly 1981). To date, approximately 197 countries have signed on to the Code. However, as of 2011, only thirty-three countries have enacted domestic legislation implementing all or nearly all of the Code's provisions; thirty-four countries had implemented many but not all provisions, forty-two countries had implemented a few provisions of the Code, seventeen regarded the Code as a voluntary measure that infant formula companies may choose to follow, five countries incorporated a few provisions of the Code into already existing laws, twenty-three countries adopted few voluntary provisions which are generally not enforced, twenty countries had draft laws, and fourteen countries had taken no action at all (International Baby Formula Action Network 2011). In total, as of 2011, eighty-nine percent of countries that signed onto the Code took some action to implement it. The United States is among the countries that have taken no action to implement the Code (International Baby Formula Action Network 2011).

The Code applies to the marketing, quality, information about, and access to, all breast-milk and breastfeeding substitutes, such as infant formula, teats, bottles, nipple shields, follow-up formula, gruels, and baby foods. The Code recommends a ban on promotion to the general public, a ban on distribution of free samples, discounts, and gifts, and a ban on promotions that suggest superiority to natural breast-milk (Resolution World Health Assembly 1981: Article 5). The Code even goes so far as to ban those who work within the industry from having any contact, direct or indirect, with pregnant women or mothers (Resolution World Health Assembly 1981: Article 5). The Code addresses the relationship allowed between the breast-milk substitute industry and the healthcare industry and attempts to ensure that mothers receive information regarding breastfeeding and substitutes from healthcare workers who are well informed of the risks and are not biased by improper influence of the breast-milk substitute industry (Resolution World Health Assembly 1981: Article 6, 7). It also attempts to regulate marketing by prescribing the specific information that must (and must not) appear on the packaging of infant formula and other breast-milk substitutes (Resolution World Health

Assembly 1981: Article 9). The Code was adopted as a recommendation and not as a regulation, and each Member State is free to interpret the Code and enact national legislation, regulations, or policies to enforce its elements (Resolution World Health Assembly 1981: Article 11).

Although approximately 197 countries are signatories to the Code and numerous governments, non-government organizations, and international bodies have undertaken activities to promote the Code, it is estimated that there are 1.4 million excess infant deaths per year that could be prevented through exclusive breastfeeding (Black et al. 2008: 243-260). In 1990 the Innocenti Declaration was drafted and adopted by participants of the WHO/UNICEF meeting, "Breastfeeding in the 1990s: A Global Initiative," held in Florence, Italy. The Innocenti Declaration was issued to reaffirm the superiority of breastfeeding and the need for governmental policy and law to support the practice. In concert with the numerous international bodies working to achieve the Millennium Development Goals, fifteen years later, in 2005, on the anniversary of the Innocenti Declaration, UNICEF issued a press release wherein it affirmed that exclusive breastfeeding is the leading preventive child survival intervention. Nearly two million lives could be saved each year through six months of exclusive breastfeeding and continued breastfeeding with appropriate complementary feeding for up to two years or longer (UNICEF Press Report, 2005). Such an unequivocal pronouncement was intended to draw international attention to recognition of the value of breastfeeding, not merely as the preferred method of infant nutrition, but as one of the best methods of decreasing infant mortality.

BREASTFEEDING AND HUMAN RIGHTS

Several conventions define universal human rights and articulate both legally binding and optional guidelines for promoting and protecting those rights. There is one convention in particular that has direct relevance to breastfeeding and the rights affected by the Code. This convention is the Convention on the Rights of the Child ("the CRC"), which is legally binding on all States that are signatories, and includes all nations except Somalia and the United States. The CRC articulates four basic principles, one of which is devotion to the best interests of the child (Convention on the Rights of the Child 1989: Article 3a). The CRC, enacted to protect children, acknowledges the interconnectivity of children's health to a mother's education and acknowledges that parents should be offered education allowing them to make an informed decision regarding whether or not to breastfeed (Convention on the Rights of the Child 989: Article 24e).

The CRC does not require that the best interests of the child be given complete priority over the rights of a parent, but rather that parental rights be considered in determining the best interests of the child (Convention on the Rights of the Child 1989: Article 3). Additionally, the CRC supports a parent's right to make informed decisions regarding whether or not to breastfeed: "States Parties shall pursue full implementation of this right and, in particular, shall take appropriate measures . . . [to] ensure that all segments of society, in particular parents and children, are informed, have access to education and are supported in the use of basic knowledge of child health and nutrition, [and] the advantages of breastfeeding" (Convention on the Rights of the Child , 1989: Article 24). Parents and children not only have the right to access basic knowledge about breastfeeding, but also the right to assistance in utilizing this knowledge or breastfeeding support. If parents and children are denied these rights and denied accurate information about breastfeeding, or are not supported in their breastfeeding, they are unable to exercise those rights.

STATE-LEVEL LEGISLATIVE REGULATIONS

Prior to the adoption of the Code in 1981, many countries took action to regulate the infant formula industry and its promotional activities on their own. Among these countries were Papua New Guinea, Venezuela, and Jamaica. Papua New Guinea passed the Baby Feed Supplies Control Act in 1977, banning advertising for feeding bottles and making bottles and teats available by prescription only (Friesen, Vince, Boas, and Danaya 1999). Such items can limit a child's ability to return to breastfeeding after using formula. Instead, the use of cups and spoons to feed infants formula is advocated to ensure children do not become habituated to a bottle teat and lose the ability to suckle from a breast. Thus, Papua New Guinea balances child and maternal health by limiting the use of products that contribute to the cessation of breastfeeding, but without limiting access to the formula itself, so that parents may choose how to meet their child's nutritional needs.

After the adoption of the Code, many countries followed suit, passing legislation focusing on regulating the infant formula industry. For example, India passed the Infant Milk Substitutes, Feeding Bottles, and Infant Foods (Regulation of Production, Supply and Distribution) Act in 1992 (amended in 2003). This act regulates the infant formula market without limiting access for mothers who choose not to breastfeed. It allows prosecution of manufacturers that violate the act with subversive promotion and outlines the potential consequences for corporations convicted of violations. The act also mandates education for pregnant women regarding the superiority of breastfeeding in the first two years of life. The legislation attempts to guide parents to make the choice to breastfeed, while still allowing the choice (Infant Milk Substitutes, Feeding Bottles, and Infant Foods 1992).

State regulation of the infant formula industry, such as the Indian legislation, most often attempts to regulate infant formula manufacturers without restricting access to substitutes. Furthermore, these laws increase mothers' and families' access to unbiased information about the benefits and drawbacks of breastfeeding and using infant formula by restricting the information provided by infant formula companies, and the contexts within which that information may be provided. Under this type of legal framework, the focus of the regulation is on curbing unethical industry practices that can harm the health of children, while still allowing women and families to decide how to apply that information to their personal lives.

Some critics argue that the Indian legislative model does not promote breastfeeding sufficiently. They emphasize that while the law regulates the practices of the industry and encourages education, it does not create adequate support for breastfeeding women. Providing support for women who choose to breastfeed is essential to promote and maintain exclusive breastfeeding and to help women overcome difficulties in initiating and continuing to breastfeed a child. A lack of sufficient and unbiased information and support are not the only impediments to breastfeeding; economic, physical, and societal barriers must be considered and addressed as well. Furthermore, as was the case in India, if appropriate funding for monitoring and addressing violations of the Code does not support legislation, there are no repercussions, and thus no incentive for manufacturers to abide by its mandates ("Nestlé tackled on human rights at Croydon demo" 1997).

Iran passed legislation regarding the Promotion of Breastfeeding and Supporting Lactating Mothers in 1995. In addition to regulating the infant formula industry, Iran's legislation goes further than the Code proscribes, limiting access to infant formula and making it available only by prescription from a medical professional. The Iranian law assigns healthcare providers the role of gatekeepers to alternative methods of infant feedings. Under its provisions, prescriptions for breastfeeding substitutes may be issued only in narrow enumerated situations. A prescription may be written in the case of a child's need, such as if a problem is observed in the child's growth. Additionally, a prescription may be written if there is a parental concern, such as if the mother is ill, deceased, or on medication that impacts her ability to breastfeed, or if the father is the primary caregiver. The legislation provides no possibility for a mother to exercise her self-determination and choose not to breastfeed on her own terms; she must always have a reason that fits within one of the limited exceptions and she must convince a doctor of her need.

The goal of this law is to establish a regime under which mothers must exclusively breastfeed their children aside from exceptional circumstances, without considering the hardship this could cause mothers. Indeed, Iran's rates of breastfeeding during the first six months are extremely high with approximately ninety percent of mothers breastfeeding their infants during the first twelve months and as many as fifty-seven percent continuing through the first two years of life (Olang, Farivar, Heidarzadeh, Strandvik, and Yngve 2009). This policy technically regulates the infant formula industry and the sale of breast-milk substitutes, rather than the actions of parents. However, in its application the Iranian law removes a mother's right to choose infant formula rather than to breastfeed and delegates control over parenting decisions and a mother's body to healthcare professionals.

While it is clear that breastfeeding is the best source of infant nutrition and a strong case has been made for the regulation of the infant formula industry, the Iranian strategy of prohibiting the use of infant formula without medical approval infringes upon the autonomy of families and, in particular, the self-determination of mothers to make well-informed decisions about infant nutrition and their own participation in social and economic spheres. In the course of promoting children's rights to nutrition, the Iranian legislation has failed to consider the rights of the mother, and overstepped its bounds from the public sphere into the private sphere. The implicit message in the Iranian legislation is that Iranian women are neither capable of nor entitled to make informed decisions regarding their bodies or how to nourish their children. Such a legislative strategy eschews the internationally recognized best practices for breastfeeding promotion and places Iran at odds with multiple international agreements to which the state is a party.

ETHICS OF LEGISLATION LIMITING ACCESS TO BREAST-MILK SUBSTITUTES

There are numerous ethical issues inherent in legislation that limit a parent's agency surrounding the decision to use infant formula rather than breast-milk for infant nutrition. A law regulating access to infant formula by requiring medical approval raises the issue of restricted opportunity to obtain such approval. The ability to access healthcare depends on factors such as location, access to transportation, ability to afford care, and comfort interacting with healthcare providers. In Iran, as in most areas of the world, rural locations have fewer physicians and healthcare centers per capita (Amir 2007). In such areas, women often must travel long distances to access formal medical care and frequently may not do so because they cannot absent themselves from family, household duties, or employment. Access to high quality, unbiased care is not something that every woman enjoys, and linking a woman's access to infant formula to access to medical services is unwise and unethical.

Additionally, access to infant formula is not automatically granted upon request, so the physician must choose to prescribe it based on the restrictive grounds specified in the Iranian legislation. Women may encounter doctors unwilling to prescribe infant formula, just as the health community has seen doctors unwilling to prescribe other things, like contraception. While limiting access to infant formula is intended to protect infants and ensure that they receive optimal nutrition, the legislation impacts both mother and child, and has the potential to lead to various unintended consequences.

In addition to issues of physical access to medical gatekeepers, the next concern is that of access to economic resources. Although Iran does have legal protections for breastfeeding government employees, such as maternity leave and paid breaks for breastfeeding, there are no similar protections for privately employed mothers and those without insurance (Olang, Farivar, Heidarzadeh, Strandvik, and Yngve 2009). Without such protection, the Iranian law unduly burdens families of low socioeconomic status and increases the likelihood of health risks for infants of those families, if they can neither breastfeed nor access infant formula. Even if there is a healthcare center available, physical access to a health center, and a physician who will prescribe infant formula, limited economic resources may prevent a patient from visiting available healthcare providers. Parents, particularly women, of low socio-economic status are less likely to be able to spend the time or have the money or healthcare coverage to visit a healthcare center to obtain a prescription for infant formula. Women who work outside the home to support their families require access to infant formula, yet they are among the least likely to have the economic resources and time to obtain the medical approval and to have the health literacy and self-advocacy skills to persuade doctors to write the required prescriptions.

While women who are initially denied access to infant formula may choose to breastfeed, they also may choose alternatives that are less nutritionally adequate for their children, such as grain-based or animal-based milk substitutes, discussed above. The choice of less nutritional breast-milk substitutes creates a greater risk of infant malnutrition and infectious disease. Additionally, as with any regulated substance, it is not implausible that a black market in infant formula and/or breast-milk could develop, creating a possibility that, without quality assurances, infants could be subjected to even greater risk of poor health from diluted, contaminated or counterfeit substitutes. One must also consider that making infant formula available only by prescription may contribute to making those using it the targets of social stigma. If "good" mothers follow the law and breastfeed, then those who choose infant formula may be considered outside the social norm: "bad mothers."

This stigma ostensibly could result in some mothers adopting secrecy as a protection. Such mothers may avoid healthcare providers, and not request formula although it is needed for the adequate nutrition of their infant. Furthermore, pursuant to the CRC, it is possible that Iranian-style regulation of access to infant formula could lead to human rights violations if women are forced to choose breastfeeding without being given the proper education or the option to make a decision regarding the best interests of their children as it relates to infant feeding.

Beyond the practical issues of whether women and their families have physical and economic access to prescribed infant formula, there are systemic issues regarding the patriarchal attitudes of control of women's bodies inherent in the Iranian government's attempt to regulate breastfeeding. Notably, this legislation was drafted by a parliament wherein women held only nine of the 261 seats, or 3.4 percent of the vote. This legislation was then approved by an all-male Council of Guardians; the same governmental body with the authority to vet presidential candidates that has consistently, to date, blocked all female hopefuls from running due to their alleged incompetence. Given the lack of female participation in the government structures that assert control over women's bodies, it is not shocking that women are valued more as child bearers than as economic and political contributors in the legislation produced therein. The Iranian model intrinsically regards women's bodies as the place for regulation and state control, preferring to regulate women's conduct rather than imposing a regime of corporate accountability and instituting appropriate legislative controls over infant formula marketing, education, and sales.

Women's bodies should not be a situs for government regulation that does not apply equally and fairly to all citizens, nor should women's bodies be colonized as a situs of regulation and control. Women have the right to control what they do, and do not do, with their bodies. Denying women access to infant formula takes away women's very personal choice about how to use their breasts and breast-milk. In so doing, such laws violate a mother's right to self-determination. This and similar laws set an alarming precedent by prioritizing the rights of children over the rights of their mothers when other, more equitable legislative alternatives, which respect female autonomy, could have been adopted.

At the core of the Iranian infant formula law is the premise that it is a legitimate use of the law to regulate women's personal conduct in all manners in order to prevent harm to children.[1] The law appears to regard mothers' rights as mutable and capable of diminishment by the state. While the health and legal rights of mother and child are interconnected, in this instance the state effectively has placed those rights into a frame of diametrical opposition by derogating from the rights of the mother in order, ostensibly, to protect the child. From a human rights perspective, appropriate state action would be to regulate the infant formula industry, which is the source of much of the problem, rather than to regulate women's self-determination as expressed in a choice or the necessity to feed her child with infant formula.

Rather than separating the rights of mother and child and symbolically placing mother and child in opposition, Kent argues that a mother and child should be viewed as a unit deserving of rights; that the mother has the right to appropriately feed her child, while at the same time that child has the right to adequate nutrition (Kent 2006). Kent argues that rather than restricting the choices of a mother and family regarding how to nourish their children, the rights of the mother and child as a unit should be enhanced, providing them with societal support and education necessary for the healthiest outcomes. The government does not need to force women to do what is best for their children; this is the goal of almost all mothers; they simply need the knowledge and support to be able to do so. Women's bodies are not the government's to deign as the only acceptable source of food for an infant; this is a mother's choice, and it must not be infringed upon.

Despite the fact that the Iranian law does not directly legislate women's bodies, its de facto result is to do precisely that. The raising of children is a collection of many personal, and often difficult, private choices in which the government should play a limited role, aside from ensuring that children are safe from the types of harm from which the rest of society also is protected by law. Limits on parental discipline operate to control parental behavior so that children are protected within the family from the types of assault that are not permitted in society at large. However, when the government essentially mandates breastfeeding, it engages in an unwarranted and unwelcome interference in the parent-child relationship by defaulting to regulation of women's bodies instead of implementing appropriate government regulation of corporate interests and effective programming for parental education. The government does not interfere in the day-to-day nutrition of the majority of society, and therefore should not over-extend its role by becoming involved in parental decisions about infant feeding. Rather than holding women hostage to their biology, efforts should be focused on creating societies that support parenthood, and motherhood in particular, by making resources and systems available so that parents may make the best choices for their children and have access to appropriate education, safe water, and balanced, ethical promotion of breastfeeding alternatives.

Children have the right to be breastfed by a mother who is willing and capable of doing so, and women have the right to be free from government interference in their personal choices about infant nutrition. All citizens, including mothers, must have the right to informed consent over all decisions that affect their bodies; the government of Iran should not presume the right to interfere in the autonomy of the maternal relationship. The fact that breastmilk is undeniably better for a child should not supersede a woman's right to consent to provide it. The Iranian legislature apparently considered it more expedient to legislate women's breastfeeding behavior than to require fair and ethical corporate accountability. Even then, legislating breastfeeding behavior does not take the place of effective measures to educate women about the consequences of their infant nutrition choices, to provide clean water, and to subsidize the availability of infant formula when necessary. While the desire to provide infants with safe and healthy nutrition is understandable and laudable, the Iranian legislation is paternalistic and unethical as an interference with the autonomy of the maternal relationship and an unacceptable patriarchal interference with women's self-determination as mothers.

CONCLUSION: TRUST WOMEN

It is undeniable that breastfeeding is the best choice for the health of mothers and children and particularly important in developing countries, given the additional risk of child morbidity and mortality due to infectious diseases. However, by enacting laws that control maternal access to breast-milk substitutes rather than limiting inappropriate marketing strategies by the infant formula industry, governments breach the boundary between legitimate social control and legitimate personal autonomy. Forcing women to breastfeed is not the answer. Government has a role as a regulator, defining the boundaries of acceptable behavior (Kent 2006). However, the use of infant formula should not be defined as legally unacceptable behavior. While the decision not to breastfeed may not be the most advantageous, or optimal, choice in most circumstances, it should not be forbidden and should always remain with the mother and those with whom she chooses to share her decision-making power.

Women make daily parenting choices throughout a child's life, yet their bodies are only legislated during this brief period of infancy under the Iranian law. A certain diet is considered optimal for a fetus's development. To that end, pregnant women are encouraged to avoid certain foods during pregnancy, such as fish contaminated with mercury. However, the government does not require a pregnant woman to obtain a prescription in order to eat a tuna fish sandwich. Instead, doctors provide prospective mothers with the knowledge they need to make informed decisions about how to use their bodies to provide nutrients to a developing fetus. No governmental intervention is necessary, nor is it considered appropriate to extend the reach of the state into these private choices.

The rationale behind a law such as Iran's is that women may not always make the best choices about feeding their children and therefore it is necessary to control the choice. However, prioritizing the health of a child over the rights of a mother is not a guarantee for better health or nutrition. The authors respectfully suggest that a more ethical approach would be for the Iranian government to function as a proactive agent of public health and work to educate women, create a positive social environment for breastfeeding, ensure that women have the support systems to begin and continue breastfeeding, and ensure that all jobs offer sufficient maternity leave, breastfeeding breaks, and child care. Further, marketing and advertising by infant formula purveyors should be closely regulated, and women should be included in the political structures and invited to participate in drafting and administering policies that affect their bodies and families. These measures would support women as productive members of society by providing information and support to make autonomous decisions in the best interests of the maternal-child unit proposed by Kent.

Rather than legislatively disenfranchising women in their choices about the maternal-child unit and infringing upon maternal bodily autonomy, governments should approach the issue of access to infant formula as an opportunity to promote education about breastfeeding, nutrition, health, and perinatal care. Governments should trust women to use their education to make the decisions that are best for their health and the health of their families. Government also has a role to play in enhancing existing healthcare systems to ensure that women and their children have access to quality healthcare near their homes and support during the inception and continuation of breastfeeding. When governments ensure that all businesses not only abide and tolerate mothers in their midst, but protect and value maternity and ensure sufficient paid maternity leave so that mothers have the option to exclusively breastfeed and care for their children without sacrificing vital income, governments will increase the economic capacity and equality of women. Women should not face punishment or dismissal for needing time to breastfeed and they should have access to high-quality childcare at or near their place of employment.

Governments should encourage women to participate in their political, economic, and social spheres rather than limiting them to the home by mandating exclusive breastfeeding. Only by encouraging female participation in government can states ensure that women's voices are incorporated into the regulations that affect their bodies and lives. Only by actively promoting the rights of both women and children can states reap the rewards of valuing women as mothers, caretakers, earners, and educators of their children. It is when women participate fully in society, and are educated as equals capable of cogent decision-making, that they are more likely to be equipped with all they need to make the best choices for their children and themselves.

REFERENCES

American Academy of Pediatrics. Work Group on Breastfeeding 1997 "Breastfeeding and the use of human milk." *Pediatrics* 100(6): 1035-1039.

Amin, R., Z. Said, R. Sutan, S. Shah, A. Darus, and K. Shamsuddin. 2011. "Work-Related Determinants of Breastfeeding Discontinuation Among Employed Mothers in Malayasia." *International Breastfeeding Journal* 6(4). Available at http://www. internationalbreastfeedingjournal.com/content/6/1/4.

Amir, A. B. 2007. "Infant feeding, poverty and human development." *International Breastfeeding Journal.* 2 (14).

Baby Milk Action. (n.d.). History of the Campaign. Available athttp://www.babymilkaction.org/pages/history.html.

Baby Milk Action. 1997. Nestlé tackled on human rights at Croydon demo. Available athttp://www.babymilkaction.org/press/press17may97.html.

Bahl, R., C. Frost, B.R. Kirkwood, K. Edmond, J. Martines, N. Bhandari, P. Arthur. 2005. "Infant Feeding Patterns and Risks of Death and Hospitalization in the First Half of Infancy: Multicentre Cohort Study." *Bull World Health Organ* 83(6).

Black, M.R., Allen, P.L., Bhutta, M.Z., Caufield, P.L., de Onis, M.M., Ezzati, P.M., et al. 2008. "Maternal and child undernutrition: global and regional exposures and health consequences." *The Lancet.* pp 243-260.

Food and Nutrition Board: Committee on the evaluation of the addition of ingredients new to infant formula. 2004. Infant Formula: Evaluating the Safety of New Ingredients. *Institute of Medicine of the National Academies.* Washington, DC: The National Academies Press.

Frank D.A., S.J. Wirtz, J.R. Sorenson, and T. Heeren. 1987. "Commercial Discharge Packs and Breast-feeding Counseling: Effects on Infant-feeding Practices in a Randomized Trial." *Pediatrics* 80, pp. 845-854.

Friesen, H., J. Vince, P. Boas, and R. Danaya. 1999. "Protection of Breastfeeding in Papua New Guinea." Bulletin of the World Health Organization: 271-274.

Gibson, R.S., E.L. Ferguson, and J. Lehrfel. 1998. "Complementary Foods for Infant Feeding in Developing Countries: Their Nutritional Adequacy and Improvement." *European Journal of Clinical Nutrition* 52(10): 764-770.

Habicht J.P., J. Davanzo, and W.P. Butz. 1986. "Does Breastfeeding Really Save Lives, or are Apparent Benefits due to Biases?" *American Journal of Epidemiology* 123: 279-290.

Infant Milk Substitutes, Feeding Bottles, and Infant Foods (Regulation of Production, Supply and Distribution) Act (1992), G.S.R. 528(E) (amended in G.S.R 726(E), dated 2nd December, 1993, G. S.R 50(E), dated the 22nd January, 1999, and G.S.R. 959(E), dated 19th December, 2003).

International Baby Formula Action Network. 2011. State of the Code by Country 2006. International Code Documentation Center.

Joint statement by the World Health Organization and UNICEF. 2006. Iron supplementation of young children in regions where malaria transmission is intense and infectious disease highly prevalent. Available at http://www.who.int/nutrition/publications/WHOStatement_%20iron%20suppl.pdf.

Kent, G. 2006. "Child Feeding and Human Rights." *International Breastfeeding Journal* 1(27).

Lamontagne, C., A.M. Hamelin, AM, M. St-Pierre. 2008. "The Breastfeeding Experience of Women with Major Difficulties who use the Services of a Breastfeeding Clinic: A Descriptive Study." *International Breastfeeding Journal* 3(17). Available at http://www.internationalbreastfeedingjournal.com/content/3/1/17

Nathan, R. 2008. Realising Children's Rights to Adequate Nutrition through National Legislative Reform. Geneva: UNICEF.

Nestlé. (n.d.). Baby Milk Issue Facts: History. Available at http://www.babymilk.Nestlé.com/History/.

Olang, B., K. Farivar, A. Heidarzadeh, B. Strandvik, and A. Yngve. 2009. "Breastfeeding in Iran: Prevalence, duration and current recommendations." *International Breastfeeding Journal,* 4(8).

Post, James E. 1978. The International Infant Formula Industry. Pp. 215-41 in Marketing and Promotion of Infant Formula in the Developing Nations: Hearing Before the Subcommittee on Health and Scientific Research of the Committee on Human Resources. U.S. Congress, Senate, 95th Congress.

Scott J.A., M. Robertson, J. Fitzpatrick, C. Knight, S. Mulholland. 2008. "Occurrence of Lactational Mastitis and Medical Management: A Prospective Cohort Study." *International Breastfeeding Journal* 3(21).

Thompson, J.F., L.J. Heal, C.L. Roberts, D.A. Ellwood. 2010. "Women's breastfeeding experiences following a significant primary postpartum haemorrhage: A multicentre cohort study." *International Breastfeeding Journal* 5(5).

UNICEF Executive Director Ann M. Veneman (November 22, 2005). Press report released on the 15th anniversary of the Innocenti Declaration on the Protection, Promotion and Support of Breastfeeding.

United Nations, 1989. Convention on the Rights of the Child.

United Nations Protein Advisory Group. 1972. Promotion of Special Foods (Infant Formula and Processed Protein Foods) for Vulnerable Groups 2(3).

U.S. Department of Health and Human Services' Office on Women's Health. 2011. Your Guide to Breastfeeding.

World Health Assembly, Resolution 34.22 (1981).

World Health Assembly, Resolution 35.26 (1982).

World Health Assembly, Resolution 37.30 (1984).

World Health Assembly, Resolution 39.28 (1986).

World Health Assembly, Resolution 41.11 (1988).

World Health Assembly, Resolution 43.3 (1990).

World Health Assembly, Resolution 45.34 (1992).

World Health Assembly, Resolution 47.5 (1994).

World Health Assembly, Resolution 49.15 (1996).

World Health Assembly, Resolution 54.2 (2001).

World Health Assembly, Resolution 55.25 (2002).

World Health Organization. n.d.. "Promoting Proper Feeding for Infants and Young Children." Available athttp://www.who.int/nutrition/topics/infantfeeding/en/index.html.

World Health Organization. 1985. The Quality and Quantity of Breast-milk: Report on the WHO Collaborative Study on Breastfeeding. Geneva: World Health Organization.

World Health Organization. 1998. Postpartum Care of the Mother and Newborn: A Practical Guide.

World Health Organization. 2006. Home-modified animal milk for replacement feeding: Is it feasible and safe? Available at http://whqlibdoc.who.int/hq/2006/a91064.pdf.

UNICEF Executive Director Ann M. Veneman (November 22, 2005). Press report released on the 15th anniversary of the Innocenti Declaration on the Protection, Promotion, and Support of Breastfeeding.

United Nations, 1989. Convention on the Rights of the Child.

U.S. Department of Health and Human Services' Office on Women's Health. 2011. Your Guide to Breastfeeding.

NOTE

1. While there is general recognition that certain behaviors are not acceptable between mother and child, such as murder, those behaviors are prohibited amongst the general population and pose great risk to the victim. Breastfeeding does not fall within such a category.

Chapter Seven

Ethics and Global Health Promotion

Katherine Ba-Thike and Ayushi Gummadi

With India currently accounting for a quarter of the world's unattended deliveries and a great proportion of maternal mortality as well, the government is currently seeking to address the problem by encouraging facility-based care with financial incentives. As a result, they have implemented the Janani Suraksha Yojana (JSY) financing plan in partnership with the National Rural Health Mission. Designed as a safe motherhood intervention, the system looks to reduce maternal and neonatal mortality by promoting institutional delivery in the form of a cash incentive given to mothers who deliver in facilities. The method also provides for reimbursement of transportation costs, which is a large contributing factor to the low rates of institutional deliveries. The scheme's success is assessed on the overall increases in institutional deliveries among low-income families; while awareness of JSY ranged from seventy-six to eighty-seven percent among all the states, the highest percentage of institutional births in 2008 was seventy-three percent (Madhya Pradesh and Orissa), while percentages for other states were fifty-nine percent in Rajasthan, forty-nine percent in Bihar, and fifty-eight percent in Uttar Pradesh, all showcasing great degrees of success. The idea behind the JSY financing scheme is to incentivize institutional deliveries because they often decrease the risk of both maternal and neonatal deliveries and allow access to better care and resources.

The success of JSY since its initial implementation showcases a bold public health measure undertaken in a lesser-developed country. The continuing success of the method supports the concept that cash incentives can successfully be applied to enhance the use of the public health system. The overall findings show an unprecedented increase in the number of institutional deliveries. However, there is still the need to intensify efforts to improve access to the best available quality obstetric care in order to achieve the goal of significantly reducing maternal and neonatal deaths.

INTRODUCTION

Consider the world context: an estimated 358,000 maternal deaths occurred worldwide in 2008. Although this was a thirty-four percent decline from the 1990 levels of 500,000, developing countries continued to account for nine-ty-nine percent (355,000) of the deaths, with Sub-Saharan Africa and South Asia contributing to eighty-seven percent (313,000) of global maternal mortality. Significant numbers of maternal deaths are in populous countries in Asia: India, Indonesia, and Bangladesh. These nations are among the eleven countries where sixty-five percent of all maternal deaths occurred in 2008 (Trends in Maternal Mortality 1990–2010).

With more than ninety-nine percent of the global maternal mortality rate attributable to the developing world, India carries much of the global burden, as it is individually accountable for twenty-two percent of the global total. These statistics show a lack of sufficient progress towards Target A of Millennium Development Goal Five, and meeting this target requires more than a seventy percent reduction from 2005 to 2015. While the global neonatal mortality rate declined by twenty-five percent from 1980 to 2000, this decline was much slower than the overall Under 5 mortality rate, which fell by one-third of its 1980 level. Neonatal deaths currently constitute a much higher proportion of Under 5 deaths now than in previous years, with deaths in the first week of life rising from twenty-three percent in 1980 to twenty-eight percent in 2000. Moreover, for every newborn baby who dies, another twenty suffer complications arising from preterm births or other neonatal conditions.

The Indian government has been addressing the problem by encouraging facility-based care through financial incentives (Kumar et al. 2005). Since 2005, the JSY financing scheme has been implemented in partnership with the National Rural Health Mission. Janani Suraksha Yojana is literally translated as "Pregnant Women Safety Scheme." With a financial outlay of over 1000 crore rupees (approximately $1.86 billion), JSY is the world's largest conditional cash transfer mechanism in terms of the number of beneficiaries. The objective of the design is to address financial barriers to maternal care services, particularly for mothers from below poverty line (BPL) households. Ultimately, JSY aims to promote deliveries in health facilities with skilled health personnel who can provide a package of basic and comprehensive care for mothers and their newborns (*JSY Guidelines for Implementation*).

INDIA AND JANANI SURAKSHA YOJANA

According to India's Ministry of Health and Family Welfare in 2001, an estimated 67,000 maternal deaths occur per year. Twenty-six out of 28 million pregnancies end in delivery and fifteen percent of those deliveries are likely to develop complications (Prasad n.d.). In response to the high level of maternal and neonatal mortality, low institutional delivery rates, and a large inequality in maternal health between more socially advanced and less socially advanced states, the government launched JSY in April 2005 (International Institute for Population Sciences and Macro International 2007). The scheme is under the umbrella of the National Rural Health Mission (NRHM), which was initiated to improve basic healthcare services for rural populations. The mission of the NRHM is to "provide effective, equitable, and affordable quality healthcare services focusing particularly on the needs of women and children." JSY is an action plan to contribute to that mission, focusing particularly on pregnant women below the poverty line and of scheduled caste and scheduled tribes.

JSY was designed specifically to reduce the maternal mortality ratio and the infant mortality rate by increasing the number of institutional deliveries in BPL families. It would therefore contribute to the achievement of Millennium Development Goals (MDG) Four (to reduce child mortality) and Five (to improve maternal health). This centrally sponsored design integrates cash assistance with antenatal care during the pregnancy period, institutional care during delivery, and immediate post-partum period care in a health center. It does so by establishing a system of coordinated care by field-level health workers. The conditional cash transfer program utilizes demand-side financing to reduce financial barriers to institutional delivery and improve access to skilled birth attendants and healthcare services.

JSY is a 100 percent centrally sponsored system and is implemented to varying degrees in all states of India. It has been substantially scaled up in the past few years since its establishment and now has a budget allocation of 15.4 billion rupees (*JSY Guidelines for Implementation*).

There is variation in the number of maternal deaths between states: in Kerala, the average maternal mortality is 110 deaths per 100,000 live births, while in Uttar Pradesh it is 517 deaths per 100,000 live births (Devadasan et al. 2008). States are classified into two categories: high-performing and non-high-performing. JSY focuses on poor pregnant women specifically in states that have low rates of institutional delivery—the eight empowered action group states of Bihar, Madhya Pradesh, Uttar Pradesh, Rajasthan, Jharkhand, Chhattisgarh, Orissa, and Uttaranchal. It also provides for partnerships with the private sector by offering accreditation to private hospitals and nursing homes that provide delivery services. Eligibility for the financial packages extends to all pregnant women belonging to households below the poverty line, provided they are above the age of nineteen years and have had no more than two live births. Funding from the program is expected to cover 9.5 out of 26 million women giving birth during the year (*JSY Guidelines for Implementation*).

Eligibility for JSY varies based on the predetermined statuses of the states: in non-high-performing states, all pregnant women who deliver in government health centers are eligible for the cash assistance. In high-performing states, JSY is extended to all pregnant women below the poverty line who are at least nineteen years of age (*JSY Guidelines for Implementation*). The program is also offered to all scheduled caste and scheduled tribe pregnant women and applies universally to up to two live births.

Accredited Social Health Activists (ASHAs) are a critical element to the implementation of JSY (see subsequent section), as they act as the link between the health system and the community in which they are located. ASHAs also benefit from the program and receive cash payments in exchange for their assistance (Garg et al. 2007).

In the rural areas of low-performing states, mothers receive approximately US$28 and ASHAs US$12. In urban areas mothers receive US$20 and ASHAs US$4. By contrast, in the rural areas of high-performing states, mothers receive US$14 and ASHAs receive US$4. The payment to mothers in urban areas of high-performing states decreases to US$12. Furthermore, the original provisions of the design also provided for a benefit of US$10 per delivery for home deliveries. Finally, JSY has a special provision for caesarean sections, which extends up to US$30 per case. This sum is used in order to hire the services of private experts to carry out the surgery if government doctors are unavailable or not capable of performing the necessary operation (Prasad n.d.).

ASHA: A CRITICAL ELEMENT IN COMMUNITY-LEVEL IMPLEMENTATION

The ASHA is a strong element in ensuring the success of the JSY program. ASHAs are all female, and between forty-two percent and sixty-eight percent of ASHAs belong to Other Backward Castes and were trained specifically to be community health activists. Their major role is to manage the interface between the community and the public health system (United Nations Population Fund [UNFPA] 2009). The ASHA is typically selected from her own village, and the average stay of the worker is 18.9 years. Villagers are highly aware of the work of ASHAs, up to a ninety-seven percent awareness level in Orissa (UNFPA 2009). Each village with a minimum population of 1000 is required to have at least one ASHA or equivalent health worker who is registered with the village's sub-center and primary healthcare facility.

The ASHA is intended to work under the supervision of the Auxiliary Nurse Midwife (ANM) and in tandem with the Aganwadi Worker (AWW). Under JSY, the main roles of the ASHA are:

To organize delivery-care services for the registered expectant mother,
To assist in immunization of the newborn, and
To act as a propagator/motivator of family planning services.

One of the major responsibilities of the ASHA is to disseminate information regarding JSY to the community, focusing specifically on motivating pregnant women to have institutional deliveries. In addition, the ASHA is required to arrange for transport, accompany pregnant women to the place of delivery, and remain with the pregnant woman at the institution. In return for her work, she is paid an honorarium of at least Rs. 200 per delivery. However, this honorarium is available only if she assists the pregnant woman (Kumar et al. 2005).

In terms of the services provided, the ASHA offers expectant mothers services such as registration for antenatal care, assistance in obtaining BPL benefits and certifications, and arrangements for TT injections. She also provides the three required antenatal checkup visits, supplies Iron Folic Acid (IFA) tablets, makes sure the newborn is immunized, provides civil birth and death registration, arranges for postnatal care, promotes family planning services, and treats minor ailments. The ASHA is also expected to create a micro-birth plan for each beneficiary. This plan includes identification of the beneficiary, completion of the JSY card, and registration of the pregnant mother at the appropriate health center. Additionally, the ASHA must record the birth plan on the JSY card, collect the BPL certification if necessary, and motivate women to have institutional deliveries. Finally, the ASHA must submit a completed JSY card for verification (*JSY Guidelines for Implementation*).

On average each ASHA supports between four and five pregnant women in JSY-related services. Essentially, the ASHA is intended to be the key link to JSY's success at the community level.

GUIDELINES FOR IMPLEMENTATION

JSY was originally established as a means of improving the National Maternity Benefit Scheme, which was linked to providing better diet to pregnant women in below poverty line families (Sarkar et al. 2004). JSY is implemented completely in ten low-performing states: Uttar Pradesh, Uttaranchal, Madhya Pradesh, Chhattisgarh, Rajasthan, Bihar, Jharkhand, Orissa, Assam, and Jammu & Kashmir. The program is especially focused in eight of the ten low-performing states—all except Assam and Jammu & Kashmir. These states are referred to as the Empowered Action Group states. However, as mentioned, JSY extends to women below the poverty line and living in rural areas even in high-performing states (Lahariya et al. 2009).

With an underlying strategy of linking cash assistance to institutional delivery, JSY has several features to ensure successful implementation. These features include early registration of beneficiaries, early identification of complicated cases, provision of three antenatal care visits and at least one postnatal care visit, organization of appropriate referrals and transport for the pregnant mothers, collaboration with Integrated Child Development Services workers, and the timely disbursement of the cash incentives to the beneficiaries and the ASHAs with funds available under the ANM. The strategy also involves provision of 24/7 delivery services at the primary healthcare level to provide basic emergency obstetric care, operationalization of First Referral Units (FRUs) also to provide emergency obstetric care, and the building of partnerships with doctors and hospitals/nursing homes/clinics from the private sector, especially in the rural areas, to provide obstetric services to the JSY beneficiaries (*JSY Guidelines for Implementation*). With regard to building these partnerships with the private sector, the technicalities would be left to each state to devise appropriate mechanisms of accreditation and recognition of private sector facilities.

Regarding the disbursement of cash assistance, the goal is to dispense the financial package in the shortest possible time period. The original guidelines of the program called for a disbursing authority that would provide a Rs. 5000 imprest package to every auxiliary nurse, midwife, or health worker and allow the nurse, midwife, or health worker to distribute payment conditional on the beneficiaries meeting the JSY requirements.

With respect to implementation of the program from a governmental perspective, a Mission Steering Group chaired by the Minister of Health and Family Welfare oversees the program at the national level. A State Health Mission chaired by the Chief Minister has oversight at the state level. In addition, each State Health Mission nominates a State Nodal Officer who is primarily responsible for implementation of JSY. The original guidelines of the program provided for an implementation committee to ensure that the state's action plan specifically incorporated the funding requirements based on the number of beneficiaries. Furthermore, governmental provisions also call for a District Health Mission responsible for completing JSY initiatives at the district level with the assistance of the District Implementation Committee (*JSY Guidelines for Implementation*).

Chandrakant Lahariya in *The Indian Journal of Community Medicine* reviewed the progress of the JSY program after its initial implementation. His report resulted in the following changes to the program's operation: removal of the age restriction in low-performing states, lifting of the restriction on birth order, and removal of the need for a BPL or marriage certificate.

The rationale behind these changes was that a large portion of maternal deaths in low-performing states occurred among mothers aged less than nineteen or with high birth order (Lahariya 2009).

FINANCIAL MANAGEMENT OF JSY

As a completely centrally sponsored financing scheme, JSY creates its budget requirements based on its administrative costs at both the national and state level. In addition, this budget covers the requirements of staffing and infrastructure, including medical supplies, hospital beds, and operation theaters. From the state level, the demand is converted to fund requirements. Beneficiaries are expected to receive their cash payments at the time of delivery; the expectant mother receives her payment in one lump sum and the ASHA usually receives the payment in two installments. Furthermore, any delay in receiving benefits is required to be recorded in order to improve the system and prevent future delays. Delays in receiving benefits can be attributed to the unavailability of JSY funds at the service-unit level, the non-submission of required documents by facilities, or the unavailability of a cheque book (Mohapatra et al. 2007–2008).

OUTCOMES OF THE PROGRAM

Social Impact

JSY has had a strong socio-cultural impact as evidenced by the high levels of awareness concerning the program. This awareness stemmed from many sources, including word-of-mouth through relatives and friends, posters, TV and radio campaigns, health workers, and newspaper advertisements. An 2009 assessment supported by UNFPA in five high-focus states found that awareness of the program was high, usually ranging from seventy-six to eighty-seven percent, and up to ninety-five percent in Rajasthan. Between seventy-five percent and eighty percent of citizens in Bihar, Madhya Pradesh, Orissa, and Rajasthan were aware of the continuous twenty-four-hour health facilities available to them and the involvement of private hospitals. Furthermore, with the exception of Uttar Pradesh, knowledge of JSY among community health leaders was universal. The widespread understanding of the program came from health workers and posters, yet the assessment also indicated that awareness in women stemmed from government publicity campaigns, which in turn reflects the need and demand for institutional deliveries (UNFPA 2009).

Increased Access to Services and Institutional Deliveries

Utilization of antenatal care has increased since JSY was implemented. JSY provides for three antenatal check-up visits, and institutional deliveries have shifted from district hospitals to community healthcare centers and primary healthcare centers, thereby easing the load on district hospitals. Post-natal care coverage has also increased to rates of more than eighty percent in Rajasthan, Uttar Pradesh, and Orissa, and more than sixty percent in Madhya Pradesh and Bihar. As a positive side effect, Polio 0 and BCG coverage has increased to more than ninety percent in Uttar Pradesh, Orissa, Bihar, and Madhya Pradesh and more than eighty percent in Rajasthan. Additionally, the ASHAs regularly received their payments, particularly in Rajasthan where seventy percent were paid on time and Orissa where seventy-three percent were paid on time (Prasad n.d.).

DELIVERY IN HEALTH FACILITIES

With respect to the beneficiaries of JSY, in 2008, seventy-three percent of births in Madhya Pradesh and Orissa were conducted in a health facility. Roughly sixty-seven percent were conducted in government centers and accredited private hospitals. This indicates the success of JSY in promoting institutional deliveries. The combined estimate was that fifty-five percent of births in 2008 occurred in institutions while the direct beneficiaries of JSY totaled forty-seven percent of pregnant mothers. However, there were still marked disparities in institutional deliveries: in Bihar, scheduled caste members living in *katcha* houses[1] had lower levels of institutional deliveries compared to their counterparts. The rate of institutional delivery was similarly low for those living in *katcha* houses belonging to the scheduled tribe community and the illiterate in Orissa. The majority of pregnant mothers were attended to immediately; a small percentage reported waiting more than fifteen minutes. Between sixty-eight and ninety percent of deliveries were conducted by nurses with the exception of Orissa where doctors supervised eighty-one percent of deliveries.

The recommended guideline for hospital stay is a minimum of forty-eight hours after delivery. Findings indicate that a disparity exists in the duration of the stay as well. In Bihar, eighty-four percent of mothers giving births in institutions stay for less than one day. By contrast, forty-three percent of mothers observed in Orissa and Rajasthan stay for the recommended forty-eight hours, and in Madhya Pradesh, sixty-seven percent of mothers stay for the recommended period of time.

In summary, JSY has been at least partially successful, based on the overall increase in institutional deliveries among low-income families. Awareness of the program ranged from seventy-six to eighty-seven percent in all states. Institutional birth rates in 2008 in several of the high-focus Empowered Action Group states were high: seventy-three percent in both Madhya Pradesh and Orissa, fifty-nine percent in Rajasthan, forty-nine percent in Bihar, and fifty-eight percent in Uttar Pradesh.

Issues with Quality of Care

The Countdown 2015 impact evaluation report indicated that most public sector facilities were understaffed and could not meet all desired functional standards. As a result, many deliveries are carried out by unskilled support staff rather than trained doctors. Best practices like neonatal resuscitation and kangaroo care are not commonly followed. Furthermore, JSY lacks an adequate system of referral to higher levels in case of emergencies or complications. Mothers are often discharged within hours of delivery instead of the recommended forty-eight-hour post-delivery stay (Lim et al. 2010).

Beneficiaries

According to an impact evaluation conducted by researchers from the Institute for Health Metrics and Evaluation and the Public Health Foundation of India (funded by the Bill and Melinda Gates Foundation), implementation of the program from 2007 to 2008 was highly variable from state to state. Depending on the state, anywhere from five to forty-four percent of pregnant women living below the poverty line received cash payments from JSY. Furthermore, the poorest and least educated segments of the target population, although positioned to benefit the most from JSY, were not necessarily the most likely to take advantage of the program. The study also found that the cash payment was directly associated with a reduction of 3.7 perinatal deaths per 1,000 pregnancies and 2.3 neonatal deaths per 1,000 live births. Additionally, JSY was found to have a significant effect on the amount of antenatal care and number of in-facility births, emphasizing the success of the program thus far (Lim et al. 2010).

Countdown 2015's impact evaluation indicated that the number of beneficiaries multiplied eleven-fold in four years, from 0.74 million women in 2005–2006 to 8.34 million women in 2008–2009 (Lim et al. 2010). Furthermore, the amount of government budget allocated to the project also increased, from US$8.75 million to US$275 million over the same four-year period. The study also showed a reduction of four perinatal and two neonatal deaths per 1,000 live births as a direct result of the program, indicating success in both promoting institutional deliveries and reducing infant mortality. However, the organization was unable to detect a direct association between JSY and a reduction of maternal deaths in the district-level analysis. The estimated effect of JSY was higher in the high-focus areas at the national level, yet the effect of JSY on skilled birth attendants was smaller than on institutional births. Furthermore, JSY had a smaller effect than anticipated on antenatal coverage as well, perhaps because antenatal care was not explicitly linked with the financial assistance provided.

Receipt of Benefits

The lack of timely receipt of the financial benefits was a cause of concern to government officials and recipients alike. A combined total showed that seventy-six percent of JSY beneficiaries around the country did ultimately receive the cash payment, with ninety-three percent in Rajasthan, eighty-nine percent in Orissa, and eighty-three percent in Madhya Pradesh receiving payment. Unfortunately many of the payments were delayed, sometimes for more than four weeks. In Madhya Pradesh, only thirty-nine percent of pregnant women received the payment at the time of discharge, while in Bihar, twenty-seven percent faced problems and had to contact officials several times in order to receive money (UNFPA 2009).

ANALYSIS AND POLICY RECOMMENDATIONS

Assessments of the program acknowledge the success of JSY but recognize the current limitations of the design and provide recommendations to improve it.

Services and Quality of Care

Conditional cash transfers throughout the world have several potential shortcomings. Since they are established as demand-side interventions, constraints on the supply side limit the quality and availability of services. If the supply of health services is simply not sufficient to meet the need, there is an inherent limit to the improvement possible. Furthermore, if health services provided are low quality or not up to standard, there will be little impact on improving overall maternal and neonatal health. Demand-side interventions such as conditional cash transfer programs cannot have much impact if there are supply-side problems, such as services being low quality or unavailable.

The Institute of Public Health in Bangalore conducted a study on process evaluation results and found a lower quality of care in heavily burdened institutions due to the increase in institutional deliveries resulting from JSY (John 2008). The length of post-delivery stay in the healthcare institution was found to be less than the recommended forty-eight hours. This is a cause for concern since almost half of maternal deaths take place in the postpartum period (UNFPA 2009).

To achieve the goal of eighty percent institutional deliveries while addressing these issues, a suggestion was made to leverage spare capacity in the private sector in order to provide more institutional services. In order to improve quality of care and sustain increases, partnerships with accredited private sector facilities should be further developed and improved (UNFPA Report).

A report by the World Health Organization's South East Asia Regional Office (SEARO) noted the increase in institutional deliveries and recommended expansion of the scope of care. Future areas of focus should include newborn healthcare, specifically the training of healthcare personnel to handle birth asphyxia and other common health complications among newborns. Efforts should also be made to ensure early breastfeeding and zero dose immunization. In addition, JSY should begin integrating post-partum counseling for family planning services, including limiting and spacing methods (Prasad n.d.).

The Role of ASHA

JSY has succeeded in empowering the ASHA in terms of outreach and status within society. This empowerment of the ASHA has resulted in making health systems more accessible, and improving facilities for healthcare at all levels (Prasad n.d.).

However, the WHO SEARO report also concluded that JSY is far too dependent on the ASHA; since the activist works on an honorarium basis, the program might in fact be detrimental to the ASHA's overall duties. Since JSY is more lucrative than the other responsibilities of the ASHA, the design could lead the ASHA to neglect other assignments. Thus, the report recommends limiting her role to that of a facilitator and informant. Furthermore, her performance should not be judged solely on the basis of institutional deliveries but should also include antenatal and post-natal care. This will ensure that the ASHA is motivated to pay attention to all aspects of delivery (Lahariya et al. 2009).

Payments to Beneficiaries

The MOHFW noted that several areas regarding the basic operation of JSY still need to be strengthened; these include transportation reimbursement, the timeliness of cash receipt by beneficiaries, the regular payment to ASHA, and a reduction of out-of-pocket expenses due to incidental costs incurred during delivery (Prasad n.d.).

The evaluation conducted by the Public Health Foundation of India focused on improving the targeting of the program. JSY still tends to not reach the poorest and least educated women in India despite the fact that they stand to benefit the most from the program. The foundation advocates investigating approaches to raise awareness and encourage the poorest and least educated women to take advantage of JSY. For example, the foundation proposes implementing communication strategies that do not depend on literacy in order to promote more universal accessibility to JSY's services.

Physical access is another barrier that must be addressed, as JSY payments can only be administered in accredited health facilities. Madhya Pradesh, which has one of the highest levels of participation in JSY, has made a point of accrediting remote health facilities in order to allow access to pregnant women living in rural areas. Other states need to expand their accreditation network to similarly reach out to rural populations.

This report by the Public Health Foundation also found that antenatal care is not being afforded the same level of attention as institutional deliveries. This is most likely since antenatal care is not linked to the financial assistance that JSY provides. The report suggests dividing cash payments into three segments: the first twenty-five percent after three antenatal care visits, the second fifty percent after in-facility delivery, and the final twenty-five percent after provision of post-partum care (Lim et al. 2010). This division will ensure proper care and attention is given to all stages of the delivery process.

The Institute of Public Health in Bangalore conducted a study on process evaluation. Their results found issues with the level of awareness and with dishonesty in the cash distribution. They also discuss the lower quality of care in heavily burdened institutions due to the increase in institutional deliveries resulting from implementation of JSY. The report shows a wide discrepancy in the level of care between states, from low levels in Chhattisgarh and Karnataka to high levels in Maharashtra and Orissa. Furthermore, some dishonesty existed within the cash distribution mechanism: some beneficiaries did not receive the entire amount of payment that was at times instead distributed among facility staff.

It is agreed that the strength of JSY lies in the fact that the government has made appropriate budgetary allocations for its poorest citizens. However, the lack of awareness in some states is an issue that needs to be addressed; ideally, all states will ultimately have the same levels of awareness as the Empowered Action Group states. Furthermore, the provision to give incentives to home deliveries directly contrasts with the goals of the program and is therefore also a major cause of concern. The Institute of Public Health in Bangalore also found that the documentation process is long and burdensome and could at times delay benefits to those in greater need. Several recommendations were made to address these concerns. These recommendations include extending coverage up to three live births and to all women, making payments in a timely fashion to cover indirect and incidental costs, and simplifying the documentation process. They also recommended that assistance be provided for the treatment of newborns, and that the reasons for rejecting certain applications must be clearly explained (Devadasan et al. 2008).

Monitoring

The UNFPA evaluation recommended that the management of JSY be strengthened by monitoring all components of the program, increasing interaction by developing a communication activity plan in order to mobilize the community, and strengthening financial planning (UNFPA 2009). Consistency in reporting has also been recommended. In some reports, sub-centers were referred to as institutions, thus inflating figures of institutional births and potentially giving rise to corruption in money distribution. If sub-centers are classified as institutions, then efforts need to be made to ensure the availability of a skilled auxiliary nurse midwife at the sub-center to assist with delivery. Additionally, it will be important to strengthen and equip the centers with appropriate facilities so that beneficiaries receive proper care and attention throughout the delivery process (Lahariya et al. 2009).

Other Factors

Cultural barriers against institutional deliveries are another area of concern that must be addressed. As ASHAs are primarily from Hindu backgrounds, their poor reach to Muslim and Christian communities leads to a lower uptake of the program by these minorities. As such, JSY should incorporate cultural awareness into the training of ASHAs such that they understand the imperatives of reaching out to other religious minorities. Furthermore, the design originally provided for payments to poor women giving birth at home. Continuing this clause is a partial disincentive for institutional births and should be entirely discontinued (Prasad n.d.). Many women may be initially reluctant to counteract the long-standing tradition of home-birth, particularly in rural areas. Moreover, many are under the influence of their husbands and other male figures in their family who may stand against institutional delivery. To combat this issue, JSY must continue to educate and improve outreach within rural communities to increase its effectiveness and customer base, and consequently its success will improve within those very regions.

ETHICAL ASPECTS OF JSY

In both developed and developing countries, governments have become increasingly centrally involved in health regulation and provision, particularly with regard to public health measures. Governments are intimately involved in the provision of preventive, promotive, and curative health services. The scope and range of responsibilities of health authorities have broadened over the past years. Due to this growth, there has been an increasing interest in the ethics of public health. It is acknowledged that public health ethics must look beyond health care to consider the structural conditions and social and economic determinants that promote or inhibit the development of healthy societies. In considering all these factors, a major tenet of public health ethics is providing equity in access to health care. The concept of equity in access to health regardless of status anywhere in the world is an innately ethical and moral question. Achieving the objective of equal access is a major part of the efforts of governments, the WHO, and other international organizations. (WHO 2005)

Maternal and neonatal health in India provides an interesting case study on the ethics of access to healthcare. As discussed, maternal healthcare is a major problem in much of the developing world, and particularly in India. Despite efforts over the past decades by the Indian government and other organizations, access to healthcare in India is still extremely asymmetrical, especially with regard to class and location. Institutional delivery is clearly safer for the mother and infant, no matter their situation. With the ethics of global health in mind, an important goal of any initiative in maternal and neonatal health should be to increase the number of institutional deliveries across the board.

Several tenets of JSY make it a program specifically designed to increase access to maternal health to underserved groups. First and foremost, the cash incentive is only given to those below the poverty line. By offering cash incentives to receive maternal care, there exists an additional economic incentive for those living in poverty to deliver in an institution. Additionally, mothers in poorer states receive a greater cash payment to further incentivize institutional delivery in poorer locations. As mentioned, in the rural areas of low-performing states, BPL mothers receive approximately US$28 in contrast to BPL mothers in urban areas of high-performing states—US$12. The financial incentive can also partially function to overcome cultural barriers that exist more prominently in those from more uneducated and poorer backgrounds (Uba 1992). Physical access is a barrier in rural India where the nearest healthcare facility can be very distant, so JSY specifically provides for transportation to the nearest delivery facility (Banerjee et al. 2004). Lastly, the use of a female ASHA as the face of JSY to the community overcomes a cultural barrier to delivering in a hospital. Since the ASHA is a local resident and member of the community, advice and education from her perspective is a better method of communicating to the poor.

JSY is clearly an initiative with the goal of increasing access to maternal healthcare for the poor and underserved. The program incentivizes the poor and those without access to healthcare and assists them in overcoming financial, cultural, and logistical barriers to receiving improved maternal and neonatal care. Given its success thus far in increasing institutional deliveries, similar programs elsewhere in the developing world can go a long way towards the ideal of access to maternal health regardless of class, socioeconomic status, or location.

CONCLUSION

As the case of JSY indicates, state policies, particularly in developing countries, have tremendous potential to assist or debilitate the status of women's health. Long-standing cultural traditions of male superiority in India have resulted in the diminished importance given to women's health. However, programs such as JSY have intended to give more attention to the status of women's health while also combating the issue of neonatal mortality, of which India carries much of the global burden. The success of the government-backed JSY project indicates the potential which governments throughout the world have to positively impact women's health.

Just as the creators of JSY did, policy-makers should consider long-standing cultural traditions and policies that may negatively impact women's health and then seek solutions to fix the resulting problems. Officials in states that have traditions of masculine superiority should particularly pay attention to women's health, as male dominance may be a negative factor contributing to the low standards of women's health. As such, government officials should make a conscious effort to improve standards and better access to healthcare for women, particularly in disadvantaged or impoverished areas that may lack necessary resources or healthcare providers. They should seek affordable, culturally acceptable solutions to the issues at hand: for example, training community-based ASHAs in rural areas who are aware of the village traditions.

Women's health should not be afforded sub-standard attention and should meet global standards, particularly in relation to pregnancy, childbirth, and neonatal health. Developing countries should look to global standards such as the Millennium Development Goals for guidance in achieving greater access to healthcare. Governments should assess their quality of healthcare based on universal standards supplied by the United Nations and hold themselves accountable to providing the best quality of healthcare to their female population, even if doing so requires initiating new projects like JSY.

REFERENCES

Banerjee, A. et al. 2004. "Health, Healthcare, and Economic Development: Wealth, Health, and Health Services in Rural Rajasthan." *Health, Health Care and Economic Development* Vol. 94, No. 2 p. 326–330. http://www.princeton.edu/rpds/papers/Banerjee_Deaton_Duflo_ Wealth_Health_and_Health_Services_in_Rural-_Rajasthan_AER.pdf.

Countdown to 2015 Maternal Newborn and Child Survival—the 2010 Report, 2010.

Devadasan, Narayanan, M.A. Elias, D. John, S. Grahacharya, and L. Ralte. 2008. "A Conditional Cash Assistance Program for Promoting Institutional Deliveries Among the Poor in India: Process Evaluation Results." Pp. 257-275 in *Reducing Financial Barriers to Obstetric Care in Low-Income Countries*, edited by F. Richard, S. Witter, and V. D. Brouwere. Antwerp, Belgium: ITGPress.

Garg, S., et al. 2007. "Current Status of the Rural Health Mission." *Indian Journal of Community Medicine* Vol. 32, No. 3, p. 171-172.

International Institute for Population Sciences (IIPS) and Macro International. 2007. *National Family Health Survey (NFHS-3), 2005–06: India: Volume I*. Mumbai: IIPS.

Janani Suraksha Yojana—Features and Frequently Asked Questions. (Government of India—Ministry of Health and Family Welfare, 2006). http://jknrhm.com/PDF/JSR.pdf.

John, Denny. 2008. "Utilization, Expenditure and Financing of Obstetric Services." *Journal of Health Studies* 1(1): 57-67.

JSY Guidelines for Implementation. Ministry of Health and Family Welfare, Government of India.

Kumar et al. 2005. "Challenges of Maternal Mortality Reduction and Opportunities Under the National Rural Health Mission—A Critical Appraisal." *Indian Journal of Public Health*. XXXXIX No 3 July–September 2005, p. 164-167.

Lahariya et al. 2009. "Cash Incentives for Institutional Delivery: Linking with Antenatal and Post Natal Care May Ensure 'Continuum of Care' in India." *Indian Journal of Community Medicine*. Vol. 34 Iss. 1, January 2009, p. 15-18.

Lim, Stephen S., L. Dandona, J.A. Hoisington, S.L. James, M.C. Hogan, E. Gakidou. 2010. "India's Janani Suraksha Yojana, a conditional cash transfer program to increase births in health facilities: an impact evaluation." *Lancet* 375: 2009–23.

Ministry of Health and Family Welfare, Government of India 2009 http://mohfw.nic.in/layout_09-06.pdf (accessed October 2010).

Mohapatra, B., et al. 2007–2008. An Assessment of functioning and impact of JSY in Orissa. http://nihfw.org/pdf/RAHI-I%20Reports/Orissa/ORISSA.pdf.

Operational Guidelines for Implementation of Janani Suraksha Yojana. http://angul.nic.in/JSY.pdf.

Prasad. *Janani Suraksha Yojana: A demand side intervention for promoting safe delivery*. n.d. Ministry of Health & F.W. Government of India. Available at http://www.searo.who.int/LinkFiles/Meetings_DAY1_P9_Mr_Prasad.pdf.pdf.

Sarkar et al. 2004. "Extending social security coverage to the informal sector in India." *Social Change* 34(4): 122-130.http://sch.sagepub.com/content/34/4/122.short.

Trends in Maternal Mortality 1990-2010. WHO, UNICEF, UNFPA, The World Bank estimates (2012).

Uba L. 1992. "Cultural barriers to health care for southeast Asian refugees." *Public Health Reports*. September–October, 1992. Vol. 107, No. 5 p. 544-548. http://www.ncbi.nlm.nih.gov/pmc/articles/PMC1403696/pdf/pubhealthrep00071-0058.pdf.

United Nations Population Fund. 2009. *Concurrent Assessment of Janani Suraksha Yojana (JSY) in Selected States*. New Delhi, India: UNFPA Development Research Services. Available at http://india.unfpa.org/drive/JSYConcurrentAssessment.pdf .

WHO Task Force on Research Priorities for Equity in Health and the WHO Health Equity Team—Priorities for research to take forward the health equity policy agenda. WHO Bulletin 2005 83: 948-953.

NOTES

1. A katcha is a "temporary" house made from wood, hay, and mud.

Chapter Eight

"Beyond Reproduction" — A New Shift in Women's Health in Modern Sri Lanka?

Darshi Thoradeniya

This chapter asks and answers the following question: What was at stake in the establishment of the Well-Woman Clinic (WWC) program in Sri Lanka in 1996? As a consequence of the International Conference on Population and Development (ICPD) in 1994 (also known as the Cairo Conference), the Family Health Bureau (FHB) of Sri Lanka launched an island-wide Well-Woman Clinic (WWC) program in 1996 by introducing the concept of reproductive health in the aim of enhancing women's health in Sri Lanka (*Suvanari Seva Athpotha* 2003). The WWC initiative presents an apparent about-face within women's health in modern Sri Lanka, because it disturbs the orthodoxy of women's health as necessarily reproductive health, with its new focus on screening women who are past their reproductive age, which is 35 years, against "common non-communicable diseases such as hypertension and diabetes, breast malignancies and cervical cancers" (i.e., women's health "beyond reproduction") (*Annual Report on Family Health Sri Lanka* 2004–2005).

According to the demographic history of Sri Lanka, this shift from family planning to reproductive health and rights is convincing, because population was no longer a "problem" for development by 1996 as Sri Lanka had reached the replacement level fertility.[1] So establishment of WWCs appeared as the best and logical step forward within the development and demographic discourses. Although it is so from the point of view of health experts, demographers, and the state, how logical was it from a woman's point of view?

129

How would women respond to submitting their bodies (most likely a post-reproductive body) for screening tests within the WWCs? What are the ethical considerations involved in this process? It is the responsibility of the state to read women's health and women's bodies in mutual intelligibility in order to formulate an ethical women's health policy where traditional and cultural understandings and perceptions of women's bodies are respected.

These two concepts, women's health and women's bodies, have generally been studied in exclusion to one another—as separate entities. In Sri Lanka women's health is predominantly a territory confined to policy-makers and medical professionals where they rule their territory with numbers, statistics, and projections. Woman's body is the territory of social scientists, anthropologists and feminists who use ethnographic research methods to rule theirs. Very few have dared to trespass these boundaries. As researchers, we are trained to remain rooted within our own epistemic province or comfort zone.

Studies on Sri Lankan women's sexuality, maternal body, social and cultural reproductive bodies have made significant contributions.[2] However, women's bodies and experiences about their bodies have not come up as categories and were hardly problematized within medical research on women's health in Sri Lanka. Medical research in Sri Lanka focuses more on issues of reproduction such as pregnancy, delivery choices, use of contraception, infertility, clinic attendance, and nutrition.[3] Both of these categories—women's health and women's bodies—should be brought into one analytical framework in order to formulate an ethical women's health policy. Thus two tasks become priorities (1) a re-reading of WWC policy documents in order to understand how the new women's health concept of "beyond reproduction" was framed at policy level; and (2) an ethnographic study of WWC attendees in order to understand how women perceive and understand their bodies "beyond reproduction." In other words, to understand what was at stake in the establishment of WWCs, both historical and ethnographical methodologies should be employed. While challenging, this work has produced rewarding results.

METHODOLOGY

Since women's health inherently requires looking at institutions and statistics, I have traced it through archival research. I have pursued ethnographic research because the topic of women's bodies entails understanding at a personal level of experience. Women's health is not an innocent concept; it is very well interconnected to eugenics, population control, family planning, and development discourses. Women's bodies are not neutral objects either. They are political objects of the state and, at the same time, political subjects with an agency—constantly negotiating, contesting, and bargaining with the state, culture, religion, and market forces. I have tried my best to do justice to the research by engaging in a conversation with archival and ethnographic methods as it demands a multi-disciplinary methodology. The archival research entails primary and secondary sources on women's health and establishment of the WWC program in Sri Lanka. The ethnographic research entails in-depth interviews with fifteen women attending two WWCs in Dehiwala Medical Officer of Health (MOH) area in Colombo, most attended WWC in a suburban setting.

After a discussion with a Public Health Nursing Sister (PHNS) and Assistant MOH of the Dehiwala MOH Office, I selected two out of seven WWCs in the Dehiwala MOH area at Attidiya and Kothalawalapura. I was first introduced to women at the Attidiya area by two of the Public Health Midwives (PHMs) of Attidiya. Through them, I formed my link to one of the Public Health Midwives at Kothalawalapura who introduced me to Kothalawalapura women. I randomly selected my sample of fifteen women (between the ages of thirty-five to fifty-five) from the WWC registers that PHMs maintain. My sample of eight women in Attidiya was selected from twenty-five women who attended the WWC during 2009 to 2010. My sample of seven women in Kothalawalapura was selected from twenty women who attended the WWC during the same period.

Attidiya WWC was started in 2002 and Kothalawalapura WWC in 2003, but the registers were not maintained in an orderly manner at the very beginning. Both Attidiya and Kothalawalapura WWCs function once a month and two to four women attend the clinic at a time.[4] Since this is an ethnographic study, I concentrated on paying more visits to them in order to get a glimpse into their lives and also the sensitive nature of the research made me spend more time with them to build up a rapport prior to broaching the topic of their bodies. When the PHMs went on house visits, I accompanied them and got myself introduced to my chosen sample of women in these two areas. Apart from that I interviewed two doctors from the Sri Lanka Family Health Bureau (FHB), three doctors from the faculty of medicine, University of Colombo, the Chief Medical Officer of Health Dehiwala, PHNS's of Dehiwala and PHMs from Attidya and Kothalawalapura as my key informants.

I have used in-depth interviews as a primary methodological tool to interview my sample. I interviewed my sample women at their houses and conducted interviews in narrative style. Discussion focused particularly on their sense of hygiene, child care, illness, and preventive health. This type of narrative style helped women to bring out the possibly unspoken views regarding their bodies. This is a crucial way forward in Sri Lanka, since there is no space for women to voice their thoughts, especially about their bodies within medical discourse. As Burns and Walker (2005) point out, it helps "challenging the silencing of women's voices in society and research and in challenging a narrow, gendered kind of science, which cast women in passive and subordinate roles" (Somekh and Lewin 2005:66). Thus I consider my research as a contribution to the feminist perspective on women's bodies in Sri Lanka.

In-depth interviews were held during morning hours (9 a.m. to 1 p.m.), where I found women attending to household chores at their own pace. I spent three months in the field interviewing my sample. I visited them at least four times during my fieldwork. I have shared some of my experiences as a researcher below in order to bring out the effectiveness in amalgamation of archival and ethnographic research methods in this study.

Most women who have attended WWCs are between the ages of thirty-five to forty-four, but I did not come across a single unmarried woman or a childless woman attending WWCs in these two areas. That hints at women's perception of WWCs and reproductive notions in these communities. This point is analyzed in relation to women's understanding of the concept of well woman below.

When I went to their houses, the women always welcomed me with a smile and spoke to me for hours about their experience at WWCs, knowledge of cancer, perception of illnesses, especially cancer, and household respon-sibilities as a mother and wife. Though it was a very sensitive, private issues that I explored, these women responded very willingly. As Van Hollen (2003) points out, women find it unproblematic to express their feelings about the body and life responsibilities to women researchers, because as women the respondents feel that there is a common experience that we all share about the body, which a male researcher or a doctor would not under-stand in the same way.

This served as my point of departure towards the sensitive nature of this research. One may ask, is it ethical for me to discuss with women how they feel and understand their bodies. Why not? If women are happy to express themselves, why not listen and talk and share their experience as a research-er? These women were quite expressive and open about their lives and feel-ings. For example, Lalani discussed her worries over her twenty-three-year old daughter's possibilities for marriage. Lalani had made her daughter break the affair that she had started at school and encouraged her to go out with someone else. Now the daughter is not very keen to get married and settle down.

I was not a passive listener as prescribed in traditional methodology text-books, but I was fully engaged with these conversations, responding to their various queries, anxieties and worries.[5] In this way it helped me to build rapport. As a mother, I also felt it was not ethical for me to evade questions which they posed with great expectations, such as how to (a) deal with a newcomer to the family; (b) manage time to spend on the elder child; and most importantly, (c) control one's temper with a new addition to the family. So I exchanged what I knew, what I have experienced, and what I have read about handling these above mentioned situations, which I think helped the women to see me as not just a researcher who wants to find out bits about their lives in order to fulfill her academic objective, but as a person with a sense of responsibility and genuineness towards them.

My research in Dehiwala was supplemented by my own body check-up at a WWC at a private hospital in Colombo. In order to experience what women go through when doing the tests at the WWCs, I went through the tests on my own. It was similar to the WWC set-up at the MCH clinic, the female doctor did not explain the Pap smear test, but she assured me that it would not be painful. Unlike earlier experiences with male gynecologists, I felt relaxed and comfortable and also believed in her when she assured me that the Pap test would not be painful. Her comforting words reminded me of the cold and cynical responses that I received six years ago from the male gynecologist to my query about how painful a normal delivery is when I was in the eighth month of my first pregnancy. He made a joke out of my query and said that he has never undergone the pain. As pointed out by Bartky (1990), when male gynecologists are questioned by a pregnant woman either they brush off the query by converting it into a joke or will use medical terms to explain the situation which she finds very difficult to understand. Thus I found myself comfortable with this lady gynecologist at the WWC; that I was able to examine the instrument—speculum—that is used to do the Pap smear test. I found it very productive during my long conversations with respondents, since I inquired how they felt about a foreign object being inserted into the body.

Prior to analysis I will briefly describe the global population, development, and women's health discourse in order to locate Sri Lanka's privileged position as "Asia's Ireland" and a "development model" for South Asia in the twentieth century, which qualifies Sri Lanka to articulate this new shift from family planning to reproductive health in a new light. Sri Lanka has gained an international reputation, beyond South Asia, due to the strategic role that women's health has played. These claims are based on relatively high rates of women's literacy and crucially low levels of fertility compared with her neighbors such as India and Pakistan. In other words it is about the ways in which Sri Lankan women were interpellated into the birth control, population control, and family planning programs advocated within the post–World War II global development discourse.

Women's Health in a Global Context

There are several analytical strands through which scientists and social scientists frame women's health. Some place it within development discourse, others in modernity, demography, economics, medicine or feminist studies. All of these, of course, are legitimate ways of approach where women's health could be placed. One crucial concept that cuts across many of these analytical strands is population.

Though population computing goes back to the time of the Roman Empire, the modern idea of a national census was ignited by the influential work of the British political economist Thomas Malthus in 1798 with the publication of *An Essay on the Principle of Population*.[6] Malthus pointed out the link between population and resources by calculating population growth trends in relation to labor force and food production. He proposed that, if the population growth continued in the same vein, the nation soon would have to face a situation of poverty and destitution. So he proposed moral restraints such as celibacy and late marriage as solutions to population checks, rather than abortion, birth control, or prostitution.

However, the growth of "problem populations" became a serious concern first within national boundaries and secondly within colonies of the British empire by the late 1800s. In this light it became an administrative necessity for the British Empire to count the populations of colonial bodies. Thus the first modern census-taking in India and Sri Lanka took place in 1871 under colonial administration in order to keep an account of its subjects.[7] A systematic census was compiled by the Dutch in the seventeenth century on Sri Lanka (then Ceylon), but as Scott suggests, the purpose was to "keep order, extract taxes, and raise armies" (Scott 1998). However, within the modern utilitarian state building project, the British wanted to make the subjects legible in order to "'take in charge' the physical and human resources of the nation and make them more productive," so they came up with a scientific framework of modern national census (Scott 1998: 51).

There is no consensus among historians and population experts as to when population emerged as a category of analysis (Bashford 2007). After World War II, the United States emerged as the leader and creator of a new world order with a new responsibility: to guard the rest of the world, especially Asia against nonalignment, Africa against independence movements, and Latin America against economic nationalism and generally all newly independent states against Communism. Population growth in a newly independent state was seen by the capitalist western society as a state of poverty, destitution, traditional, under-developed, and pro-communist. Thus demographers' assistance was sought by international planners and U.S.-policy makers to formulate a development plan for the underdeveloped world.

According to modern demographic transition theory,[8] introduced by Notestein in 1945, "the shift towards low mortality and fertility rate occurs when there is a process of overall modernisation resulting from industrialisation, urbanisation, education, empowerment of women, as well as substantial overall socio-economic development" (UNECA Report). Notestein reintroduced it as a global framework to place "all countries on a grand evolutionary scheme running from pre-transitional ('traditional') to transitional to post–transitional ('modern')" (Greenhalgh 1976; Caldwell 1976). Since it supported Rostow's growth theory, it came in as a unique explanatory model to develop the backward societies of the Third World. It not only provided a model to develop, but also helped to strengthen the Eurocentric idea of western superiority over the rest of the world. Actually it was more of a prediction based on the western experience rather than a theory, but it served as a unique justification to the contemporary political milieu, which was fashioned by Cold War politics. In other words, it was the marriage between development studies and demography with the blessings of politics.

At the 1952 population conference convened by John D. Rockefeller III, the Population Council was set up as a platform for population research and advocacy (Hartman 1995). Taking the rapid population growth in the Third World into consideration, thirty-one scientists met at the population conference in Virginia and decided to introduce population control measures to these countries prior to them being modernized and industrialized (Watkins 1998). In other words, it was a decision of intervention into less developed areas of the world in the name of modernization. According to Hartman, these demographic research findings of "Malthusian alarmists," not only caused shocking headlines but drew on "deep undercurrents of parochialism, racism, elitism, and sexism, complementing the Social Darwinist 'survival of the fittest' view" (Hartman 1995: 13). Capturing this politicization process, Susan Greenhalgh historicizes the emergence of demography as an "intellectually unprincipled" science during the Cold War period (Hartman 1995: 33). In fact, population trends in the Third World became a concern of the First World because of the new world order that was taking shape under the auspices of the United States.

Women's Health in Sri Lanka

With the economic and technical assistance of the First World (and mainly the United States), birth control and family planning initiatives were launched in Third World countries in the 1950s in order to regulate and organize the population to achieve "development." Third World populations were computed and analyzed according to the demographic transition theory and the results were used to design development plans for the region. Within the golden decades (1960s and 1970s) of American demography (Greenhalgh 1976: 33), biologist Paul Ehrlich introduced the term "population bomb" to describe the rapid population growth in Asia (Hartman 1995: 4). Population became an "object" which needs to be carefully scrutinized and planned for development purposes (Escobar 1997). As a Third World country, Sri Lanka came under the gaze of the development experts first in 1953 with the establishment of the Family Planning Association of Ceylon, in the efforts of population control, and these experts were bestowed with unquestionable authority, knowledge, expertise, and competence to formulate policies and practices to control women's health.

With the state welfare policy adopted by the post-independence government of Sri Lanka (Ceylon became Sri Lanka in 1972) and the aid of technical and financial assistance from international development agencies such as the Swedish government, International Planned Parenthood Federation (IPPF), WHO, and UNFPA, Sri Lanka soon fell in line with development policies advocated by the First World through these institutions. As development anthropologists point out, newly independent states of Asia, Africa, and Latin America entered into a new era of imperialism in the 1950s leaving behind traditional, unscientific, and superstitious knowledge systems by depending on the First World for financial aid, technical know-how, and modern scientific institutions. The danger of this dependency is ideological. As Escobar points out, this all-inclusive package of development aid encouraged the Third World to eschew possible alternate avenues of development thinking.

Sri Lanka—A Development Model for South Asia?

However, Sri Lanka stood out from the Asian demographic picture by the late 1960s, because its population growth rate came under control (nearly 3 percent per annum in the late 1950s to about 2.2 percent by the late 1960s) (Corea 1971) as a result of the improvements in the field of social indicators such as high literacy rates, rise in female age at marriage, women's employment, and family planning activities. Thus by the late 1960s Sri Lanka turned out to be a case of interest as well as a puzzle for scholars of not only demography but also economics and development studies due to unusual progress in social indicators as opposed to very poor progress in economic indicators. Though social indicators were well above the standards of other developing countries, economic progress was still alarmingly slow. Within international comparisons this has given Sri Lanka its well-known "outlier" status (Lakshman and Tisdell 2000). And by the 1970s, Sri Lanka achieved the status of a "development model," thanks to plans designed by western development experts.[9]

The 1980s was a decade of implementing population programs under the dynamic secretary of the Ministry of Plan Implementation, Dr. Wickrema Weerasuria. By 1994 Sri Lanka achieved replacement level fertility—six years before the target. Thus establishment of WWCs in 1996 seemed the most appropriate women's health decision in the eyes of demographers.

WWC PROGRAM IN SRI LANKA

Although the WWC concept was a new phenomenon for Sri Lanka in 1996, its origins go back to the 1940s in the United States.[10] It was developed essentially as an extension of preventive medical care. In other words, when preventive care engaged in routine medical monitoring in the United States, Sri Lanka had not even entered the global discourse on family planning.

However, 1996 marked a new phase in women's health in Sri Lanka with the launch, assisted by the UNFPA, of the island-wide WWC program. WWC was based on the new paradigm of sexual and reproductive health and rights put forward at the Cairo conference (*Annual Report on Family Health Sri Lanka 2007*). It signalled a significant moment in the history of women's health and body in Sri Lanka because, on one hand it marked a disjuncture in the existing nexus of women's health-reproduction-population and on the other hand Sri Lanka was the first to launch a government WWC program in South Asia. This initiative is challenging because the WWC program presents an apparent about-face by disturbing the orthodoxy of women's health as necessarily reproductive health. It is indeed a very radical shift in women's health in Sri Lanka, which up until 1996 was essentially centered within the population control paradigm. According to this new shift, women's health goes beyond its conventional understanding of biological and social reproductive roles. If placed within the ICPD rhetoric, the WWC program in Sri Lanka suggests a shift from reproduction to "beyond reproduction" or family planning to reproductive health and rights.

Out of the three UN sponsored decennial conferences, the Cairo conference made significant headway in the discourse on population control and women's health. As mentioned in the ICPD program of action, it moved away from coercive measures of population control towards a new, emancipated reproductive health agenda. Halfon suggests that ICPD is the "rhetorical shift from 'population control' to 'women's empowerment'" (Halfon 2007:4). And Simon-Kumar perceives ICPD in relation to India as a move from incentives to a targets-free approach, population control to reproductive agency, and numerical quotas to informed choices (Simon-Kumar 2006:6).

What, then, is ICPD for Sri Lanka? According to the health policy-makers of Sri Lanka, ICPD called for a paradigm shift from family planning to reproductive health, from society to individual, and from vertical health service delivery to integrated services. And the underlying element of this shift was the emphasis on women's empowerment and its inextricable link with reproductive health and rights (*Annual Report of the Family Planning Association of Sri Lanka 1998–1999*: 3).

Establishment of the WWC Program in Sri Lanka

With the financial support of the UNFPA, an island-wide WWC program was launched in Sri Lanka in 1996, promoted by international agencies at the ICPD Cairo in 1994 (*Annual Report on Family Health Sri Lanka 2002-2003*). It was incorporated into the Family Health program under the concept of reproductive health. FHB is the central institution responsible for the implementation of the WWC program in Sri Lanka. The first WWC was set up in Kaluthara District (Southern Sri Lanka) in June 1996 (Wijesinghe 2003). As the responsible authority of implementing the WWC program in Sri Lanka, the FHB, from the inception of the WWC program, has issued three circulars and published one handbook on the implementation of the WWC. These documents were addressed to all the Provincial Directors of Health Services (PDHS), Deputy Provincial Directors of Health Services (DPDHS), Medical Officers Maternal and Child Health (MOMCH), Divisional Directors of Health Services (DDHS), Medical Officers of Health (MOH), and Heads of Medical Institutions.

At the end of year 2009, 617 WWCs were functioning in the country, mostly based at MOH offices. The number of women attending has increased to 116,415 in 2009 compared to 111,789 in 2008. However, FHB notes that "it is still only a fraction of the target population" (*Annual Report on Family Health Sri Lanka 2008-2009*).

WWCs operate in four models within Sri Lanka, one within family planning clinics at Maternal and Child Health (MCH) Clinics at MOH areas, the other within government-based hospitals (both provide free access to medical services) and the third model within private hospitals, where they offer different packages to undergo the tests that are done at WWCs. The fourth model is private institutions specifically geared towards wellness, such as Ceylinco Cancer Detection Centre. Apart from these institutions the FPA of Sri Lanka established a WWC in December 1997 (*Annual Report of the Family Planning Association of Sri Lanka 1998-1999*).

When the minister of health decided to launch an island-wide WWC program in 1996, no one made an effort to understand the broader discourse of women's bodies that was taking new and critical turns in the plight of the conflict situation in 1990s Sri Lanka. The WWC program was also treated as another women's health initiative to "horn their trumpets" on performance targets, rather than understanding the new ideology, women's health "beyond reproduction," that it calls for, which in turn led to ethical issues at institutional and conceptual levels.

Institutional Issues

Under the public sector health service WWCs operate within the Maternal and Child Health (MCH) Clinics at MOH offices in Sri Lanka. Within the Sri Lankan patriarchal culture, women's bodies were essentially perceived by the society as well as by women themselves within a biological and social reproductive framework. According to my fieldwork, the MCH clinic is perceived by the public as essentially an institution providing maternal and child health care, especially family planning advice and support. Therefore I find it problematic that WWCs are placed within such a setting as it is perceived as an unwelcome space for a divorcee, an older, unmarried or childless woman. Within Sri Lankan patriarchal society, women's lives are rigidly controlled by social values and norms, so the WWC becomes a taboo for these women purely due to its location. One of my respondents, a divorcee, pointed out that one of her reasons for not attending a WWC at its inception was because of the general misunderstanding about the MCH clinics:

> People will not bother to find out the real reason for my visiting the MCH clinic; they will spread unnecessary rumours about me getting family planning treatment at a MCH clinic. So why invite unnecessary problems?

If a divorcee hesitates to attend a WWC within this context, then a widow or a childless woman would be very likely to keep away from it as well, as it is likely to generate unnecessary suspicion and talk within the community. During my fieldwork I did not come across a single divorcee, widow, or barren woman in the WWC register which both clinics have maintained since 2006. Though the national program is aimed at uplifting the health of women, the unmarried and divorced women were excluded when designing the program. Within the Sri Lankan culture, the general norm is for women to get married and raise a family. The WWC program is also geared to cater to this general category, effectively ignoring the other categories such as barren women, older unmarried women, widows, and separated or divorced women who are not socially recognized. How could the state be insensitive towards these socially excluded women when designing public health programs such as the WWC Program?

On the other hand, by situating WWCs within the MCH clinic, the essence or the logic of WWCs—beyond reproduction—is undermined. I see this as an ideal Third World scenario, where a new project (WWCs) has preceded ideology (beyond reproduction) and infrastructure (using MCH clinic premises). Of course this dilemma creates major ethical considerations with regard to women's health because it creates space for health policies to further subordinate women's bodies, which are already subordinated within patriarchal culture and the western medical system in Sri Lanka.

Public health as a welfare policy in Sri Lanka further denies women their right over their bodies. During my conversations with the policy-makers of the WWC program at the FHB, the idea of denying rights when offering a free service came up frequently, in the common Sinhala idiom *nikam dena assayage dath balanne nane*, which means "never look a gift horse in the mouth." When the WWC program is provided as a free service, the government involuntarily denies women their rights over their bodies. In other words, women's bodies become the property of the state where health policies are aimed at achieving performance targets.

Conceptual Issues

During my interviews with the doctors who were involved in the process of conceptualizing WWCs, they articulated this new shift as women's health beyond reproduction, screening as a preventive measure, and a clinic for healthy women. Thus the WWC program was clearly a step forward because it suggests freeing women's health from reproduction. I will explore how this concept (characterized by the above three features) worked or was received within the state/official rhetoric and at the grassroots level.

What Does "Beyond Reproduction" Mean in Sri Lanka?

Women's position in society as biological and social reproducer can be traced from pre-colonial times in Sri Lanka. A section of *Kavyasekaraya*, a Sinhalese narrative poem of the fifteenth century authored by Sri Rahula thero of Thotagamuwa, which contains the advice given by a father to his daughter (of a noble family) on marriage, is an epitome of patriarchal thinking. It appears even today in the Sinhala textbook of grade eleven under the national curriculum. (See Appendix I.) It defines how a woman should behave, her role at home as a dutiful wife and a mother, her limitations in social relations, and how she should express her feelings, so these ideas are still alive, within the Sri Lankan society, of course at different levels according to class, caste, and educational background (Sinhala Textbook Grade 11, 2000).

Referring to a Tamil School textbook, Maunaguru (1995) points out that this same ideology still persists within the Tamil community in Sri Lanka. All advice and responsibilities make the woman's life revolve around her family, with nurturing and caring responsibilities, without leaving space for herself to think as an independent human being. She is bestowed with reproductive functions, and her socialization process is aimed at training her to achieve her ultimate goal of reproduction. Within this process there is no space for women to think about their lives and bodies "beyond reproduction."

Similar ideology and traditions were further defined during the British period (late-nineteenth and early-twentieth centuries) through nationalist struggles in Sri Lanka. Anagarika Dharmapala was one of the leading nationalists of the day who made a great impact on the lives of the rising Sinhalese middle class in the early twentieth century. Dharmapala introduced a new Sinhalese life-style, and bestowed women with a special and rather active role within the domestic sphere. Housekeeping was her key responsibility, which he advised every woman to attend with greatest care. For attending to all the housekeeping and child-rearing duties, the middle-class mother was attributed a holy status within the Buddhist revivalist ideology; she was considered the "Buddha at home" (*Gedara Budun*). The parental responsibility was emphasized within the nuclear family unit, where mothers played the role of a teacher at home, cultivating social and moral values in children, while fathers played a social role in the society by providing for the family.

Family health is a primary duty of the wife and mother. As part of her social reproductive role, Dharmapala advised her to look into the needs of all the members (including the servants) of the household, and hygiene was one of her key responsibilities in order to ensure smooth functioning of the house. This same ideology was further established within school curriculum. Health of the family lay in the hands of women. Though she was taught the importance of health and hygiene, she was not trained to give the same importance to her own health, because as a social reproducer she is the caregiver of the family. Health education was provided to women within the social reproductive role, providing nutritious food and boiled water for the family, washing clothes of the family, inculcating hygienic habits among children, and keeping the house clean.

Women I interviewed mentioned most of these activities as their daily household chores and also as what they expect a girl child to learn. Stressing how important it is to ensure that her children eat nutritious food, 43-year-old Lalani proudly said,

> I still feed my daughter (23 years old) and son (21 years old) while they get dressed to go to work in the morning, if they don't have time to have breakfast. I make it a point that they don't eat fast junk food.

The biological and social reproductive role was clearly embedded within the educational and social upbringing of the girl child in Sri Lanka. Within this socializing process, a girl child is not given the opportunity to think of her body "beyond reproduction" and also the state is not ready to free the woman's body from the biological and social reproductive role.

Even though women's bodies seemed to be liberated from demographic goals by 1996, the youth uprising in Southern Sri Lanka in 1989-1991 and ethnic conflict which became violent during the 1990s bestowed a different manifestation to women's bodies by valorizing the concept of "brave mother-hood" propagated by both the government and the LTTE with the enlisting of women cadre in the late 1980s (Thiruchandran 1999). In other words the conflict situation could not liberate women's bodies for the new ideology— women's bodies "beyond reproduction"—to be developed.

Studying the LTTE women cadres in Sri Lanka, de Mel shows that the female body has been used by the LTTE to achieve their political agendas by training women suicide bombers. Maunaguru further points out that a popu-lar image of a woman with a child in one arm and a gun in another was used in the late 1990s by one of the militant groups in Jaffna (i.e., in Northern Sri Lanka where the majority community is Tamil), asking Tamil women "not to be fooled by the state's family planning policy on the grounds that this policy was a conspiracy to control the demographic size of the Tamil population" (Maunaguru 1995: 163).

These two events complement each other in two ways: first, by justifying the unfeminine nature attributed to the woman warrior and, secondly, by reminding women that their prime duty towards the nation is to reproduce healthy, brave children. In short, this justifies a new non-traditional role (woman warrior), but of course in terms of a need of the hour at hand, within the traditional framework. Further, the labor of women is valorized as sup-porting (both by the State and the LTTE) the national cause by protecting the mother Lanka or motherland for future generations. The poster helped wom-en to digest this new shift in gender roles, yet the new paradigm reverberated with the reproductive responsibilities and duties propagated by Dharmapala in early twentieth century.

Further, motherhood was valorized both by Sinhalese and Tamil national-ists by forming a Mothers' Front in pressurizing the state to find the missing youth (sons) during the youth uprising *Janatha Vimukthi Peramuna* (Peo-ple's Liberation Movement—JVP) in Southern Sri Lanka in the early 1990s. Thus, the State was not politically ready in 1996 to introduce the concept of "beyond reproduction" or freeing women's bodies from reproduction due to the strategies adopted in combating the ethnic conflict and the JVP uprising becoming violent in the 1990s. In other words, the concept of "beyond repro-duction" became politically meaningless within the conflict as the state was not in a position to release women's bodies from the social reproductive functions.

Within this context, introduction of an island-wide WWC program can be viewed as a conceptual misnomer with regard to women's health in Sri Lanka.

Clinics for "Screening Healthy Women"?

Circulars on implementation of WWCs clearly set out the idea that WWCs are for "healthy" women by recommending WWC test "for any woman over 35 years" (Guidelines for Implementation of the WWC program, Clause 2, 1999). The PHMs are advised to educate and inform women in the area with the help of the field officers (General Circular No. 1926, Guideline 5, 1996). Screening of healthy bodies was an innovative idea to Sri Lanka because it challenged the previously held notions of health and women's body as interconnected with traditional medical practices of Ayurvedic, Unani, and Siddha systems, religion, and women's position in the patriarchal household. All the PHMs interviewed expressed the difficulty in getting the idea of screening "healthy women" for common non-communicable diseases across to women. One of the PHMs said that she still could not convince her own mother who is aged fifty to undergo WWC tests. Her mother finds it embarrassing and difficult to show her private parts of the body to anybody now, in her old age. Also she says it seems,

> It is not worth spending money on me, even if I have a serious illness such as cancer, because I have lived my life, now it is your turn to live a good life.

Anthropologists who study notions of illness and sickness in colonial contexts perceive medicine as part of culture (Kleinman 1995). Although the western medical system in Sri Lanka is highly institutionalized, rational, and scientific, still people attend to their ailments according to the way they understand their bodies. Interpretations of disease/illness and ailments come from culture, because people perceive their bodies as part of culture and bodies are placed within culture. According to the Ayurvedic medical system, sickness is a result of an imbalance within three compositions of the body named as *Thridosha*. In order to maintain the equilibrium of these *doshas*, it is recommended to eat healthy food and exercise the body and maintain some bodily regulations. From my fieldwork I have observed that people in general and women in particular, seek medical help or advice only if there is some kind of an ailment. Even for an ailment, women try a range of home remedies prior to seeking medical help. After two to three days of such treatment, if the ailment still persists only then do they seek medical help. For medical assistance they go to the nearby dispensary or government hospital. Within their perception, medical treatment is sought only when they admit and accept that they are sick.

Within such a context there was no room for screening of healthy bodies within the general understanding of health, sickness, and bodies. But then WWCs are not for the sick but for healthy women. What does that mean? Why should a woman go to a clinic or seek medical advice when she is feeling fine and healthy? The western notion of "check ups" is not a common practice among lower-middle-class women, who largely utilize public health sector services in Sri Lanka. Generally in Sri Lanka, being healthy means not associated with clinics and medical settings. Rather, it is the opposite; they are proud to say that they have not paid a visit to any medical setting for the last couple of years or so. During my brief conversation with one mother of a respondent, who was fifty-nine said,

> "My husband and I have a good understanding about our bodies. Both of us do not seek medical help unless it is really necessary. Our life style and eating habits have given us good health and we listen to the rhythm of our bodies." I asked her what she meant by rhythm? "Rhythm is, what the body needs, for example, if I don't feel like having a bath today, I refrain from having a bath and if I feel like lying on the bed for some time I do so, because my body needs it. Now-a-days, these children (pointing towards her daughter) wash their hair just because they want to go out in the evening, without actually listening to what the body says. I think such practices cause unnecessary problems and health hazards. Proudly she said that I haven't visited a doctor for more than 3 years now" (a proud smile crossed her lips).

While WWCs are introduced for healthy women, the notion of healthiness advocated in WWCs and the general perception of healthiness have two different and contradictory connotations within Sri Lankan society and culture. WWCs are introduced for healthy women in order to continue their good health as a preventive measure, while the general understanding of healthiness means keeping away from a medical setting. Monitoring procedures of the WWCs, such as screening and periodic check-ups, did not fall in line with the general understanding of healthiness among lower-middle-class women of Sri Lanka. Of course they undergo those routine check-ups during their pregnancies because the reproductive function gives a significant status to women within the social and cultural framework. At the same time, as pointed out above, pregnancy and child birth is a responsibility of the state within the nation-building and development discourse.

However, issues about women's bodies "beyond reproduction" or reproductive health and rights are read within an entirely different text by women who utilize private health care (not even five percent of the population) in Sri Lanka. By saying so, I do not mean that these women are entirely devoid of patriarchal ideology promoted by the state. But they exercise a certain choice that women who utilize public health services do not enjoy due to their less affluent position in society.

So women in their post-reproductive age in Sri Lanka find the logic of WWCs difficult to comprehend, which makes ethically sensitive women's health policy even more challenging. According to my understanding of the WWC program in Sri Lanka, the first step is to free women's bodies from historical strangulation by giving due recognition to women's bodies beyond reproductive health, which will facilitate the development of new ideology: "beyond reproduction." A second step is to bring both women's health and bodies into one analytical framework. That will pave the way to compile an ethically sensitive women's health policy.

CONCLUSION

Keeping up with the development model in South Asia, Sri Lanka reached replacement-level fertility by 1994. In other words, 1996 seemed like the demographically correct moment for Sri Lanka to embark on the shift from family planning to reproductive health and rights or from reproduction to beyond reproduction by launching the WWC program as advocated by the ICPD in 1994. But in order for the WWC program to be ethically correct and meaningful, it is pertinent that this ideological shift is intellectually captured by policy-makers and implementers of the program. First and foremost, policy-makers should be able to read women's health and bodies as mutually intelligible concepts, because women's health is not only about health per se, but it is about women's bodies with clearly defined ethnic and cultural identities and limitations.

As a preventive health measure, the WWC initiative is quite challenging because it presents an apparent about-face within women's health in modern Sri Lanka. It disturbs the orthodoxy of women's health as necessarily reproductive health, with its new focus on screening healthy women who are past their reproductive age.

But as a practical health policy the WWC initiative is an ideological misnomer, because it fails to capture the conflict situation in the country during the 1990s, which strapped women's bodies to its biological and social reproductive roles. Further, my ethnographic study of the WWC program in Sri Lanka attests that a woman's body is enmeshed in patriarchal culture and traditional health/medical perception. This in turn created no space to develop the new ideology "beyond reproduction," which is the base and logic of the WWC program.

In order to compose an ethically correct/sensitive women's health policy, women's bodies should be freed from the notion of reproduction (both biological and social) to broaden the understanding of health, which was not possible in the 1990s. Today, after twenty-six years of ethnic violence (from 1983-2009), Sri Lanka can hope to free women's bodies from past traditions and come up with an ethically sensitive women's health policy.

REFERENCES

Annual Report on Family Health Sri Lanka 2002-2003. 2005. Colombo. Family Health Bureau, Ministry of Health Sri Lanka.

Annual Report on Family Health Sri Lanka 2004-2005. 2007. Colombo. Family Health Bureau, Ministry of Health Sri Lanka.

Annual Report on Family Health Sri Lanka 2008-2009. 2010. Colombo. Family Health Bureau.

Annual Report of the Family Planning Association of Sri Lanka 1998-1999. 1991. Colombo, FPA.

Bartky, S. L. 1990. *Femininity and Domination: Studies in the Phenomenology of Oppression*. New York and London: Routledge.

Bashford, A. 2007. "Nation, Empire, Globe: The spaces of population debate in the interwar years." In *Comparative Studies in Society and History* 49:1 (pp. 1-32).

Burns, D. and Walker, M. 2005. Feminist Methodologies; in B. Somekh and C. Lewin (eds) *Research Methods in the Social Sciences*. London and New York: Sage.

Caldwell, John. 1976. "Toward a Restatement of Demographic Transition Theory." *Population and Development Review* 2(3/4): 321-366.

Chandrarathne, S.M.P. 2004. Effect of Antenatal Body Mass Index on Maternal and Fetal Outcome. Unpublished PhD thesis submitted to the Post Graduate Institute of Medicine, Colombo.

Corea, G. 1971. "Ceylon in the Sixties." *Marga Quaterly* 1(2).

de Alwis, M. 1998. "Motherhood as a Space of Protest: Women's Political Participation in Contemporary Sri Lanka" in *Appropriating Gender: Women's Activism and the Politicization of Religion* in South Asia, edited by A. Basu and P. Jeffrey, London/NY: Routledge/ Delhi: Kali for Women, pp. 186-201.

———2004. "The Moral Mother Syndrome." *Indian Journal of Gender Studies* 11(1): 65-73.

de, Mel, N. 2004. "Body Politics: (Re)cognising the Female Suicide Bomber in Sri Lanka." *Indian Journal of Gender Studies* 11(1): 75-93

———2007. *Militarizing Sri Lanka: Popular Culture, Memory and Narrative in the Armed Conflict*, Los Angeles/London/New Delhi/Singapore. Sage.

de Silva, N. 1989. A Study of Emotional Disorders in Women Patients in General Practice. Unpublished PhD thesis submitted to Post Graduate Institute of Medicine, Colombo.

Denham, E.B. 1912. *Ceylon at the Census of 1911: Being the review of the results of the census of 1911*, Colombo, H.C. Cottle.

———1997. "The Making and Unmaking of the Third World Through Development." In *The Post Development Reader*, edited by M. Rahnem and V. Bawtree. London and New Jersey: Zed Books.

Fernando, K.N.J. 1999. Knowledge and Practices on Contraception Among Married Female School Teachers in Udunuwara MOH Area and the Use by Them of Available Family Planning Services. Unpublished PhD thesis submitted to Post Graduate Institute of Medicine, Colombo.

Gardner, K. 1983. "A well woman clinic in an inner-city general practice." *Journal of the Royal College of General Practitioners*: 711-714.

General Circular No. 1926 dated 19th August 1996, Colombo. Ministry of Health Sri Lanka.

Greenhalgh, S. 1976. "The Social Construction." *Population and Development Review* 2(3/4): 321-366.

Guidelines for Implementation of the WWC programme dated 14th July 1999. Colombo, Ministry of Health Sri Lanka.

Halfon, S. 2007. *The Cairo Consensus: Demographic Surveys, Women's empowerment, and Regime Change in Population Policy*. Lanham/Boulder/New York/Toronto/Plymouth: Lexington books.

Hartman, B. 1995. *Reproductive Rights and Wrongs: The Global Politics of Population Control*. Boston, Massachusetts: South End Press.

Jayawardena, K. 2003. *Feminism and Nationalism in the Third World*. London and New Jersey: Zed Books Ltd.

Kleinman, A. 1995. *Writing at the Margin; Discourse between Anthropology and Medicine.* Berkeley, Los Angeles, California: University of California Press.

Lakshman, W.D. and Tisdell, C.A. 2000. "Introduction to Sri Lanka's Development Since Independence." In *Sri Lanka's Development Since Independence: Socio-economic perspectives and Analysis,* edited by Lakshman and Tisdell. New York: Nova Science Publishers.

Lukumar, P. and Pathmeswaran, A. 2006. "Factors Associated With Home Deliveries in Thampalakamam, Trincomalee" *The Ceylon Medical Journal* 51(2).

Maunaguru, S. 1995. "Gendering Tamil Nationalism: The Construction of 'woman' in Projects of Protest and Control." Pp. 158-175 in *Unmaking the Nation: The Politics of Identity and History in Modern Sri Lanka,* edited by P. Jeganathan and Q. Ismail. Colombo: Social Scientists' Association.

Oakley, A. 1981. "Interviewing women: A contradiction in terms." In *Doing Feminist Research,* edited by H. Roberts. London: Routledge.

Sakar, N.K. 1957. *The Demography of Ceylon.* Ceylon govt. Press.

Scott, J.C. 1998. *Seeing Like a State: How certain schemes to improve the human condition have failed.* New Heaven and London: Yale University Press.

Simon-Kumar, R. 2006. *Marketing Reproduction? Ideology and Population Policy in India.* New Delhi: Zubaan.

Sinhala Textbook Grade 11. 2000. Colombo: Ministry of Education.

The State of Demographic Transition in Africa. Food Security and Sustainable Development Division, Economic Commission for Africa, 2001.

Suvanari Seva Athpotha (Handbook on Well Woman Clinic Services). Colombo: Family Health Bureau, 2003.

Thiruchandran, S. 1999. *The Other Victims of War: Emergence of Female Headed Households in Eastern Sri Lanka (Volume II).* Colombo: Women's Education and Research Centre, Colombo.

Turner, L.J.B. (superintendent of Census and Director of Statistics, Ceylon). 1923. Census Publications, Ceylon 1921, Report on the Census of Ceylon, 1921, Vol. 1, Part I. Ceylon: Government Printer.

Van Hollen, C. 2003. *The Birth on the Threshold: Childbirth and Modernity in South India.* Berkeley, Los Angelesm and London: University of California Press.

Watkins, E.S. 1998. *On the Pill: A Social History of Oral Contraceptives 1950-1970.* Baltimore and London: The John Hopkins University Press.

Wickramasinghe, N. 2006. *Sri Lanka in The Modern Age: A History of Contested Identities.* London: Hurts Company.

Wijesinghe, C.J. 2003. Descriptive Study on women attending WWCs in the Galle District. Unpublished PhD Thesis submitted to PGIM, Colombo.

APPENDIX I

Do not leave your house without your husband's permission;
    When you go out, do not walk fast and see that you are properly clad.
    Be like a servant to your husband, his parents and his kinsmen.
    Sweep your house and garden regularly and see that
    it is always clean. Make sure that you light the
    lamps to the gods both at dawn and dusk.
    Do not spend your time standing at your door,
    strolling about in gardens and parks and do not
    be lazy at your household duties.
    Protect the gods in your house. Do not give
    anything away even to your own children,

without your husband's consent.

If your husband's attention seems directed elsewhere,

Do not speak to him about it, let your tears be

the only indication of your sorrow.

Seek out your husband's desire in food and see that

He is constantly satisfied, feed him and ensure his

well-being like a mother.

Even if your husband appears angry and cold,

do not speak roughly to him; be kind and forgiving

Never think to look elsewhere for your comfort.

(Quoted in Kumari Jayawardena, Feminism and Nationalism in the Third World, Colombo, Sanjiva books, 2003, pp 113-114).

NOTES

1. By 1995 Total Fertility Rate has come down to 1.9, which is below population replacement level. www.statistics.gov.lk/PopHouSat/index.asp www.statistics.gov.lk http://www.un.org/depts/escap/pop/journal/v09n4a1.htm.

2. De Alwis (1998, 2004), Coomaraswamy (2003) and De Mel (2004, 2007) have analyzed how Sri Lankan women's bodies were depicted in the conflict and political settings both by the state and the Liberation of Tamil Tigers of Elam (LTTE), where they were forced to depart from traditional attire and behavior in order to fulfil political causes of the state, and the use of powerful rhetoric such as moral oriental mother, to justify their cause within the traditional lines, as women protecting their motherland for future children of the nation.

3. For example see works of Lukumar and Pathmeswaran (2006), de Silva (1989), Chandrarathne (2004) and Fernando (1999).

4. There are five Public Health Midwives in Attidiya MCH clinic, each of whom provides their service to a population of 4000, and there are six Public Health Midwives in Kothalawalapura MCH clinic and each of them provides service to a population of 4000. Ideally, a PHM should cover a population of 3000.

5. Oakley (1981) discusses methodological problems with textbook "recipes" of the art of interviewing.

6. According to Turner, the word "census" derived from the Roman enumeration by the censors in 435 B.C. and, later, the count appeared to have been taken every fifth year. Census Publications, Ceylon 1921, Report on the Census of Ceylon, 1921, Vol. 1, Part I, L.J.B. Turner, (superintendent of Census and Director of Statistics, Ceylon), Ceylon, Government Printer, 1923, p. 1.

7. The first British census of Sri Lanka (then Ceylon) took place in 1871. See E.B. Denham, Ceylon at the Census of 1911: being the review of the results of the census of 1911, Colombo, H.C. Cottle, 1912, for a concise report on the British census of Sri Lanka. Also see N. Wickramasinghe, *Sri Lanka in The Modern Age: A History of Contested Identities*, London, Hurts Company, 2006, p. 47 for an analysis of British colonial governance through census reports. According to Sakar, the quality and reliability of statistical data of Ceylon is superior to other Asian countries. "Registration of deaths was made compulsory in 1867 and failure to register births was made punishable in 1893." (N.K. Sakar, The Demography of Ceylon, Ceylon govt. Press, 1957, p. 1).

8. The demographic transition theory was founded in 1929 by the demographer Warren Thompson through his careful study of birth and death rates of industrialized countries over a period of 200 years. It was later applied by Frank Notestein.

9. See Dudley Kirk, "Natality in the Developing countries: Recent Trends and Prospects," in *Fertility and Family Planning a World View*, edited by S.J. Behrman, Leslie Corsa and

Ronald Freedman, University of Michigan Press, 1969, Caldwell, J.C., Gajanayake, I., Caldwel, B. and Caldwell, P., "Is marriage delay a multiphase response to pressures for fertility decline? The case of Sri Lanka" in *Journal of Marriage and the Family* 51 (May 1989), (pp. 337-351), Alam, I. and Cleland, J. C. (1981) *Illustrative Analysis: Recent Fertility Trends in Sri Lanka.* World Fertility Survey Scientific Report No. 25. International Statistical Institute, Voorburg and Gunnar Myrdal, *Asian Drama: An Inquiry into the Poverty of Nations, Vol. II*, New York, Pantheon, 1968.

10. Katy Gardner, "A well woman clinic in an inner-city general practice" in *Journal of the Royal College of General Practitioners*, 1983, November, p. 712. (pp. 711- 714).

Chapter Nine

What Have We Learned?

Patrick James and Lyn Boyd-Judson

OVERVIEW

Women's global health is a vast topic that can be studied from a wide range of intellectual perspectives. With thousands of international organizations and about 200 states that encompass national, regional, and local governments, the range of evidence about norms and policies that could be assembled is overwhelming. Along those lines, recall the mapping from table 1.1 in chapter 1, which identified twelve major themes, any one of which can (and does) require many volumes to explore thoroughly. The current project stands as an attempt to sample from that enormous reality regarding women's global health at the level of policies and norms. Moreover, the workshop that initiated this project included numerous references to *facilitating* rather than completing a dialogue on the subject of women's global health. Thus the present volume's case materials from the UN, Sweden, Netherlands, Germany, Mozambique, Tanzania, U.S., Iran, India, and Sri Lanka represent an effort to encourage further research through identification of tendencies within the data. As an important and rapidly expanding subject area of scholarship, women's global health obviously transcends a single-volume treatment even for state policy and norms as one subject area.

This volume takes seriously the challenge of moving closer to a multifaceted objective regarding women's global health: improvement in absolute terms, along with increasing equality with respect to level of effort in comparison to men's health. As pointed out in the chapter by Ba-Thike and Gummadi, for example, equity in access to health services regardless of status anywhere in the world is a matter for state policy *and* an innately ethical and moral issue. Thus the study began in chapter 1 with the academic objective of answering three interrelated questions that pertain to empirical reality and norms about women's global health:

- How do laws and policies of states and international organizations impact upon women's health?
- In what ways should states and international organizations consider altering their laws and policies to impact more favorably on women?
- What norms can and should guide the provision of women's global health?

This concluding chapter answers each of these questions, with implications for the interdisciplinary fields of ethics, women's studies, international studies, and beyond. It is understood that the responses provided are tentative; the contents of the volume, as summarized here, represent a highly selected sample of the available intellectual perspectives, methods and data that might be applied to the topic of women's global health. The chapter finishes up with some final thoughts and a few ideas about future directions for research.

STATES AND INTERNATIONAL ORGANIZATIONS: THE IMPACT OF LAWS AND POLICIES

Laws and policies among states and international organizations vary in their impact on women's global health. Discussion begins with the plus side and moves on to the minus as identified by findings from respective chapters.[1] While no attempt will be made to weigh the balance, significant positive examples are sufficient to establish an upward trend. The reason for such a forthright conclusion regarding a favorable direction is the virtual *absence* of attention to women's global health until the most recent decades.

Norms and actions put forward by the most prominent international organizations generally are positive with respect to women's global health. At the level of norms, the UN—the principal international organization—stands out. For example, an explicit commitment is made through one of the UN's MDGs to reduce maternal mortality seventy-five percent by 2015 (Sjoberg). It also is encouraging to see in the chapter by Perlman and Roberts how the WHO and members of the NGO community reacted to the massive public health challenge posed by unethical corporate practices regarding infant formula. In response to marketing tactics from those selling infant formula, international breastfeeding advocates and the WHO created the Code of Marketing of Breast-milk Substitutes (i.e., The Code) (Perlman and Roberts). Other examples from the present volume easily could be recounted, although the favorable mind-set and policies exhibited by international organizations toward women and global health remain at an early stage of development. Greater efforts are needed to effect sustained change, notably in the developing world.

What about states? Chapters in this volume have described a range of positive laws and policies. Levels of compliance among states with regard to at least some legal commitments already are noteworthy. For example, Perlman and Roberts observe that, as of 2011, eighty-nine percent of countries that signed onto the above-noted Code regarding infant formula had taken some form of action to implement it. India serves as a specific illustration; legislation there increases access to unbiased information about the benefits and drawbacks of breastfeeding and using infant formula by regulating information provided by infant formula companies (Perlman and Roberts).

Further positive developments in policy are highlighted in the chapters that focus on South Asia. In India the JSY aims to promote deliveries in health facilities with skilled personnel who can provide a package of basic and comprehensive care for mothers and their newborns. Ba-Thike and Gummadi report a strong sociocultural impact for the JSY as evidenced by high levels of awareness about it. In nearby Sri Lanka, the WWC program represents a step forward because it suggests freeing women's health from the more specific issue of reproduction (Thoradeniya).

What about the negative side of the ledger regarding international organizations, states, and women's global health? As revealed by DeLaet, when lost years of health are examined, superficial patterns favoring women with regard to life expectancy and HALE are reversed. Global health disadvantages for women become apparent when more precise measurements are introduced.

Consider, for instance, the financial aspects of global health. Taken together, maternal/child health, reproductive health, and health systems funding suggest a gender gap in global health aid that works against women (DeLaet). De Laet reports that funding for maternal/child care is up in recent years, but still significantly lower than global health aid for HIV/AIDS. Moreover, rather than having positive spill-over effects into other health priority categories, global funding for HIV/AIDS may have come at the expense of support for other important health initiatives, including health systems funding and population and reproductive health.

Along those lines, note that the number of women continues to be below expected value within the global population. This almost certainly is the result of gender-biased practices in areas of the developing world—a cultural preference for boys over girls in many societies (DeLaet). Other cultural problems for women's global health can be identified. For example, many cultures feature significant pressure on women to procreate; failure to do so in societies where this norm is central can lead to negative treatment (Sjoberg). Excessive reproduction is the result of such pressure and brings with it threats to physical and mental health. The problem of bias against women persists even in the domain of health-related research. In many instances, as DeLaet points out, medical research is conducted with only male subjects but practices inferred from the results assume applicability to women. This type of inference is certain to be false across a wide range of circumstances.

When a more panoramic view of global health is taken into account vis-à-vis policy issues, the problem of biased allocation of resources arguably becomes even more graphic. Consider human trafficking, a challenge to global health covered in the chapter by Marinova and James. This criminal activity, which operates on a large scale, overwhelmingly targets women, often those who are very young. It almost goes without saying that the health-related implications of human trafficking for women and girls are awful—sexually transmitted diseases, drug addiction, and violence are just the most visible and obvious by-products. Marinova and James infer that human trafficking continues because of social norms that exclude and treat some people as inferior. This problem persists even in the presumably most advanced locations in the world. Poor treatment of trafficked women by European governments, which otherwise implement extensive social safety nets, parallels the behavior of empires toward those stereotyped negatively in the past (Marinova and James).

Examples from the United States show that global health problems related to women can be aggravated by the state at the very center of the system. Efforts have been made to defund Title X, a key piece of legislation in the United States. Furthermore, family planning services have been cut in many countries because of U.S. enforcement of the GGR. HIV/AIDS services are provided at family planning clinics around the world, so the GGR hinders that as well (Baird). Instability regarding the GGR—cycles of implementation and repeal from one presidential administration to the next—also create strategic difficulties for family planning.

International organizations and states, in sum, manifest an improving but mixed record with regard to women's global health. The natural question to answer next is what might be changed in order to achieve better outcomes.

STATES, INTERNATIONAL ORGANIZATIONS AND POLICY CHANGE

Discussion here will work through general aspects and move on to specifics. Subject areas regarding potential policy change include information and data collection, administrative aspects, legality, and family planning.

Consider information and data collection as key elements in the effort to improve global health for women. Maternal mortality could be virtually eliminated—if some degree of funding and accountability can be assumed—

through legal reform that permits women's access to provision of appropriate health information and services (DeLaet). This is just one example of the well-verified point in favor of disseminating information as a path to improved health outcomes.

Accurate data is the flip side of the preceding point. In addition to providing access to trustworthy information about healthcare practices, it is important to gather valid and reliable data to assess current policies and derive recommendations for improvement of women's global health. It is known already, for instance, that leading health indicators may not capture burdens faced by women that undermine the quality of their lives without (a) necessarily constituting disease or disability or (b) being categorized as health challenges (De Laet). The most salient examples are child related, with human trafficking and prostitution causing less obvious problems that should be added to the roster of items deemed relevant to women's global health.

And how much worse is the situation for women than for men at the level of global health? This question is very difficult to answer specifically because of an inability to engage in comparative analysis that could inform policy. Failure among governments to provide comprehensive data on men's global health, as DeLaet points out, complicates efforts to ascertain the extent to which there are biologically rooted and gender-based inequities. Data are lacking for purposes of comparison.

Administration is an aspect of policy implementation that warrants further attention. The priorities here are greater coordination and expanded programming, along with introduction of structures to counteract major problems.

Compared to existing piecemeal and sometimes overlapping efforts, a central location for all international health programs would allow for a coordinated worldwide strategy (Baird). Such an institution may be a long way off in global terms, but more limited measures that build on existing examples would seem realistic in the near future. It is worth bearing in mind that a "bottom up" approach also could have value; even with greater coordination, there still is something to be said for local initiative and ownership.

Consider, as an instance of concerted action, Indian experience with the JSY. Coordination and expansion emerge as priorities here. The UNFPA evaluation recommended that management of JSY be strengthened via coordination in particular. This could be achieved by monitoring all components of the scheme, increasing communication by developing a communication activity plan in order to mobilize the community, and strengthening financial planning (Ba-Thike and Gummadi). In addition, a WHO report from SEARO notes an increase in institutional deliveries and recommends expansion of the scope of care provided through JSY. Future areas of focus should include newborn healthcare, specifically the training of healthcare personnel to handle problems of newborns (Ba-Thike and Gummadi). Similar observations can be made concerning WWC in Sri Lanka (Thoradeniya). Given JSY's success thus far in increasing institutional deliveries, analogous programs elsewhere in the developing world can go a long way towards the ideal of access to maternal health benefits regardless of class, socioeconomic status, or location (Ba-Thike and Gummadi).

Administrative structures can and should be created to increase the likelihood of evidence-based policymaking (Baird). A key concern is to work most effectively within the constraints imposed by a given culture while seeking to counteract its pernicious aspects. According to Ba-Thike and Gummadi, JSY should incorporate cultural awareness into the training of staff to understand the importance of reaching out to religious minorities. Just as the creators of JSY did, policy-makers should consider long-standing cultural traditions and policies that may negatively impact women's health and then seek solutions to the resulting problems (Ba-Thike and Gummadi).

Legality emerges as an important area in need of improvement to facilitate women's global health. What is (il)legal can matter significantly for health outcomes. Moreover, even the *degree* of legality seems to matter regarding abortion access (Sjoberg). Sjoberg points out that legalization with taboo-deconstructing grounds has the greatest health benefits for women who otherwise would have resorted to illegal abortions.

Specific examples support a contention that the degree of legality matters regarding access to health services. Tanzania, as Sjoberg observes, is a case where legalization not only failed to deconstruct the taboo against abortion, but kept it in force. In Mozambique, legal abortions are fairly readily available in hospitals to women signing a statement asking for one, yet illegal abortions continue rampantly during de facto legalization because of the continuing taboo on abortion (Sjoberg). The law also matters in terms of compliance mechanisms. Consider the example of Iran with regard to infant formula. Legislation there is definitive but not effective. The law is not supported by appropriate funding for monitoring and punishing violations of the Code, so no incentive exists for manufacturers to respect it (Perlman and Roberts).

Family planning is an area in need of improvement around the world. Relatively modest increases in resource allocations could go a long way in that sense. For example, it is estimated that, with $100 million in support for family planning, 2.1 million unwanted pregnancies could be avoided and 825,000 abortions prevented (Baird).

WHAT NORMS CAN AND SHOULD GUIDE THE PROVISION OF WOMEN'S GLOBAL HEALTH?

Analysis of existing policies and laws, along with their potential improvement, suggest the following norms for improved provision of women's global health: comprehensiveness, enhanced legality, and recognition of asymmetric needs. Each is covered in turn.

Comprehensiveness must guide the approach to women's global health (Baird). There is so much more to consider than the traditionally narrow focus on reproduction. This point is illustrated through arguments and evidence in chapters by Thoradeniya on one hand and Marinova and James on the other. State involvement in women's health, as argued by Thoradeniya, should focus on amalgamating the mutually excluded concepts of women's health and bodies, in order to formulate an ethical policy. More specifically, to compose an ethical health policy, women's bodies should be freed from the fixation on reproduction to broaden the understanding of their health (Thoradeniya). According to Marinova and James, the role of social norms in the creation of law provides an explanation for varying approaches to prostitution and trafficking of persons. Promotion of norms related to equality of opportunity, achieved through comprehensive protection of those most vulnerable in society, thereby emerges as an ideal for which to strive.

Governments should formulate informed and supportive health policies for the common good. The contents should cover "A to Z" when it comes to women's health—both obvious (e.g., reproductive) and non-obvious (e.g., human trafficking–related) aspects should be included (Sjoberg; Baird; Marinova and James).

Enhanced legality is revealed in preceding chapters as an important norm regarding women and global health. A number of studies have demonstrated that legality matters, for example, with respect to the exercise of reproductive rights. Legalization with taboo-deconstructing grounds creates the greatest health benefits for women who otherwise would have resorted to illegal abortion (Sjoberg). In addition, it is important to target the right behavior when attempting to improve health conditions. Consider the issue of infant formula: From a human rights perspective, appropriate state action would be to regulate the infant formula industry, which is the source of much of the problem. This is much better, ethically speaking, than regulating women's self-determination in a way that fails to recognize a possible need to eschew breastfeeding (Perlman and Roberts). As Perlman and Roberts point out, by enacting laws that control maternal access to breast-milk substitutes rather than limiting inappropriate marketing strategies by the infant formula industry, the Iranian government in particular breaches the boundary between legitimate social control and legitimate personal autonomy.

While equal opportunity is an obvious goal with regard to women in society, asymmetries can exist at the level of need when it comes to social services. This is clear to see with regard to women's global health. For example, the burden of contraception tends to fall primarily on women. The need for assistance in that domain therefore will continue to be unequal. Thus it makes sense in some areas to put an emphasis on *women's* global health instead of the latter issue in and of itself. To some extents that shift is taking place already. The UN's MDGs, for instance, prioritize women's issues that are pertinent to health status and outcomes. Although the core rights claims asserted in the ICESCR are made in gender-neutral language, the treaty also underscores particular health needs of women and children (DeLaet).

Comprehensiveness, enhanced legality, and recognition of asymmetric needs combine to form a normative basis for the consideration of women's global health. While all three norms are gaining traction, it would be fair to say that each is far from fully reflected within the existing range of policies and laws at the international and state levels.

FINAL THOUGHTS

This volume represents the combined efforts of a range of scholars to learn more about norms and state policies vis-à-vis women's global health. Its contents reflect various disciplinary backgrounds and geographic interests among the contributors. The overall conclusion from the theory and research contained in the preceding chapters is as follows: *The positive trend in women's global health will be sustained to the extent that norms of comprehensiveness, enhanced legality, and recognition of asymmetric needs become more established in the policy matrix of international organizations and states.*

What about future research? The agenda obviously is vast. While central issues such as reproduction have been considered, other concerns and problems such as human trafficking remind us of how much can be relevant—that even more work is needed on these and other matters under the rubric of women's global health. Further research on international organizations and states also should expand in geographic coverage and range of issues included. These points are obvious in the specific context of the present volume which, among many dimensions of women's health identified by ethnographic research in table 1.1 from chapter 1, focuses most directly on the themes related to state intervention and norms.

Table 1.1 from chapter 1, which conveys twelve major themes, can serve as a guide to expansion of the research agenda on women's global health in disciplines beyond what has been carried out in anthropology, its point of origin. For example, how does the increasing biomedical hegemony over women's health, identified through ethnographic research, stand up under scrutiny from research conducted in political science? The same could be asked about other themes in the table, such as the increasing medicalization of women's lives, which is not covered by the present volume. Moreover, some of the themes touched upon in the current study of norms and state policies—examples would include the reproductive essentialization of women's lives and the politics of women's health—deserve far more attention.

Achievement of a more integrated research enterprise on women's global health, with the potential to impact upon policy, will require research far beyond that contained in the pages of this book. If the volume facilitates further research on women's global health, with greater breadth and depth, then it will have served as a significant step toward building a body of knowledge with the potential to encourage positive norms and better state policy around the world.

NOTES

1. The plus and minus approach takes place without any desire to delegitimize the complications revealed throughout the chapters. The purpose here is to enumerate basic positive and negative findings while remaining aware of the nuances in a given chapter that might point in another direction.

Index

About the Contributors

Katherine Ba-Thike is an obstetrician and gynecologist who worked for twenty years in tertiary care hospitals in Yangon, Mandalay, Myanmar, and London, UK. She was involved in clinical care of obstetric and gynecological patients and training of undergraduate and postgraduate trainees in obstetrics and gynecology and reproductive health, both for masters degrees and short courses. She was involved in clinical and epidemiological research at the national and regional level. Dr. Ba-Thike served as Regional Adviser on Reproductive Health and Family Planning Programs, UNFPA Country Technical Services Team for East and South-East Asia (UNFPA/CST) from 1999 to 2003. From 2003 till her retirement in 2011, she served as Area Manager for Asia and Pacific, Department of Reproductive Health and Research, WHO, Geneva. She coordinated research-capacity-strengthening activities and reproductive health/maternal and child health (RH/MCH) program development for least developed and developing countries in Asia.

Karen L. Baird is associate professor of political science at Purchase College, SUNY, where she also teaches in the gender studies program. She is an author and consultant, works to reduce HIV/AIDS in the United States, and is active in a variety of social justice organizations. She has been at Purchase College since 1994 and has chaired, at various times, the political science and the gender studies programs. Her latest book is *Beyond Reproduction: Women's Health, Activism, and Public Policy* (2009, Fairleigh Dickinson University Press)

Lyn Boyd-Judson is director of the Levan Institute for Humanities and Ethics at the University of Southern California. Judson's research and teaching focus on diplomacy, ethics, global governance, and international negotiation. She has published in *International Studies Quarterly*, *Foreign Policy Analysis*, *Pew Case Studies in Ethics and Diplomacy* (Georgetown University), and *Leiden Journal of International Law.* Her book *Strategic Moral Diplomacy: Understanding the Enemy's Moral Universe* was published in 2011. Previous affiliations include RAND, the Carter Center of Emory University, the Hong Kong Legislative Council, the United States Embassy Berlin—Third Reich Document Center, USC's Center for International Studies, the Walt Disney Company Asia-Pacific, and Dow Jones News Service.

Debra L. DeLaet is professor of politics and international relations at Drake University in Des Moines, Iowa, where she teaches courses on human rights, global health, the United Nations, and gender and world politics. Her major research interests are in the area of human rights, global health, and gender issues in world politics. She has published three books: *U.S. Immigration Policy in an Age of Rights* (Praeger 2000), *The Global Struggle for Human Rights* (Wadsworth, 2006), and (coauthored with David E. DeLaet) *Global Health in the 21st Century: The Globalization of Disease and Wellness* (Paradigm Publishers, 2012). In addition to these books, she has published numerous articles and book chapters in her areas of interest.

Ayushi Gummadi is a 2012 graduate of the University of Southern California, where she studied business administration, international relations, and neuroscience. She spent the summer of 2010 working at the World Health Organization in Geneva with Dr. Ba-Thike, where she engaged her interest in maternal and reproductive health issues in developing countries. She is currently a Fulbright fellow in South Africa and hopes to pursue a career in international development and policy, particularly in the health and education sectors.

Patrick James is Dornsife Dean's professor of international relations and director of the Center for International Studies at the University of Southern California. James is the author or editor of twenty-two books and over 120 articles and book chapters. James has been Distinguished Scholar in Foreign Policy Analysis for the International Studies Association (ISA), 2006–2007, and Distinguished Scholar in Ethnicity, Nationalism and Migration for ISA, 2009–2010. He served as president (2007–2009) of the Association for Canadian Studies in the United States, vice-president (2008–2009) of the ISA and president of the International Council for Canadian Studies (2011–2013). James also served as editor of *International Studies Quarterly.*

Nadejda Marinova is assistant professor of political science at Wayne State University. She previously served as a Dornsife College Postdoctoral Distinguished Teaching Fellow at the University of Southern California (2011–2012). Her research interests include diaspora and migration, human trafficking, Middle East politics, ethnic lobbies in foreign policy, and the intersection of culture and gender. Dr. Marinova's work has been published in *Foreign Policy Analysis*, as part of George Mason University's *Global Migration and Transnational Politics* series and in the *International Studies*

Association (ISA) Encyclopedia. She is the past communications chair (2011–2013) of the Ethnicity, Nationalism and Migration section of ISA.

Leah R. Perlman, Esq. is in-house counsel with a private retail company where she specializes primarily in employment law. Before entering her current position, Ms. Perlman worked as a clinical law fellow with the Domestic Violence Institute (DVI). Ms. Perlman graduated from Northeastern University School of Law in May of 2009. While a student at Northeastern, Ms. Perlman was involved with the DVI as a clinical student based in the Dorchester Division of the Boston Municipal Court as well as serving in the DVI's Boston Medical Center Program. She interned with the Honorable Jay Blitzman of the Middlesex Juvenile Court; with Lambda Legal; with the Mental Health Legal Advisors Committee/Clubhouse Family Legal Support Project; and with the Victim Rights Law Center. Prior to attending law school, Ms. Perlman worked as a legal advocate for domestic violence victims in the South County District Court of Rhode Island. She is a member of the Massachusetts and Florida Bar associations and an alumnus of Emory University where she graduated in 2006 with a Bachelor of Arts in women's studies and psychology.

Kathryn Roberts is an international public health practitioner. She is a member of the Malaria Elimination Initiative within the Global Health Group at UCSF. Prior to this position she worked with the Columbia Group for Children in Adversity conducting evaluations and research to gauge the experiences and needs of children and families during and after conflict and disasters. Her research interests include connections between migration, conflict, social support mechanisms, and the spread of infectious diseases. She continues her engagement in child and maternal health and breastfeeding through research and advocacy. She earned her Masters of Public Health at Columbia University.

Laura Sjoberg is associate professor of political science at the University of Florida, with a faculty affiliation in Women's and Gender Studies. She holds a Ph.D. in International Relations from the University of Southern California and a juris doctorate from Boston College Law School. Her research interests include feminist theory in Security Studies, women's violence in global politics, and other intersections of gender, sexuality, and violence in global politics. Her work has been published in three dozen journals in political science, international relations, and gender studies. She is author or editor of eight books, including, most recently, *Gendering Global Conflict: Toward a Feminist Theory of War* (Columbia University Press, 2013).

Darshi Thoradeniya is attending to revisions of her PhD thesis on women's health as state strategy in twentieth century Sri Lanka submitted to the Centre for History of Medicine at the University of Warwick. She is the author of an article on oral histories in a medical setting in Sri Lanka which will be published in the *Oxford Oral History Series*. Currently she is working as the academic coordinator of the Quality Improvement Grant of the Higher Education for the Twenty-First Century project at the Open University of Sri Lanka.

CPSIA information can be obtained at www.ICGtesting.com
Printed in the USA
BVOW07*1448201213

339541BV00001B/3/P